ART
SAVES

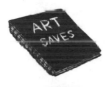

THE PLAIN JANES

Published by DC Comics,

1700 Broadway,

New York, NY 10019.

Printed in Canada.
DC Comics, a Warner Bros.
Entertainment Company.

ISBN: 1-4012-1115-1
ISBN 13: 978-1-4012-1115-8

COVER BY JIM RUGG

Special thanks to the Manhattan and Maplewood MINX Collectives.

Karen Berger, Sr. VP-Executive Editor Shelly Bond, Editor Angela Rufino, Assistant Editor
Robbin Brosterman, Sr. Art Director Paul Levitz, President & Publisher
Georg Brewer, VP-Design & DC Direct Creative Richard Bruning, Sr. VP-Creative Director
Patrick Caldon, Exec. VP-Finance & Operations Chris Caramalis, VP-Finance
John Cunningham, VP-Marketing Terri Cunningham, VP-Managing Editor Alison Gill, VP-Manufacturing
Hank Kanalz, VP-General Manager, WildStorm Jim Lee, Editorial Director-WildStorm
Paula Lowitt, Sr. VP-Business & Legal Affairs MaryEllen McLaughlin, VP-Advertising & Custom Publishing
John Nee, VP-Business Development Gregory Noveck, Sr. VP-Creative Affairs
Sue Pohja, VP-Book Trade Sales Cheryl Rubin, Sr. VP-Brand Management
Jeff Trojan, VP-Business Development, DC Direct Bob Wayne, VP-Sales

THE PLAIN JANES

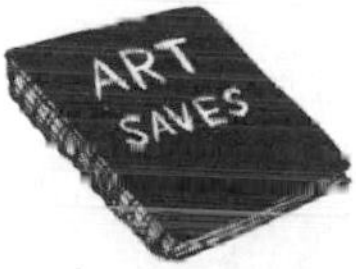
ART
SAVES

by CECIL CASTELLUCCI
and JIM RUGG

with lettering by
Jared K. Fletcher

minx

To all you Dandelions.

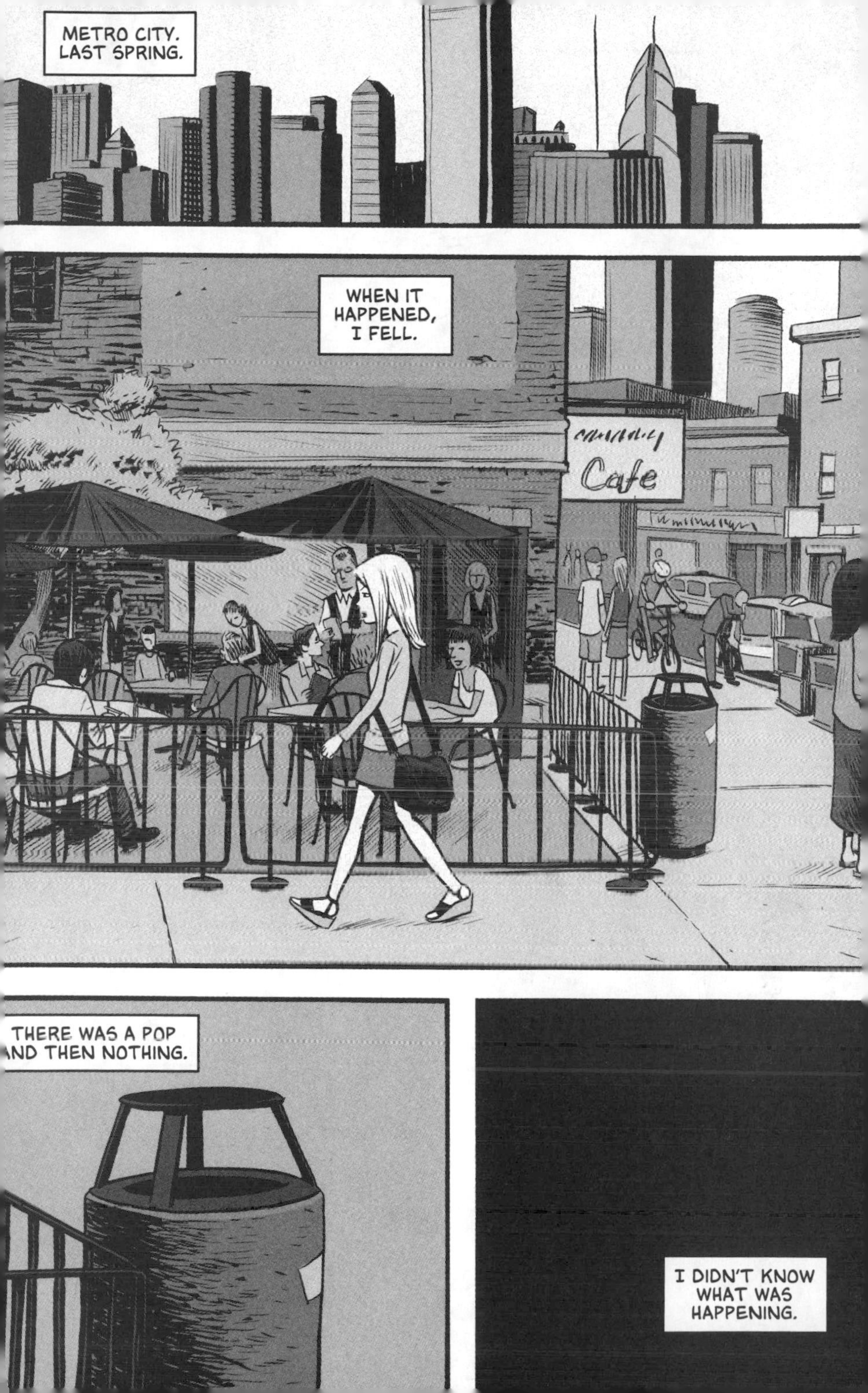
METRO CITY. LAST SPRING.
WHEN IT HAPPENED, I FELL.
Cafe
THERE WAS A POP AND THEN NOTHING.
I DIDN'T KNOW WHAT WAS HAPPENING.

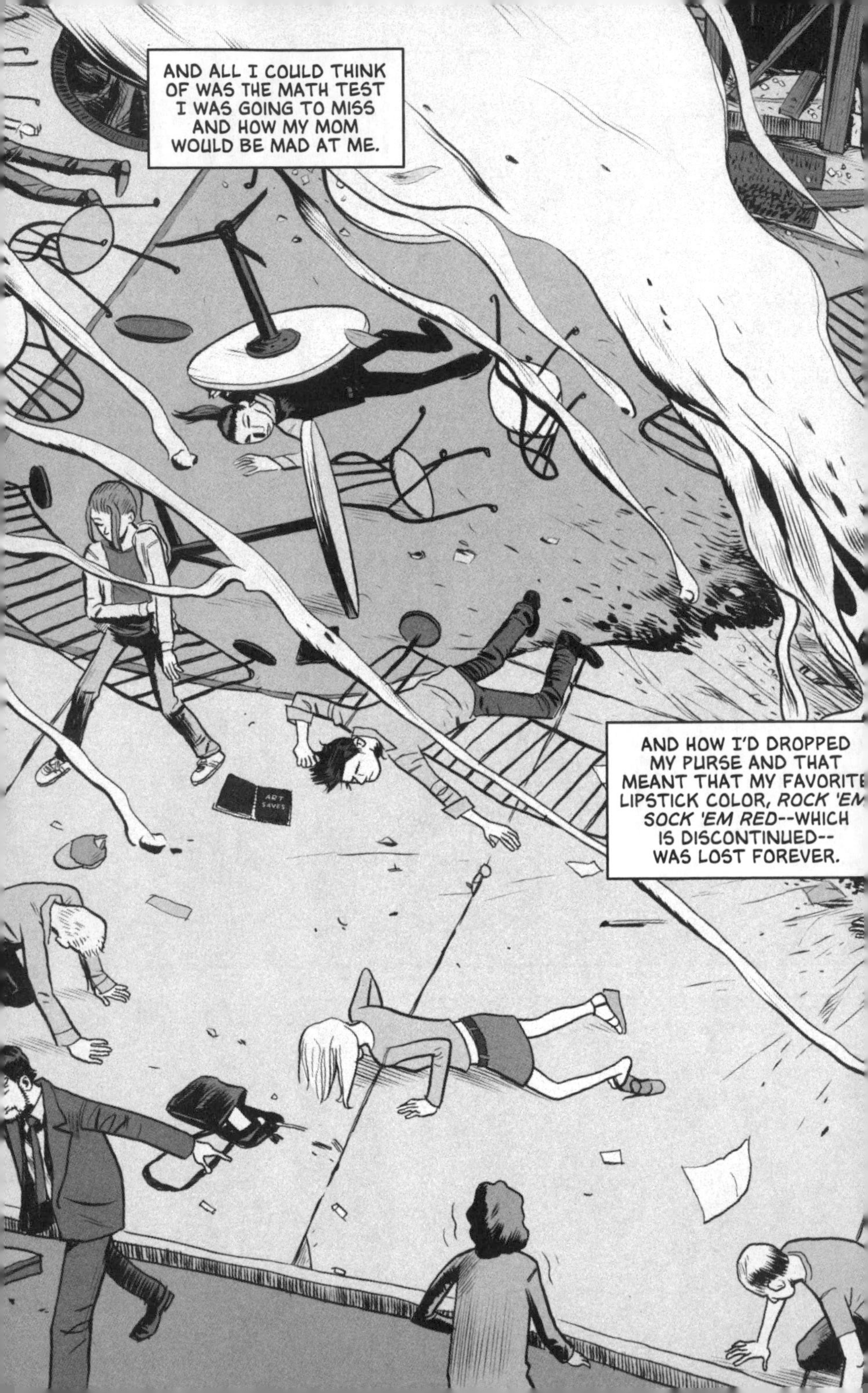
AND ALL I COULD THINK OF WAS THE MATH TEST I WAS GOING TO MISS AND HOW MY MOM WOULD BE MAD AT ME.
ART SAVES
AND HOW I'D DROPPED MY PURSE AND THAT MEANT THAT MY FAVORITE LIPSTICK COLOR, *ROCK 'EM SOCK 'EM RED*--WHICH IS DISCONTINUED--WAS LOST FOREVER.

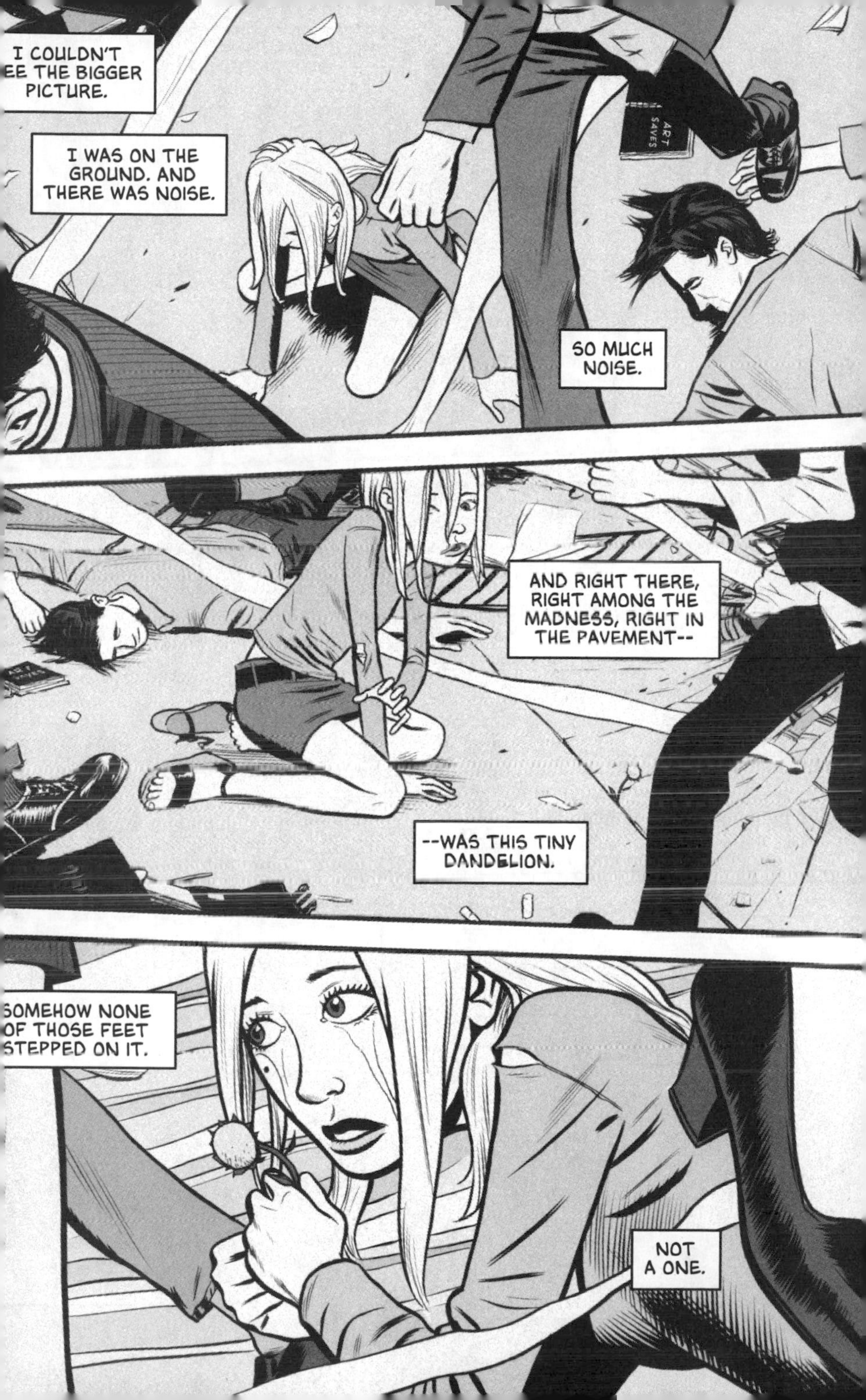
I COULDN'T
EE THE BIGGER
PICTURE.
I WAS ON THE
GROUND. AND
THERE WAS NOISE.
ART
SAVES
SO MUCH
NOISE.
AND RIGHT THERE,
RIGHT AMONG THE
MADNESS, RIGHT IN
THE PAVEMENT--
--WAS THIS TINY
DANDELION.
SOMEHOW NONE
OF THOSE FEET
STEPPED ON IT.
NOT
A ONE.

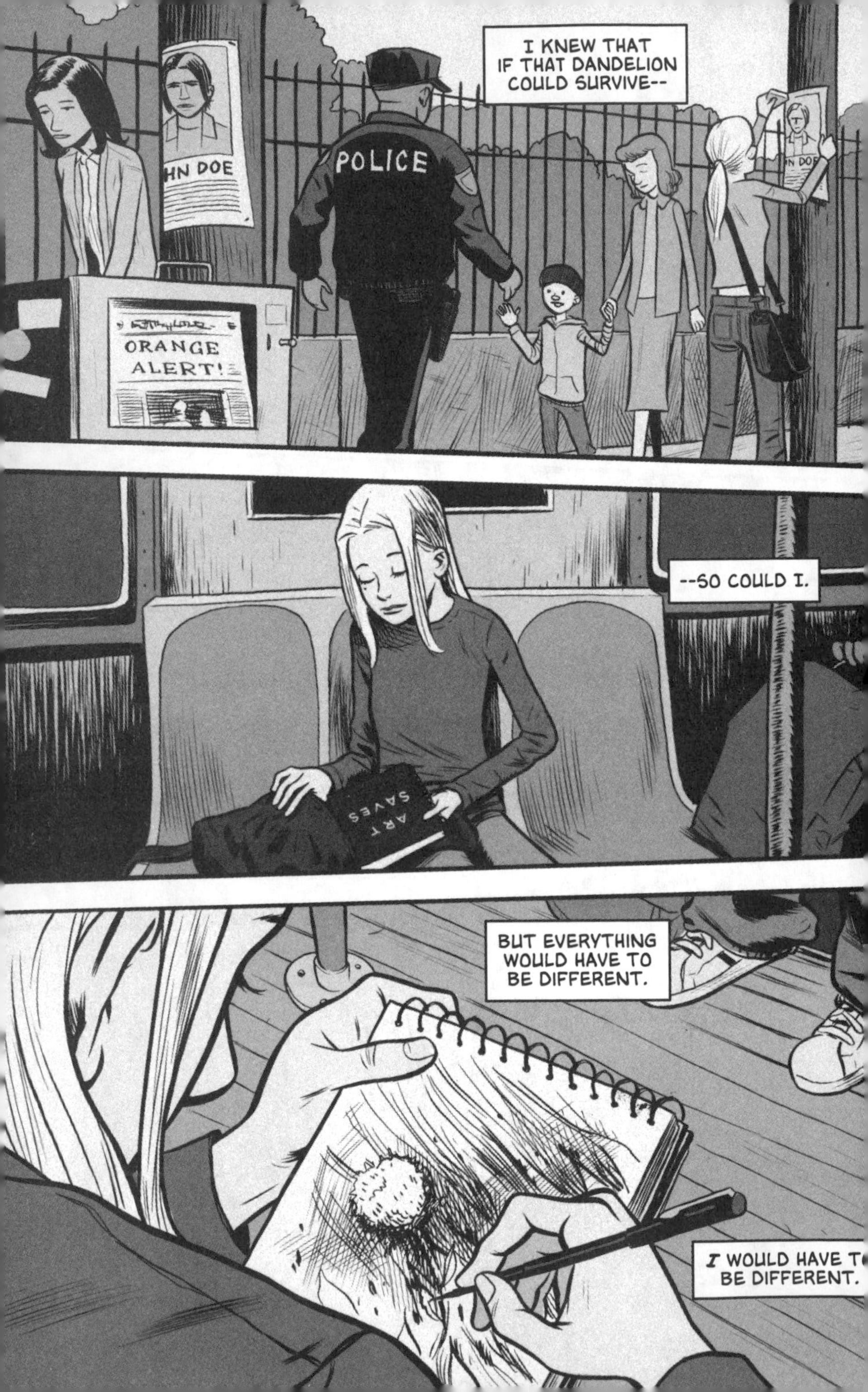
I KNEW THAT IF THAT DANDELION COULD SURVIVE--
HN DOE
POLICE
N DOE
ORANGE ALERT!
--SO COULD I.
ART SAVES
BUT EVERYTHING WOULD HAVE TO BE DIFFERENT.
I WOULD HAVE T
BE DIFFERENT.

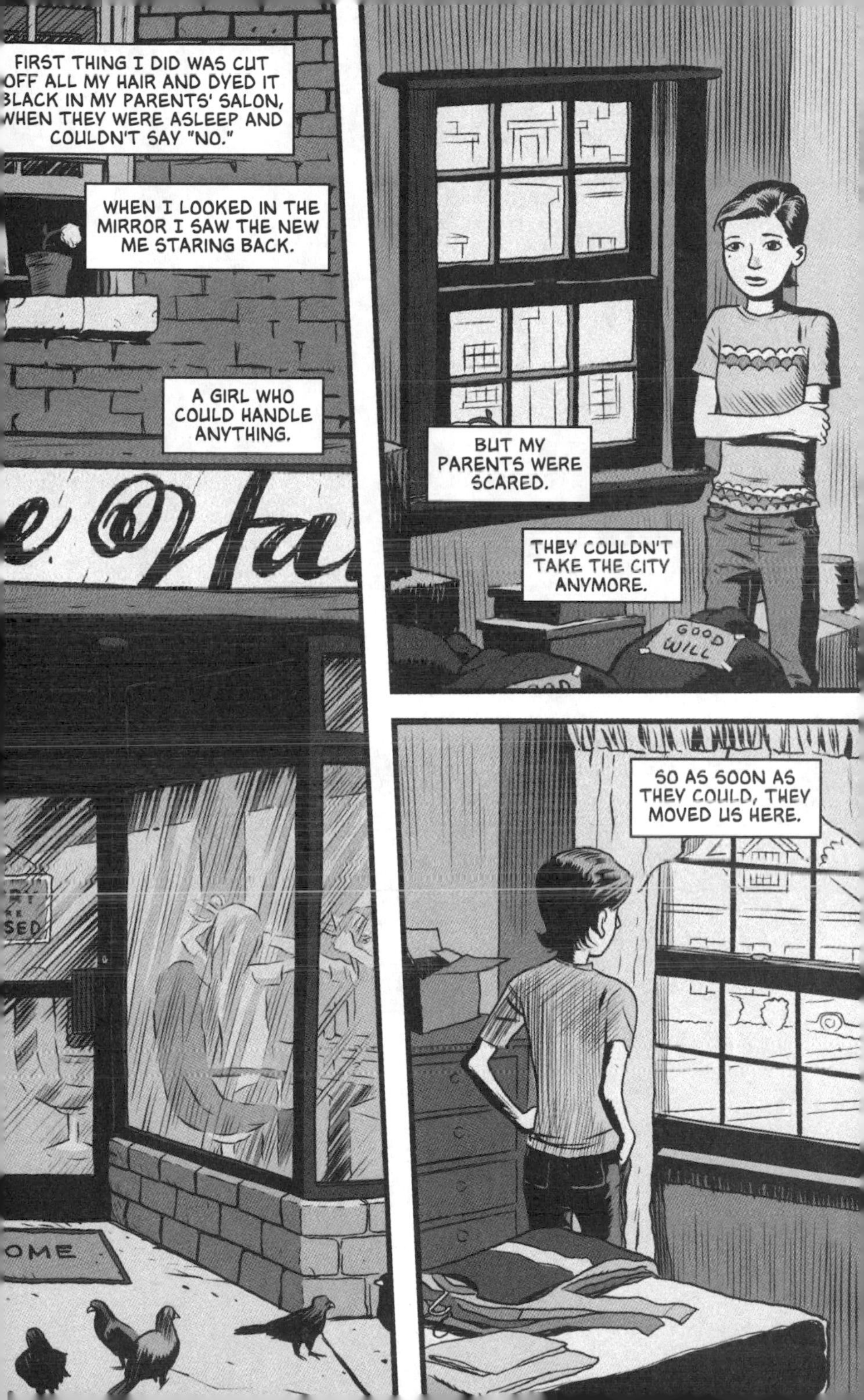
FIRST THING I DID WAS CUT OFF ALL MY HAIR AND DYED IT BLACK IN MY PARENTS' SALON, WHEN THEY WERE ASLEEP AND COULDN'T SAY "NO."
WHEN I LOOKED IN THE MIRROR I SAW THE NEW ME STARING BACK.
A GIRL WHO COULD HANDLE ANYTHING.
BUT MY PARENTS WERE SCARED.
THEY COULDN'T TAKE THE CITY ANYMORE.
GOOD WILL
SO AS SOON AS THEY COULD, THEY MOVED US HERE.

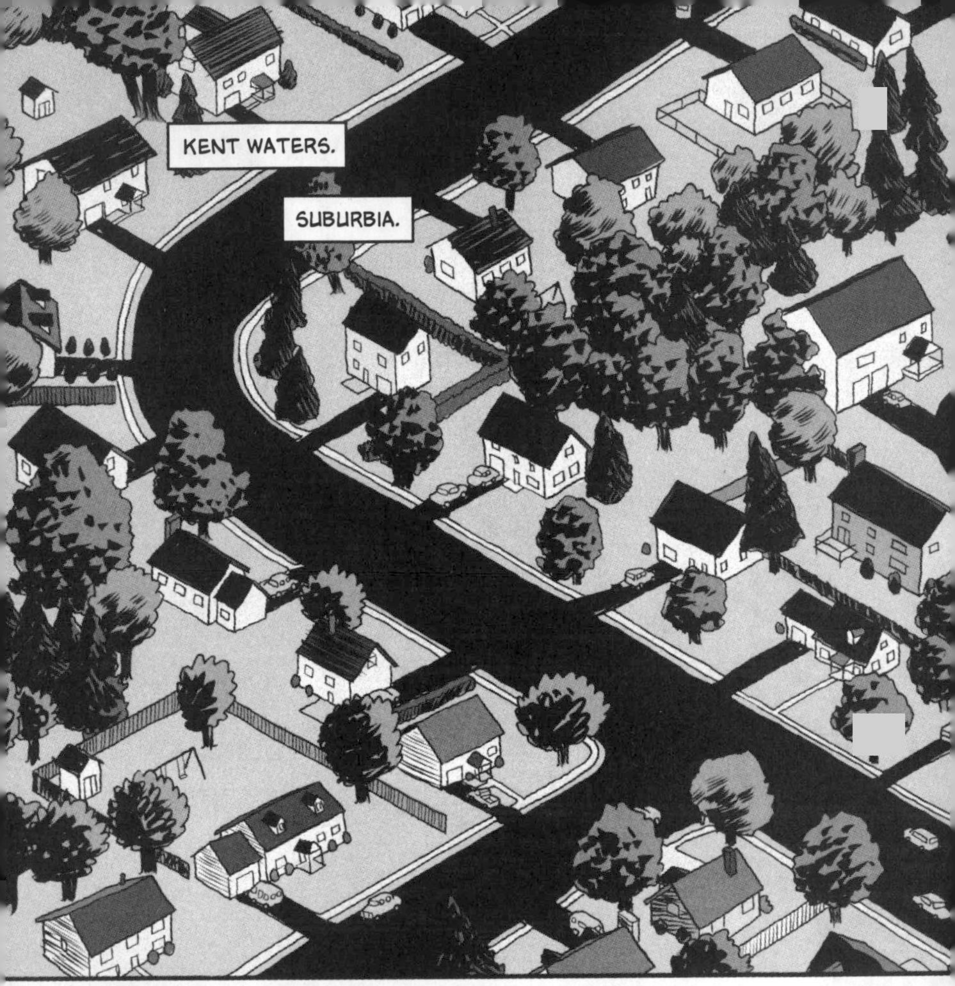
KENT WATERS.
SUBURBIA.

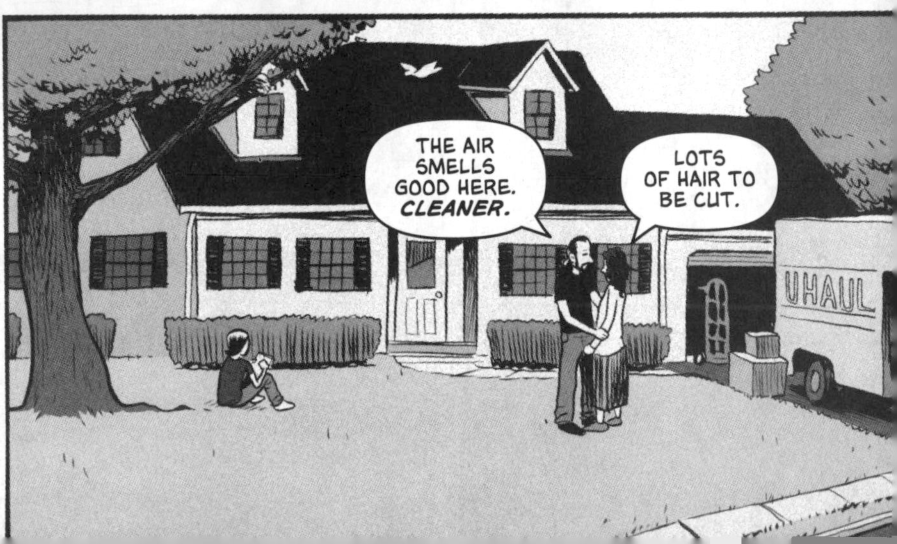
THE AIR SMELLS GOOD HERE. CLEANER.
LOTS OF HAIR TO BE CUT.
UHAUL

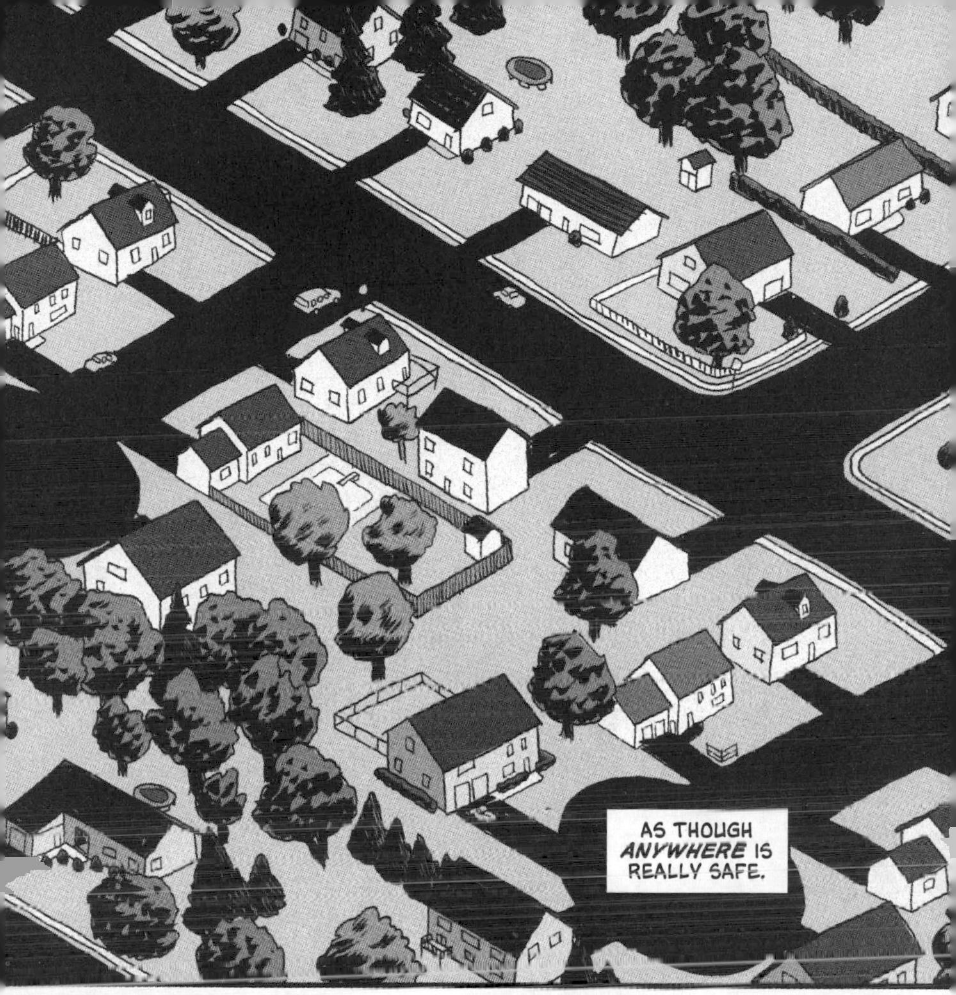
AS THOUGH ANYWHERE IS REALLY SAFE.

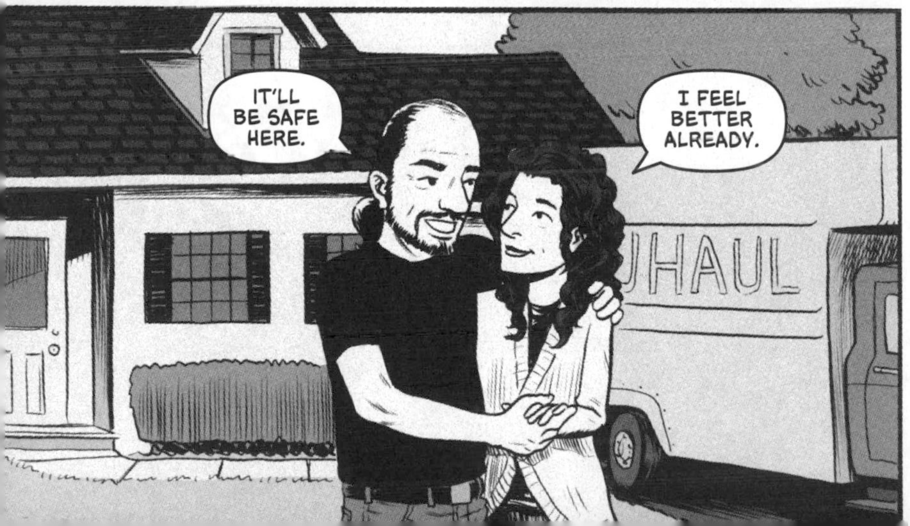
IT'LL BE SAFE HERE.
I FEEL BETTER ALREADY.
UHAUL

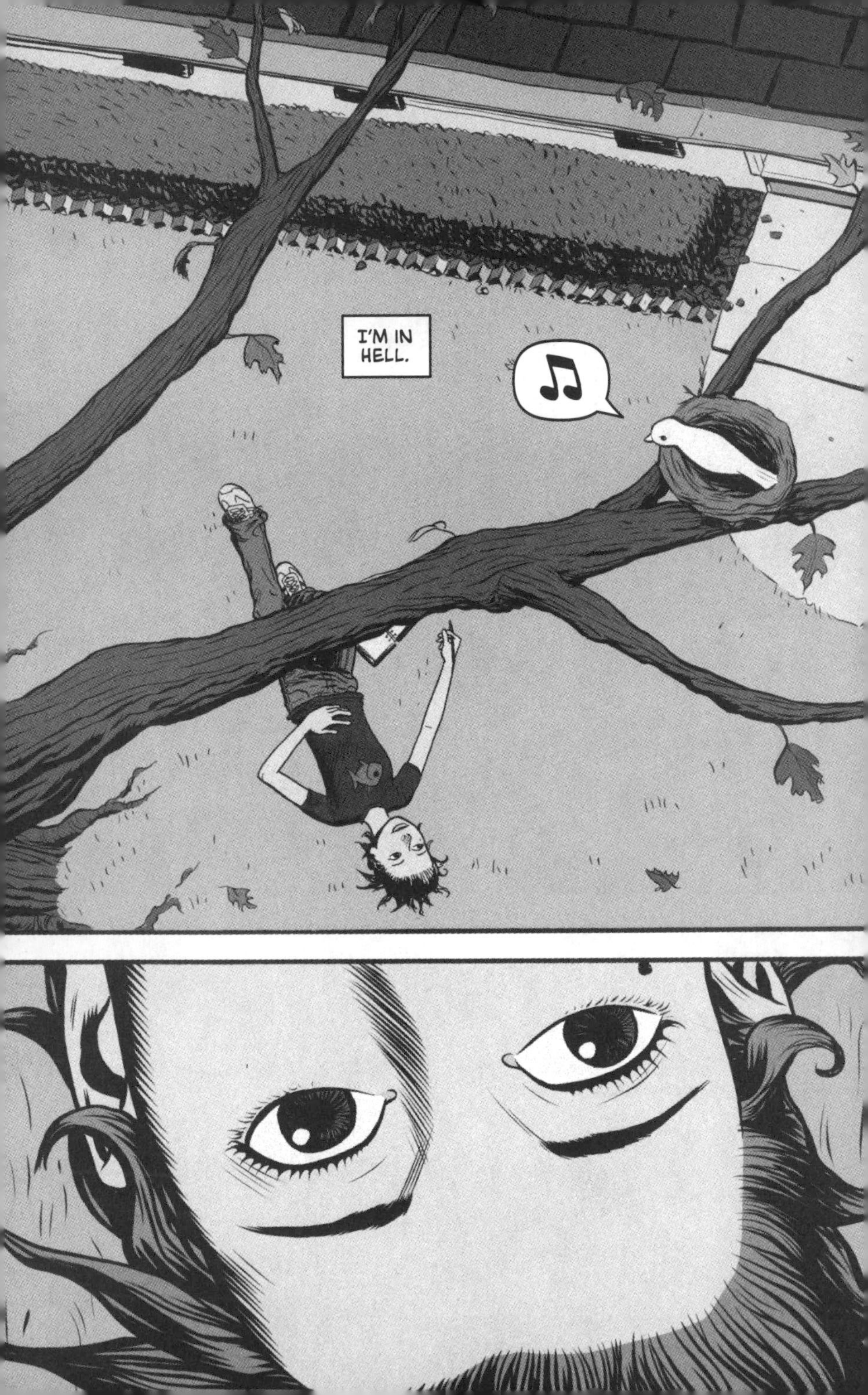
I'M IN HELL.
♫

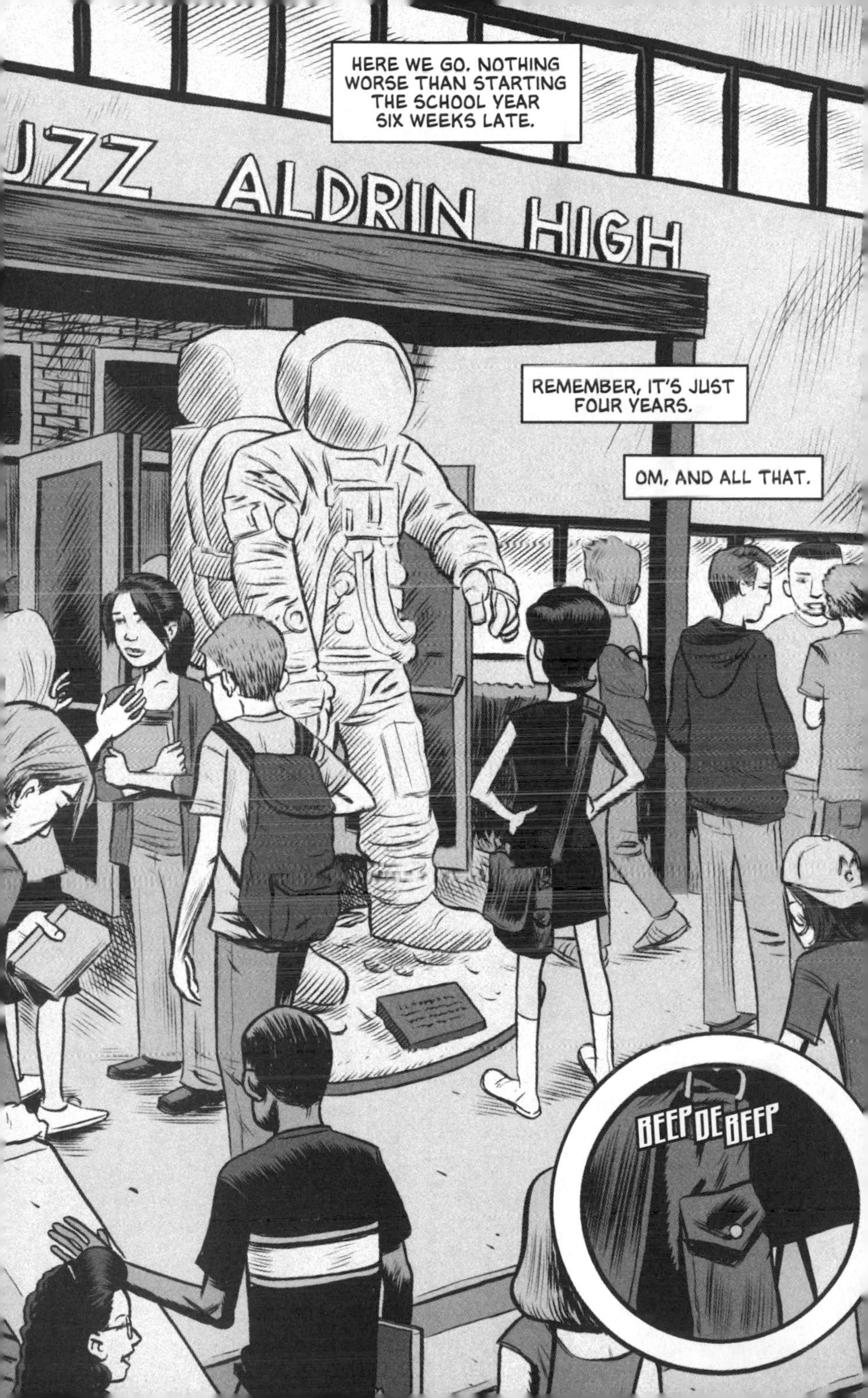
HERE WE GO. NOTHING WORSE THAN STARTING THE SCHOOL YEAR SIX WEEKS LATE.
UZZ ALDRIN HIGH
REMEMBER, IT'S JUST FOUR YEARS.
OM, AND ALL THAT.
BEEP DE BEEP

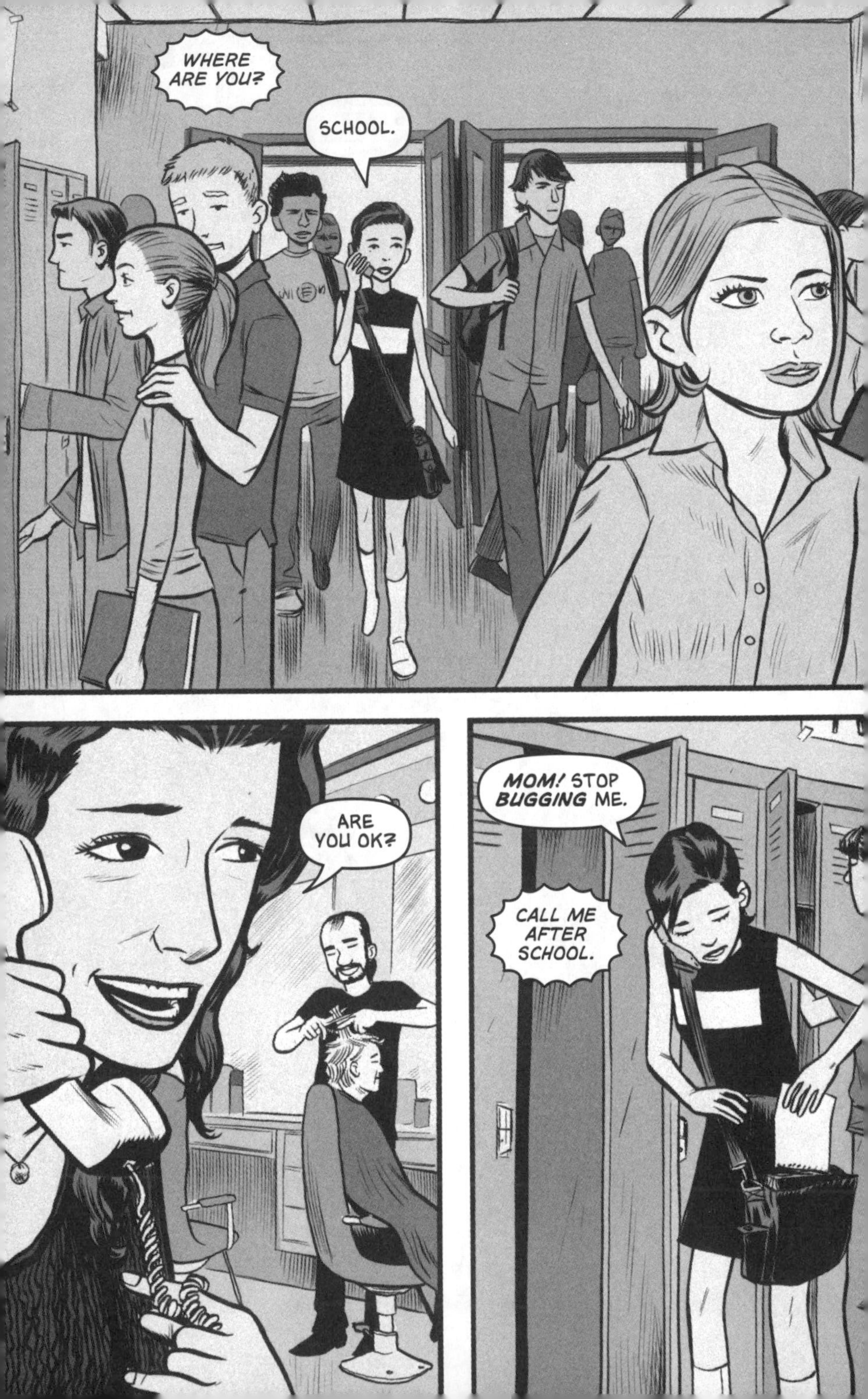
WHERE ARE YOU?
SCHOOL.
ARE YOU OK?
MOM! STOP BUGGING ME.
CALL ME AFTER SCHOOL.

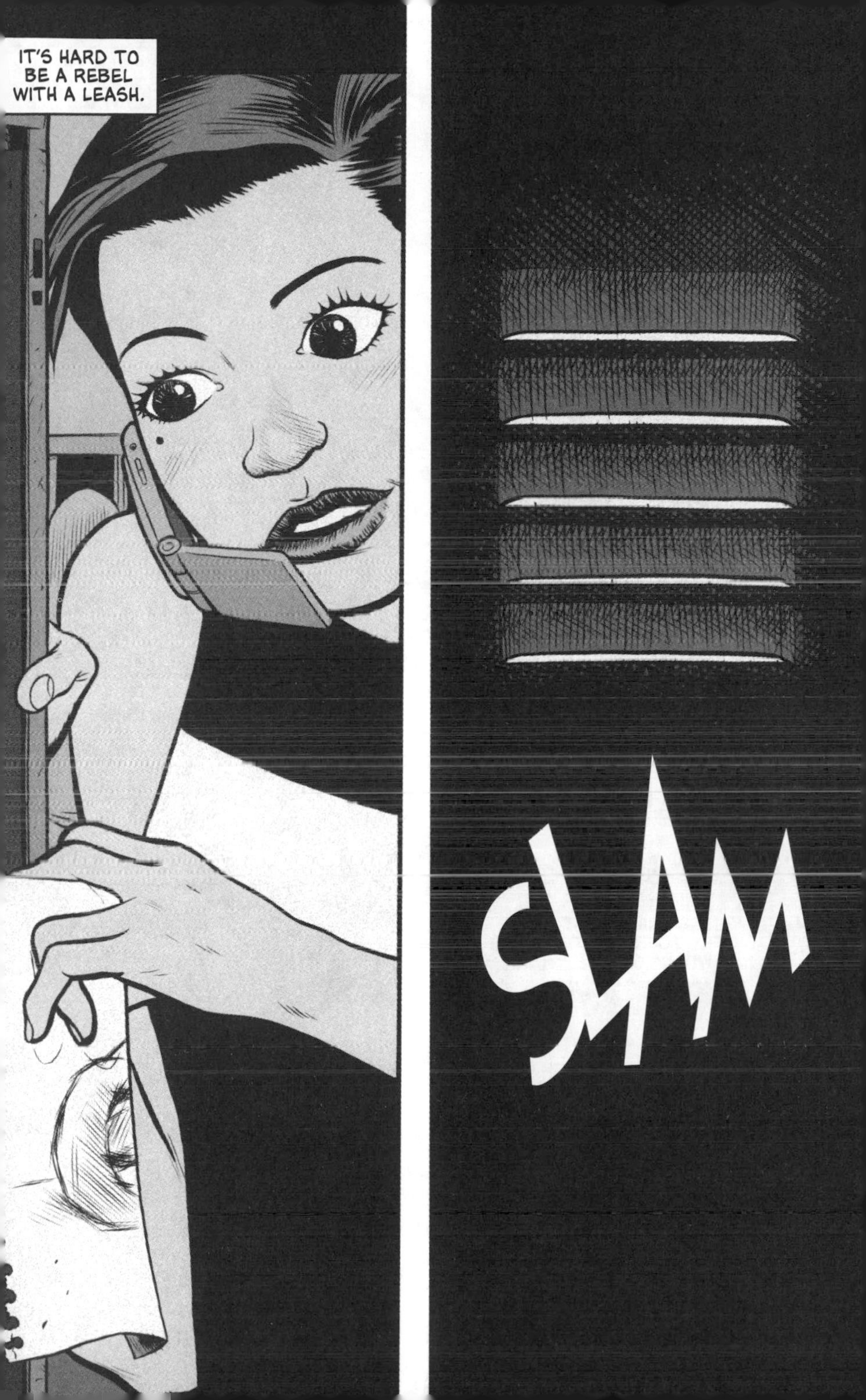
IT'S HARD TO BE A REBEL WITH A LEASH.
SLAM

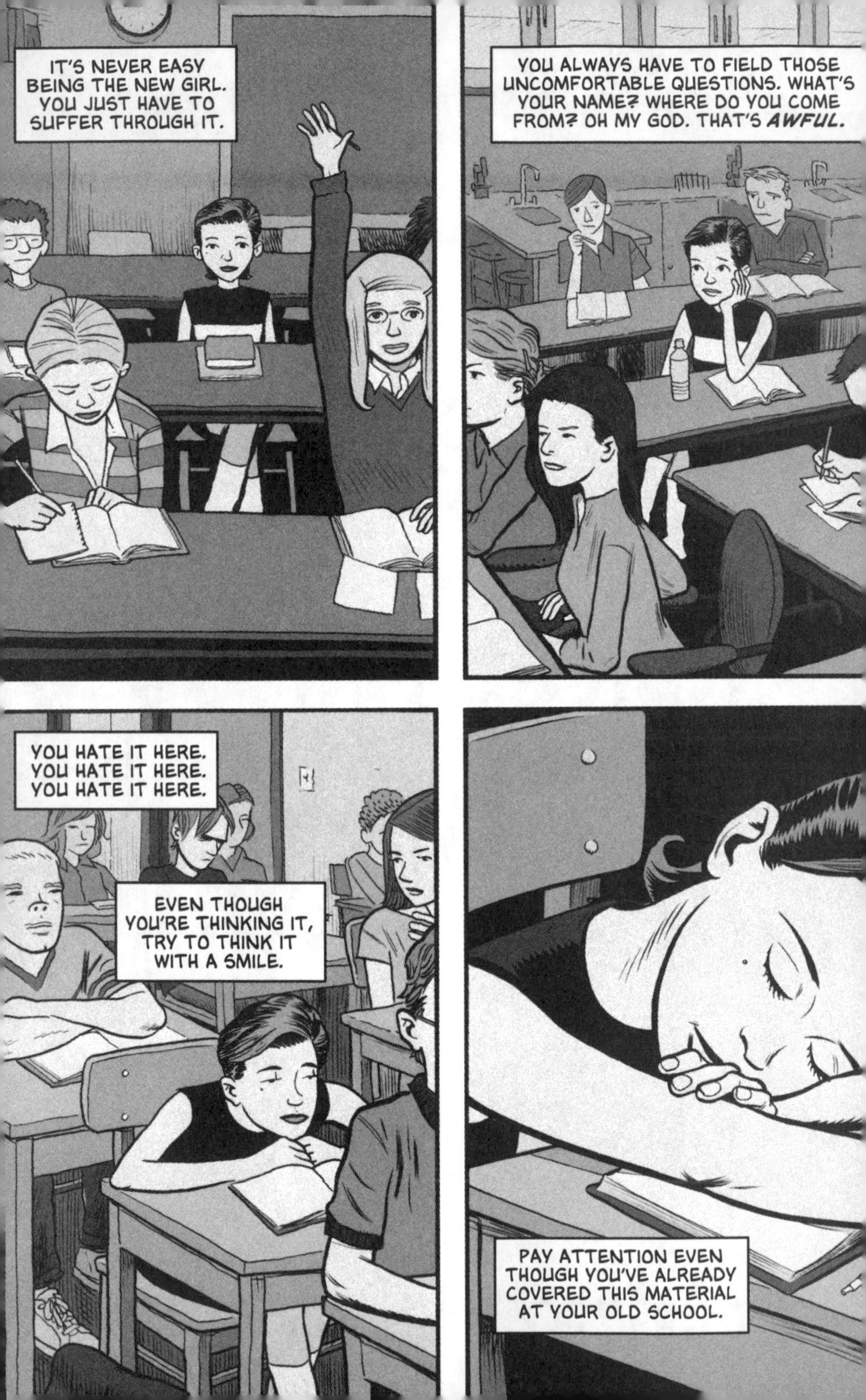
IT'S NEVER EASY BEING THE NEW GIRL. YOU JUST HAVE TO SUFFER THROUGH IT.
YOU ALWAYS HAVE TO FIELD THOSE UNCOMFORTABLE QUESTIONS. WHAT'S YOUR NAME? WHERE DO YOU COME FROM? OH MY GOD. THAT'S *AWFUL.*
YOU HATE IT HERE. YOU HATE IT HERE. YOU HATE IT HERE.
EVEN THOUGH YOU'RE THINKING IT, TRY TO THINK IT WITH A SMILE.
PAY ATTENTION EVEN THOUGH YOU'VE ALREADY COVERED THIS MATERIAL AT YOUR OLD SCHOOL.

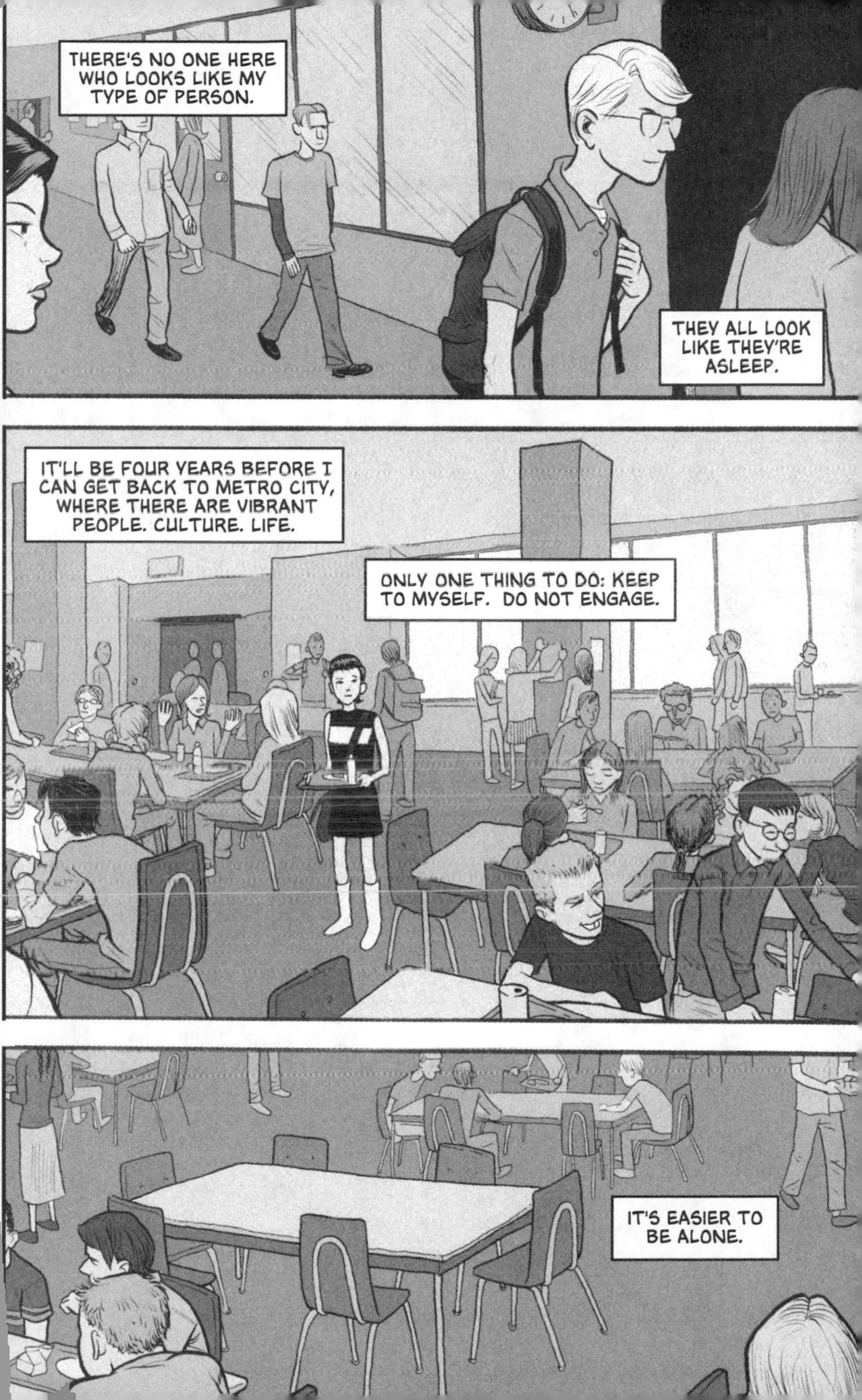
THERE'S NO ONE HERE WHO LOOKS LIKE MY TYPE OF PERSON.
THEY ALL LOOK LIKE THEY'RE ASLEEP.
IT'LL BE FOUR YEARS BEFORE I CAN GET BACK TO METRO CITY, WHERE THERE ARE VIBRANT PEOPLE. CULTURE. LIFE.
ONLY ONE THING TO DO: KEEP TO MYSELF. DO NOT ENGAGE.
IT'S EASIER TO BE ALONE.

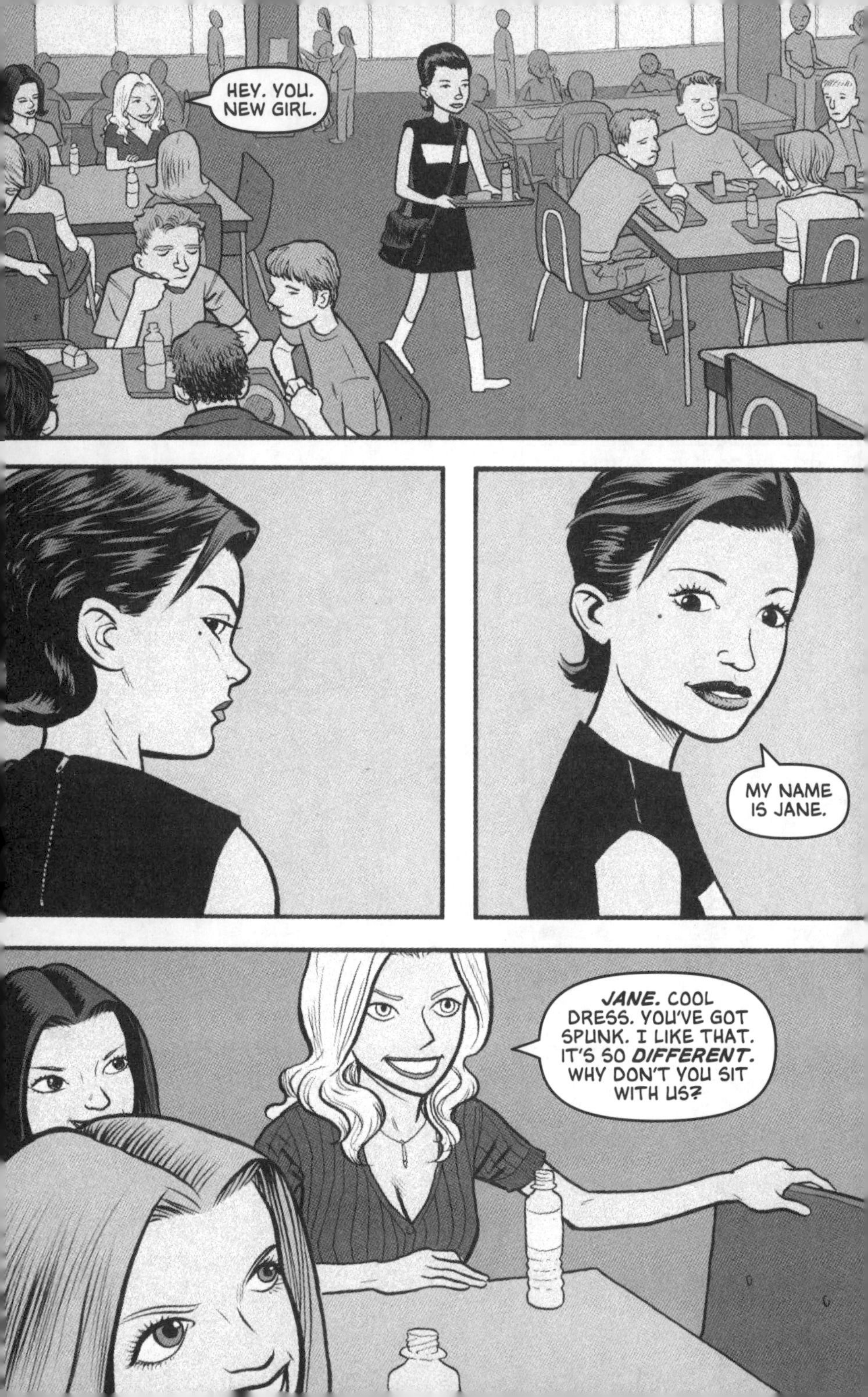
HEY. YOU. NEW GIRL.
MY NAME IS JANE.
JANE. COOL DRESS. YOU'VE GOT SPUNK. I LIKE THAT. IT'S SO DIFFERENT. WHY DON'T YOU SIT WITH US?

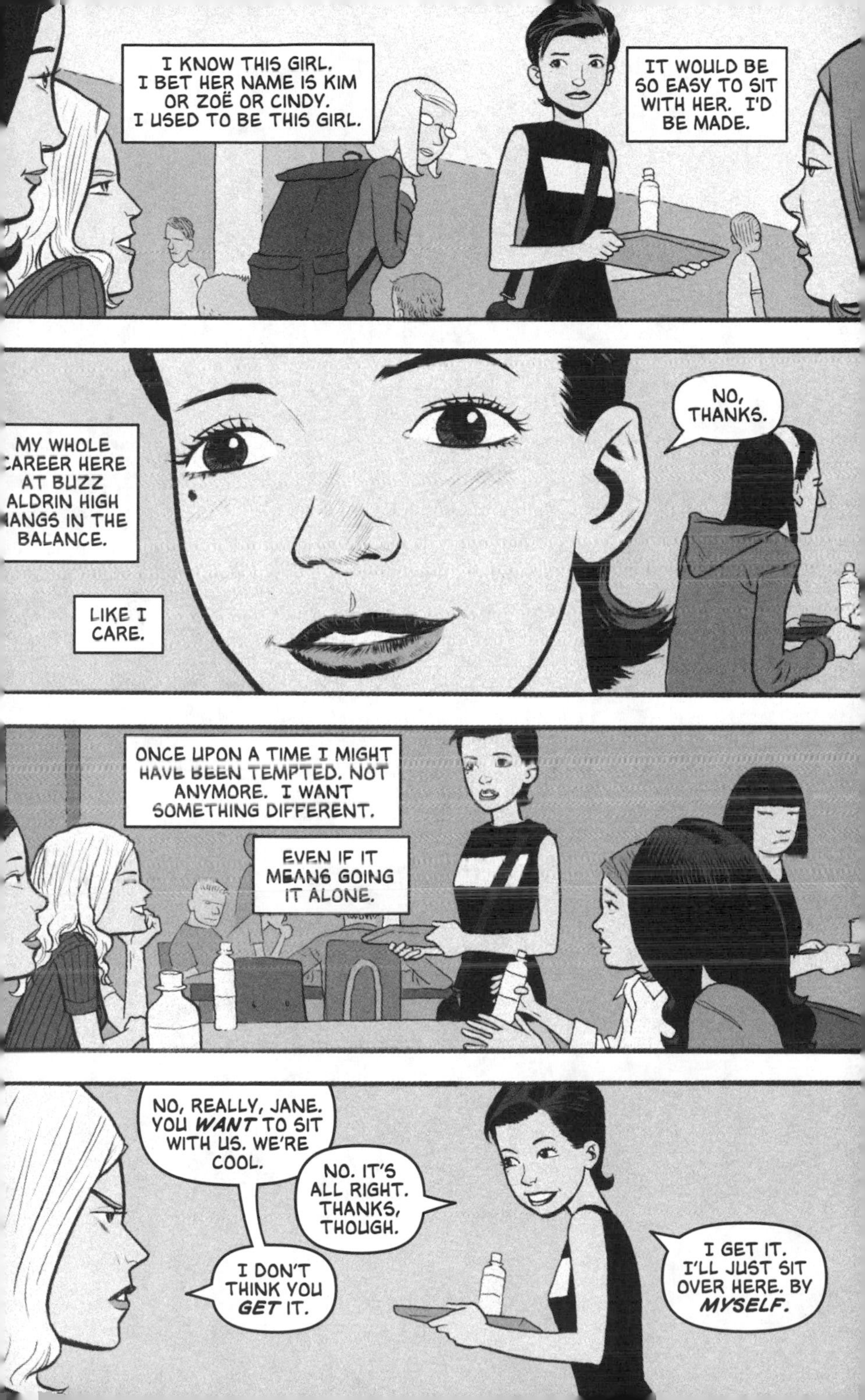
I KNOW THIS GIRL. I BET HER NAME IS KIM OR ZOË OR CINDY. I USED TO BE THIS GIRL.
IT WOULD BE SO EASY TO SIT WITH HER. I'D BE MADE.
MY WHOLE CAREER HERE AT BUZZ ALDRIN HIGH HANGS IN THE BALANCE.
NO, THANKS.
LIKE I CARE.
ONCE UPON A TIME I MIGHT HAVE BEEN TEMPTED. NOT ANYMORE. I WANT SOMETHING DIFFERENT.
EVEN IF IT MEANS GOING IT ALONE.
NO, REALLY, JANE. YOU *WANT* TO SIT WITH US. WE'RE COOL.
NO. IT'S ALL RIGHT. THANKS, THOUGH.
I DON'T THINK YOU *GET* IT.
I GET IT. I'LL JUST SIT OVER HERE. BY *MYSELF*.

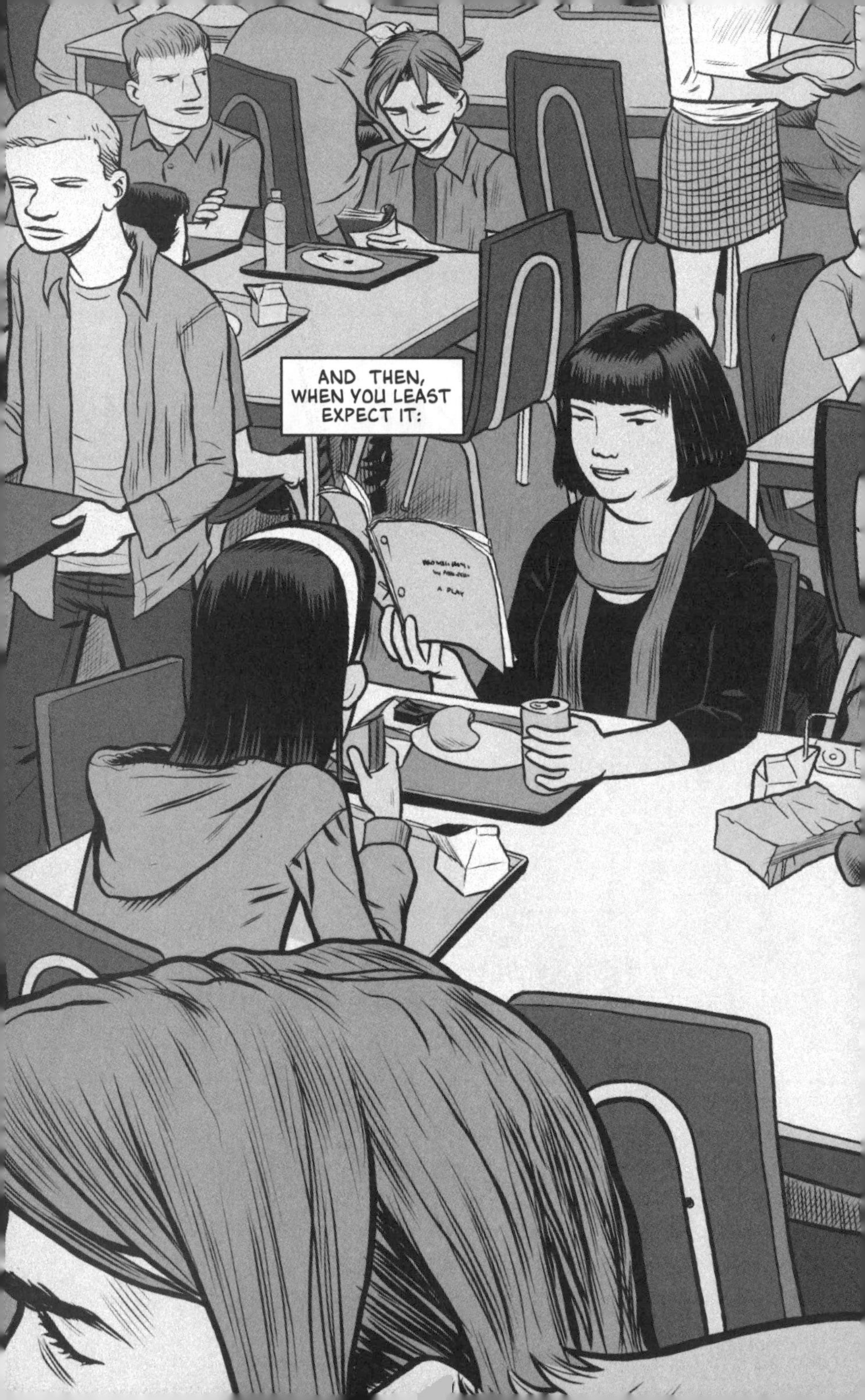
AND THEN, WHEN YOU LEAST EXPECT IT:
A PLAY

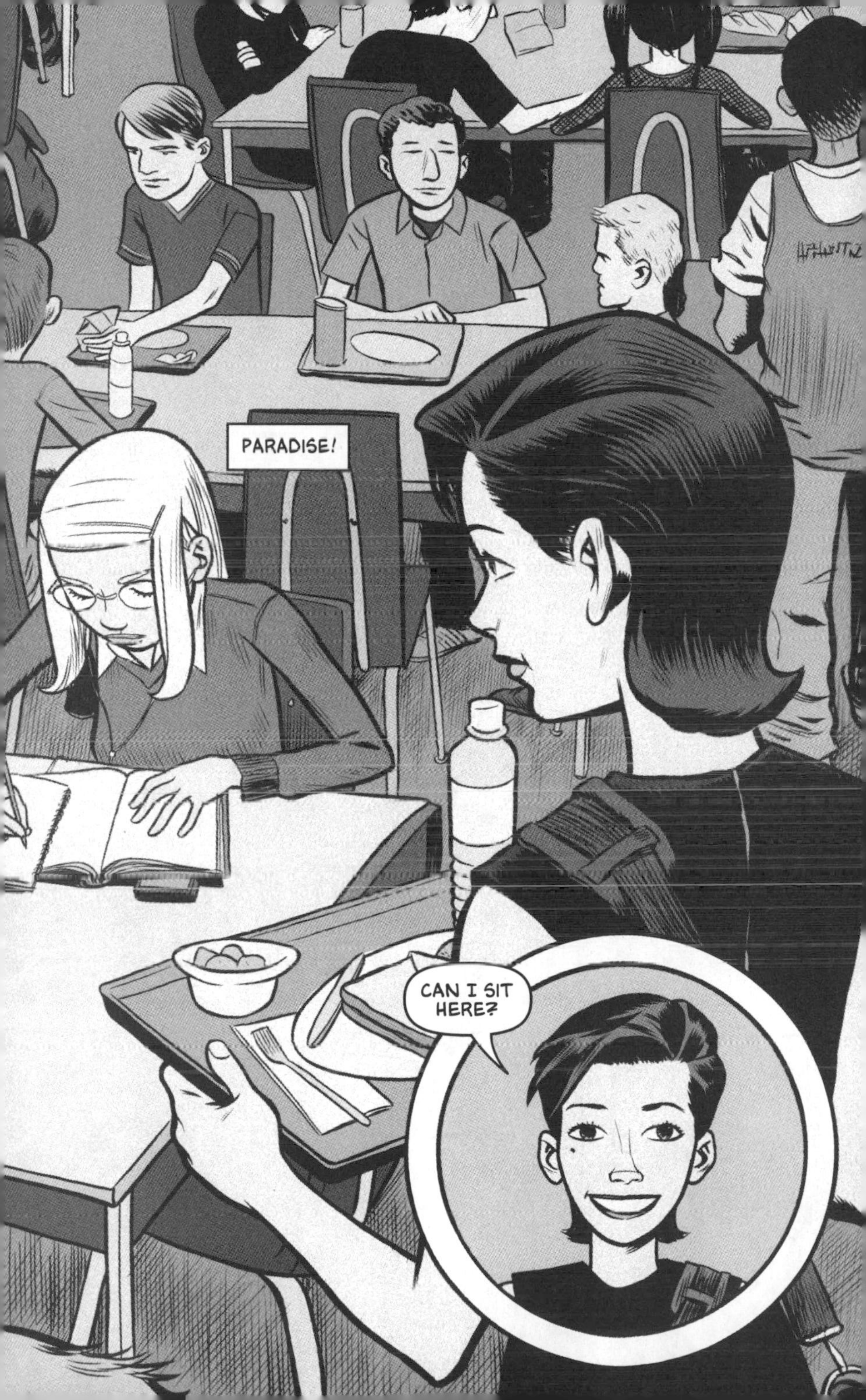
PARADISE!
CAN I SIT HERE?

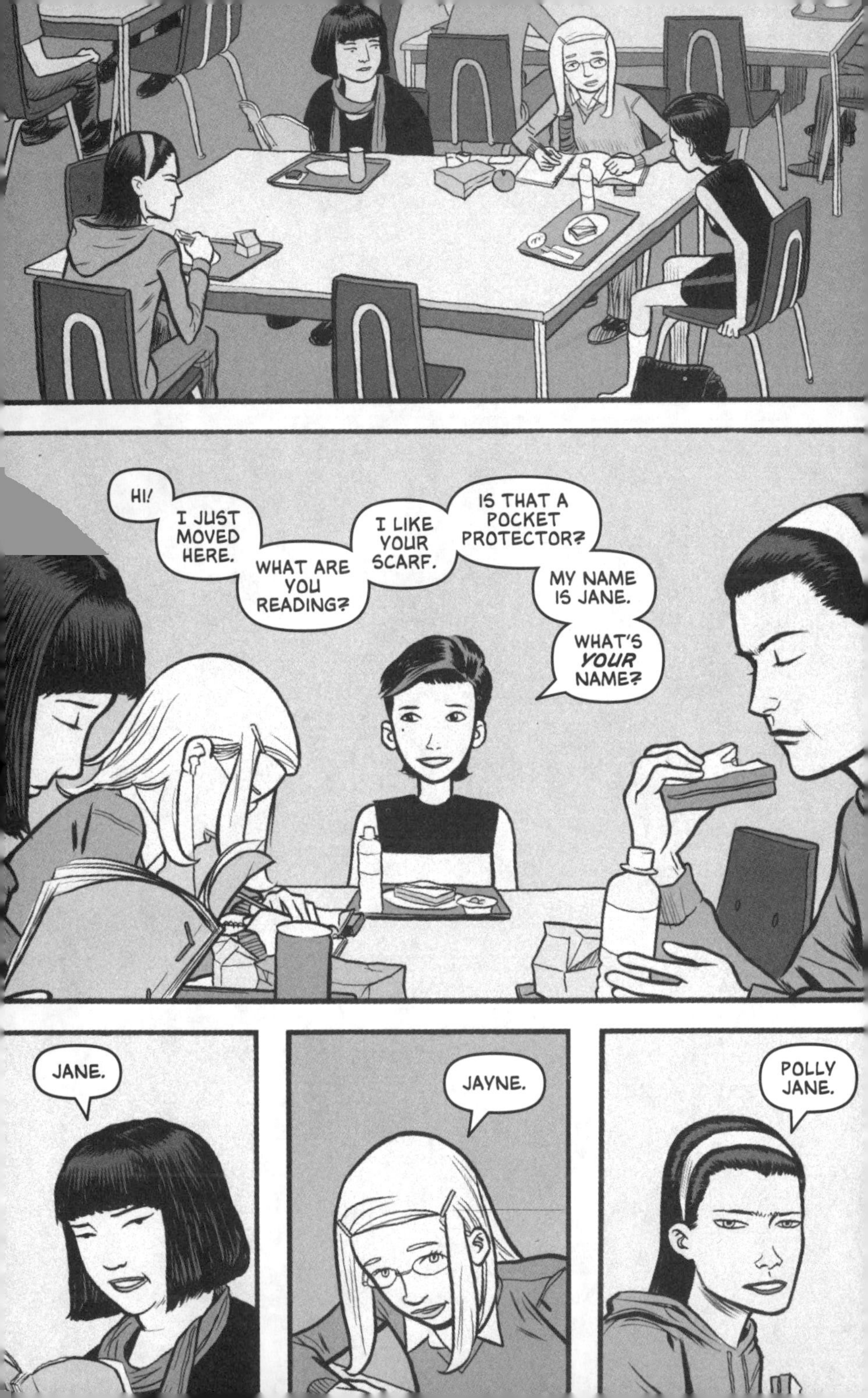
HI!
I JUST MOVED HERE.
WHAT ARE YOU READING?
I LIKE YOUR SCARF.
IS THAT A POCKET PROTECTOR?
MY NAME IS JANE.
WHAT'S *YOUR* NAME?
JANE.
JAYNE.
POLLY JANE.

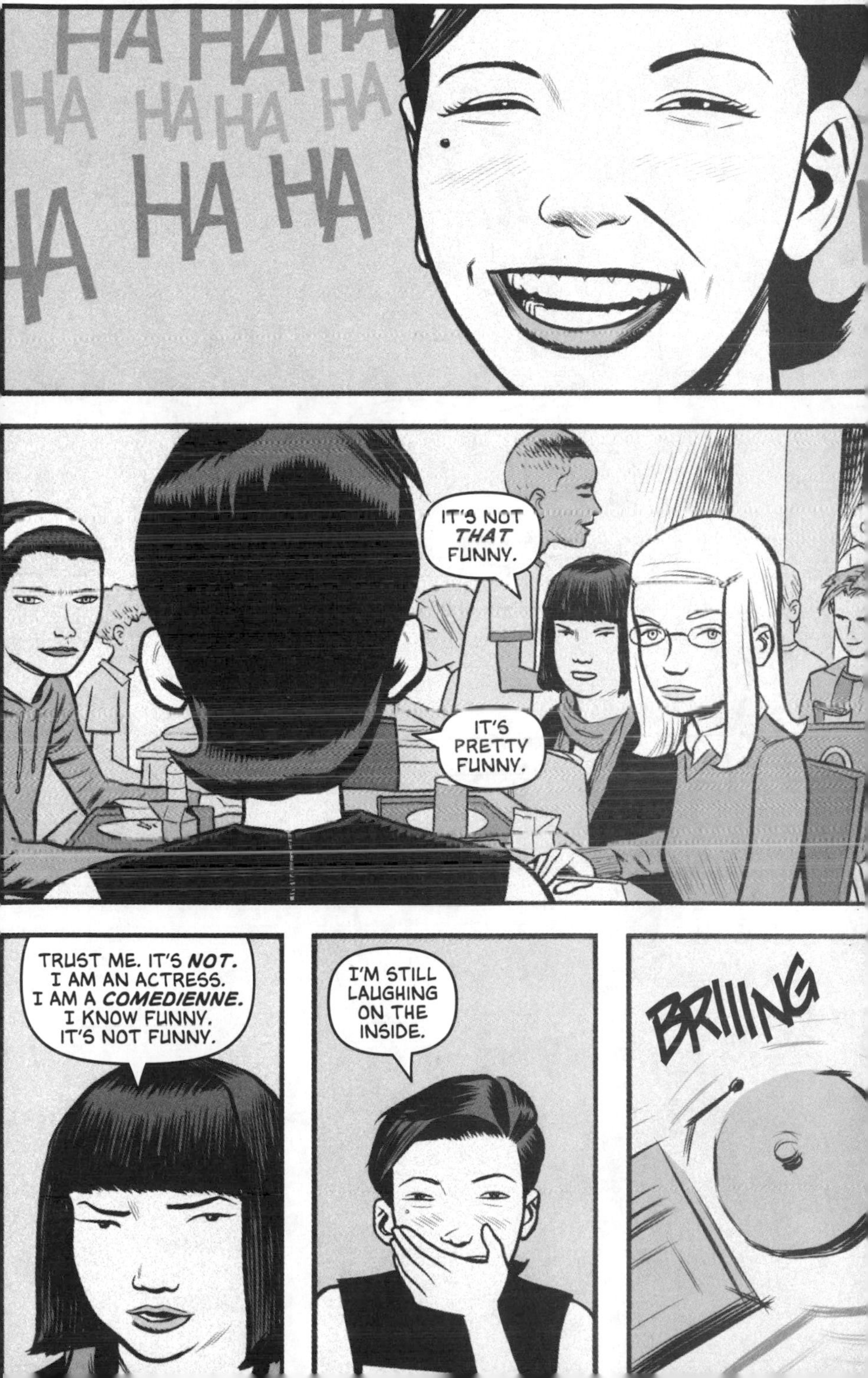
HA HA HA
HA HA HA HA
HA HA HA
IT'S NOT *THAT* FUNNY.
IT'S PRETTY FUNNY.
TRUST ME. IT'S *NOT*. I AM AN ACTRESS. I AM A *COMEDIENNE*. I KNOW FUNNY. IT'S NOT FUNNY.
I'M STILL LAUGHING ON THE INSIDE.
BRIIING

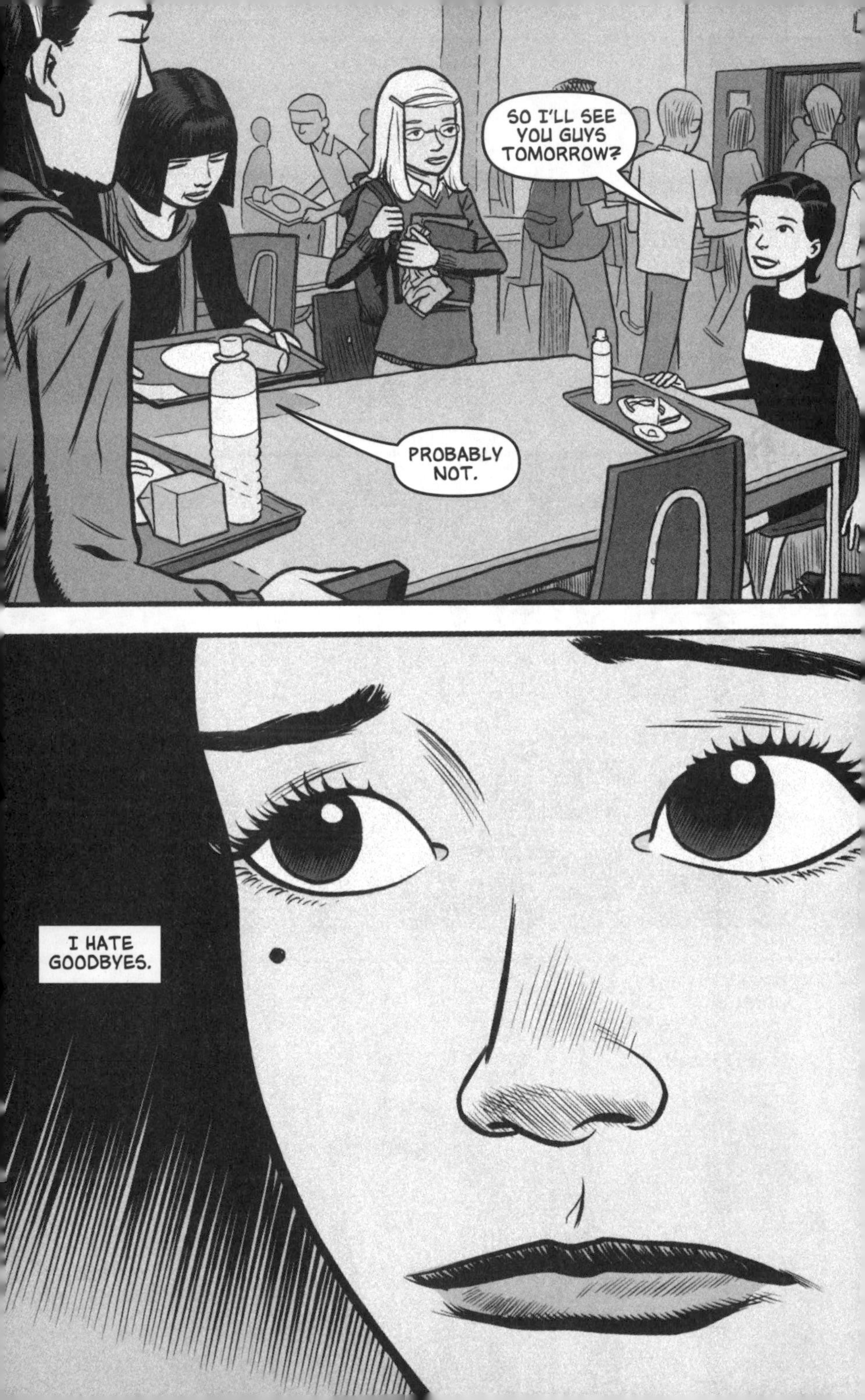
SO I'LL SEE YOU GUYS TOMORROW?
PROBABLY NOT.
I HATE GOODBYES.

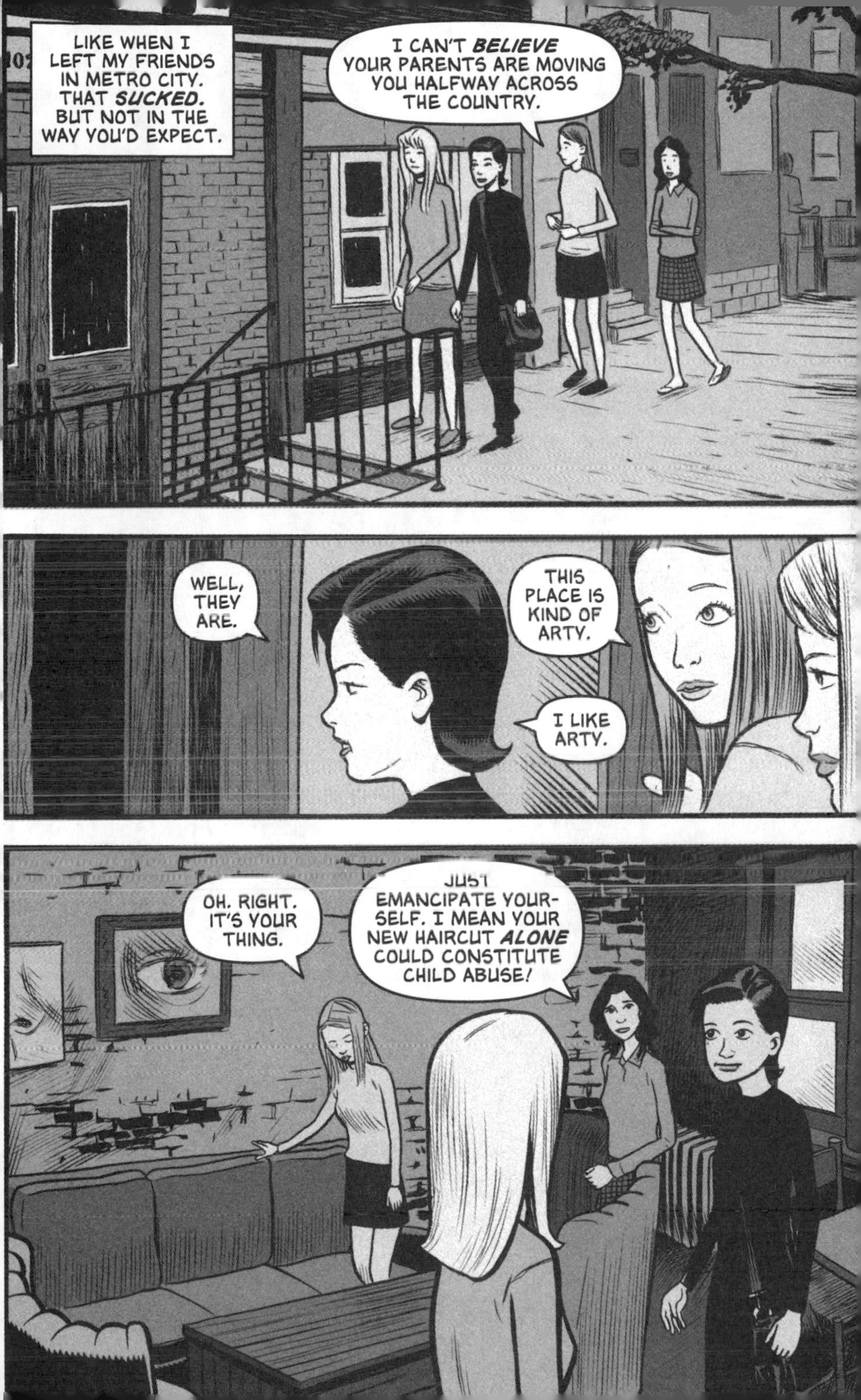
LIKE WHEN I LEFT MY FRIENDS IN METRO CITY. THAT SUCKED. BUT NOT IN THE WAY YOU'D EXPECT.
I CAN'T BELIEVE YOUR PARENTS ARE MOVING YOU HALFWAY ACROSS THE COUNTRY.
WELL, THEY ARE.
THIS PLACE IS KIND OF ARTY.
I LIKE ARTY.
OH. RIGHT. IT'S YOUR THING.
JUST EMANCIPATE YOURSELF. I MEAN YOUR NEW HAIRCUT ALONE COULD CONSTITUTE CHILD ABUSE!

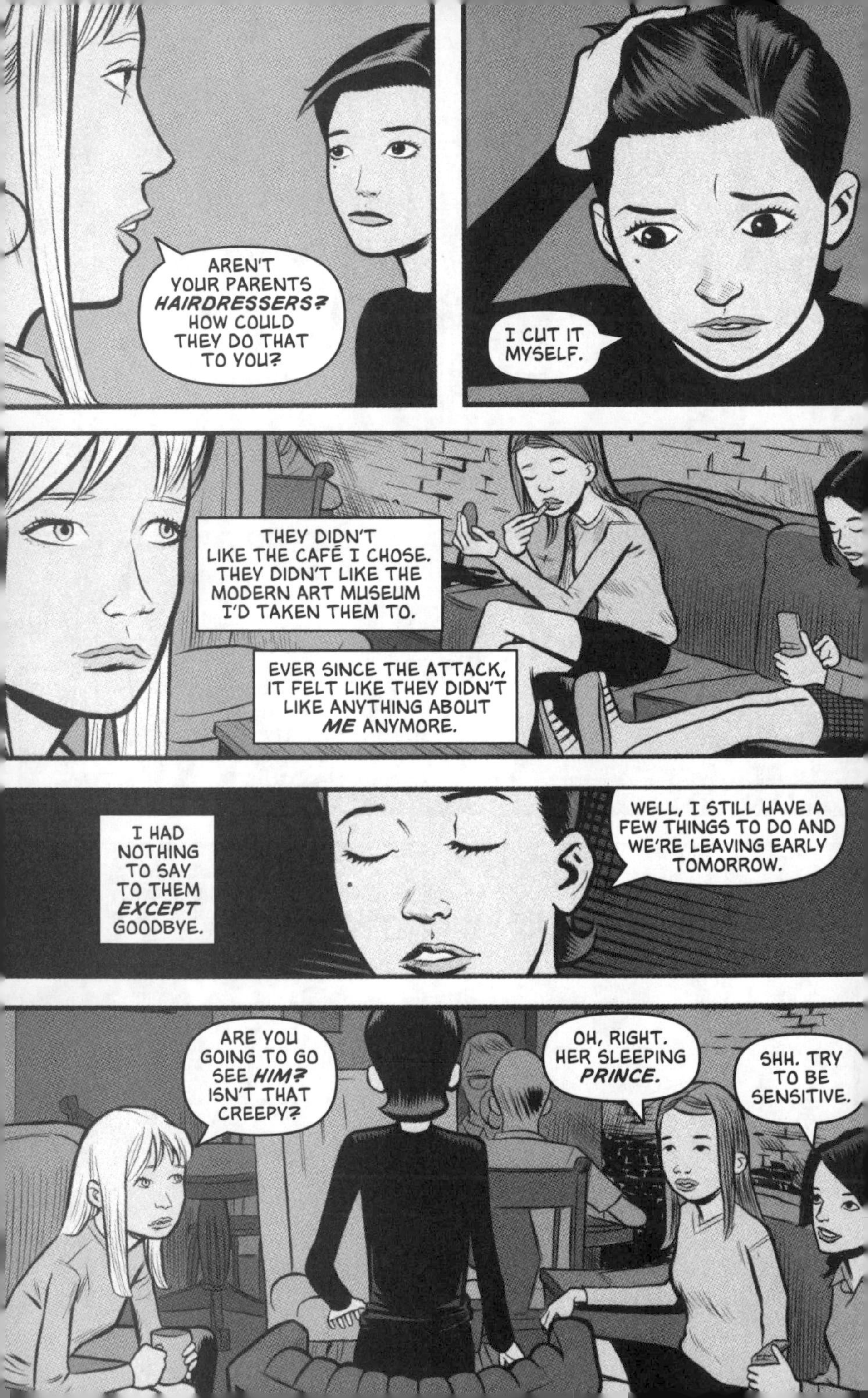
AREN'T YOUR PARENTS HAIRDRESSERS? HOW COULD THEY DO THAT TO YOU?
I CUT IT MYSELF.
THEY DIDN'T LIKE THE CAFÉ I CHOSE. THEY DIDN'T LIKE THE MODERN ART MUSEUM I'D TAKEN THEM TO.
EVER SINCE THE ATTACK, IT FELT LIKE THEY DIDN'T LIKE ANYTHING ABOUT ME ANYMORE.
I HAD NOTHING TO SAY TO THEM EXCEPT GOODBYE.
WELL, I STILL HAVE A FEW THINGS TO DO AND WE'RE LEAVING EARLY TOMORROW.
ARE YOU GOING TO GO SEE HIM? ISN'T THAT CREEPY?
OH, RIGHT. HER SLEEPING PRINCE.
SHH. TRY TO BE SENSITIVE.

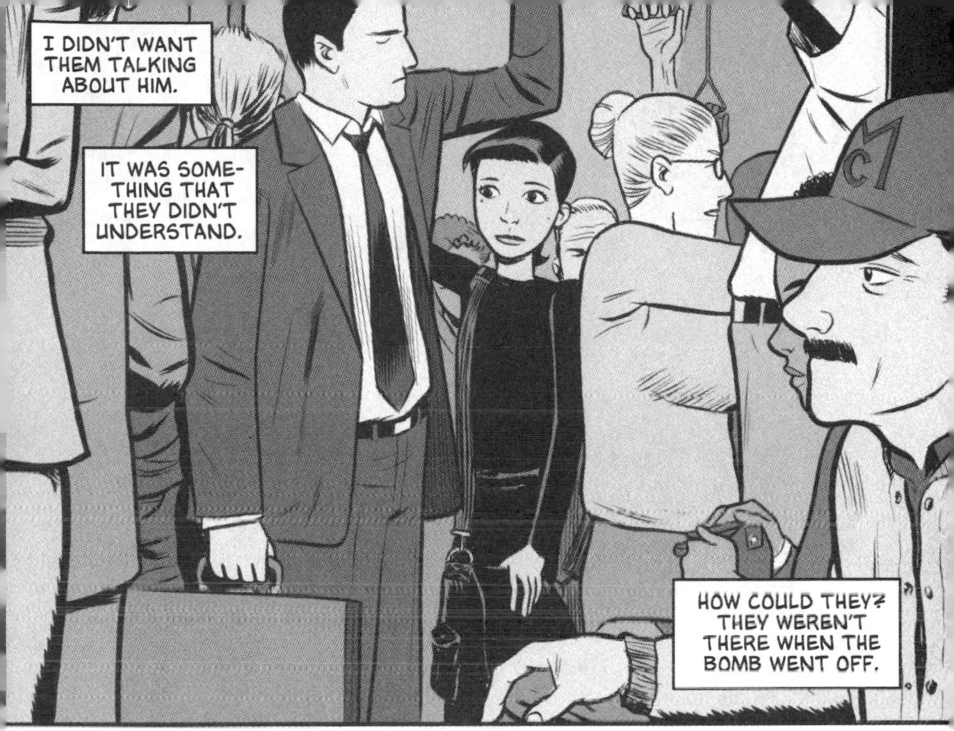
I DIDN'T WANT THEM TALKING ABOUT HIM.
IT WAS SOMETHING THAT THEY DIDN'T UNDERSTAND.
HOW COULD THEY? THEY WEREN'T THERE WHEN THE BOMB WENT OFF.

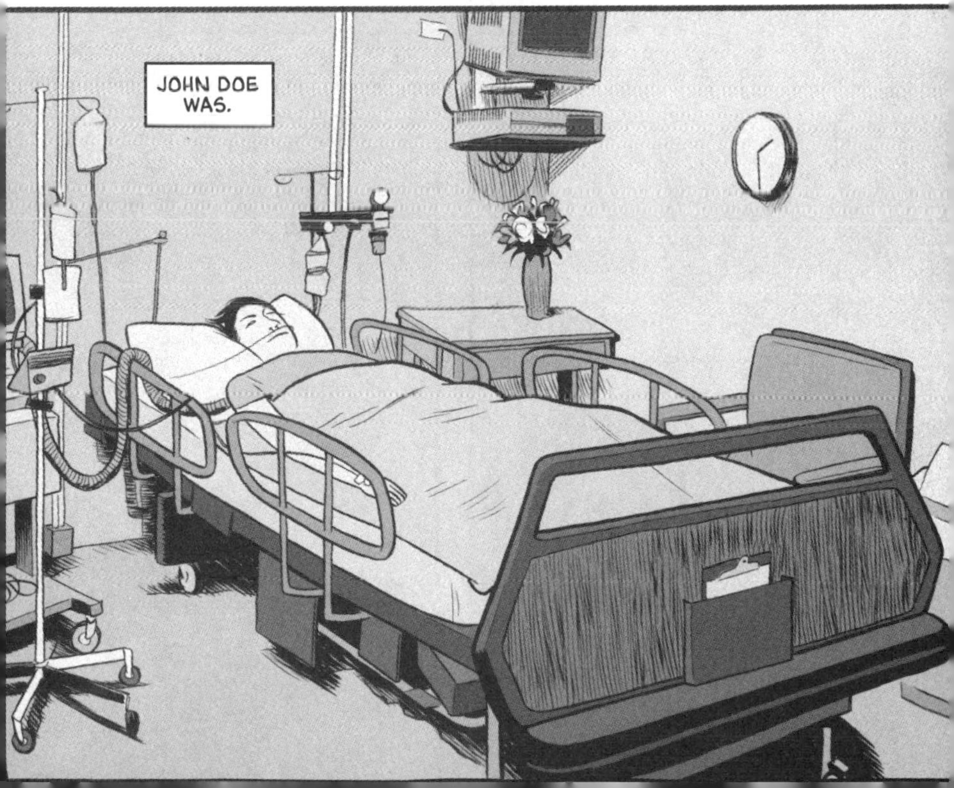
JOHN DOE WAS.

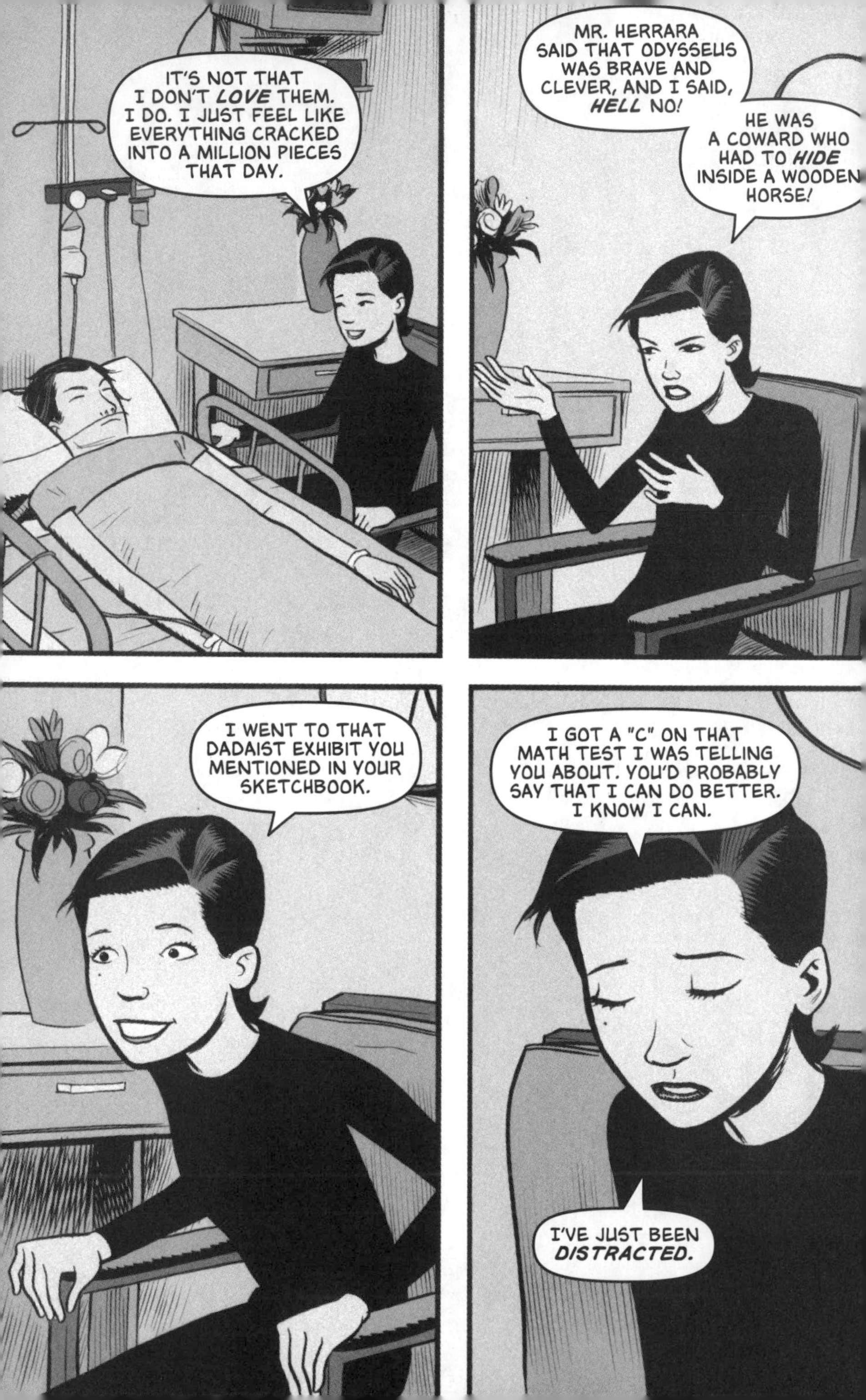
IT'S NOT THAT I DON'T LOVE THEM. I DO. I JUST FEEL LIKE EVERYTHING CRACKED INTO A MILLION PIECES THAT DAY.
MR. HERRARA SAID THAT ODYSSEUS WAS BRAVE AND CLEVER, AND I SAID, HELL NO!
HE WAS A COWARD WHO HAD TO HIDE INSIDE A WOODEN HORSE!
I WENT TO THAT DADAIST EXHIBIT YOU MENTIONED IN YOUR SKETCHBOOK.
I GOT A "C" ON THAT MATH TEST I WAS TELLING YOU ABOUT. YOU'D PROBABLY SAY THAT I CAN DO BETTER. I KNOW I CAN.
I'VE JUST BEEN DISTRACTED.

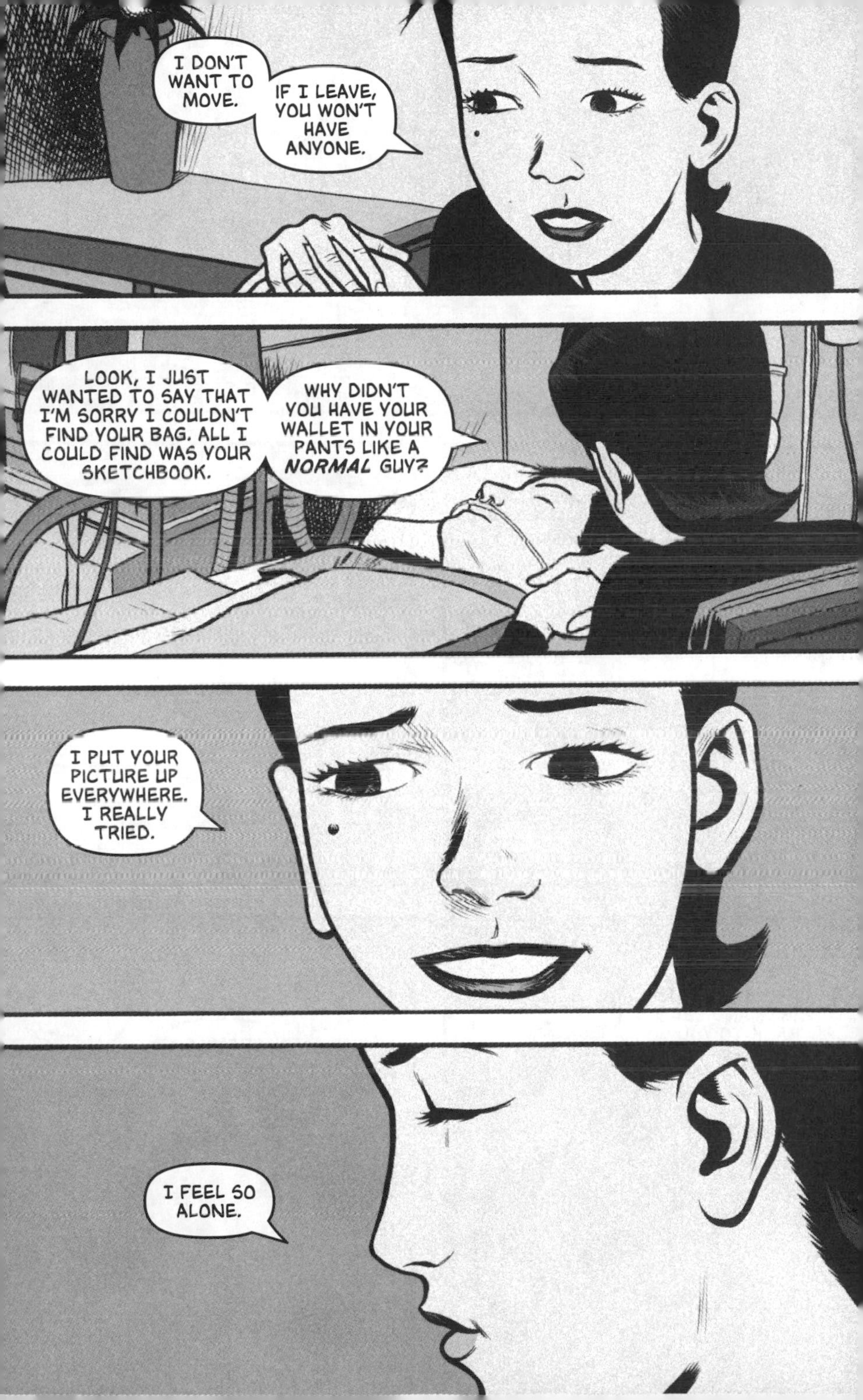
I DON'T WANT TO MOVE.
IF I LEAVE, YOU WON'T HAVE ANYONE.
LOOK, I JUST WANTED TO SAY THAT I'M SORRY I COULDN'T FIND YOUR BAG. ALL I COULD FIND WAS YOUR SKETCHBOOK.
WHY DIDN'T YOU HAVE YOUR WALLET IN YOUR PANTS LIKE A NORMAL GUY?
I PUT YOUR PICTURE UP EVERYWHERE. I REALLY TRIED.
I FEEL SO ALONE.

VISITING HOURS ARE OVER, JANE.

I'LL JUST BE A FEW MINUTES.

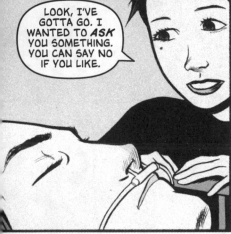

LOOK, I'VE GOTTA GO. I WANTED TO *ASK* YOU SOMETHING. YOU CAN SAY NO IF YOU LIKE.

CAN I TAKE THE SKETCHBOOK WITH ME TO KENT WATERS?

I'LL KEEP FILLING UP THE REST OF THE PAGES AND SEND IT BACK TO YOU SO YOU CAN SEE MY PROGRESS.

PROMISE.

ART SAVES

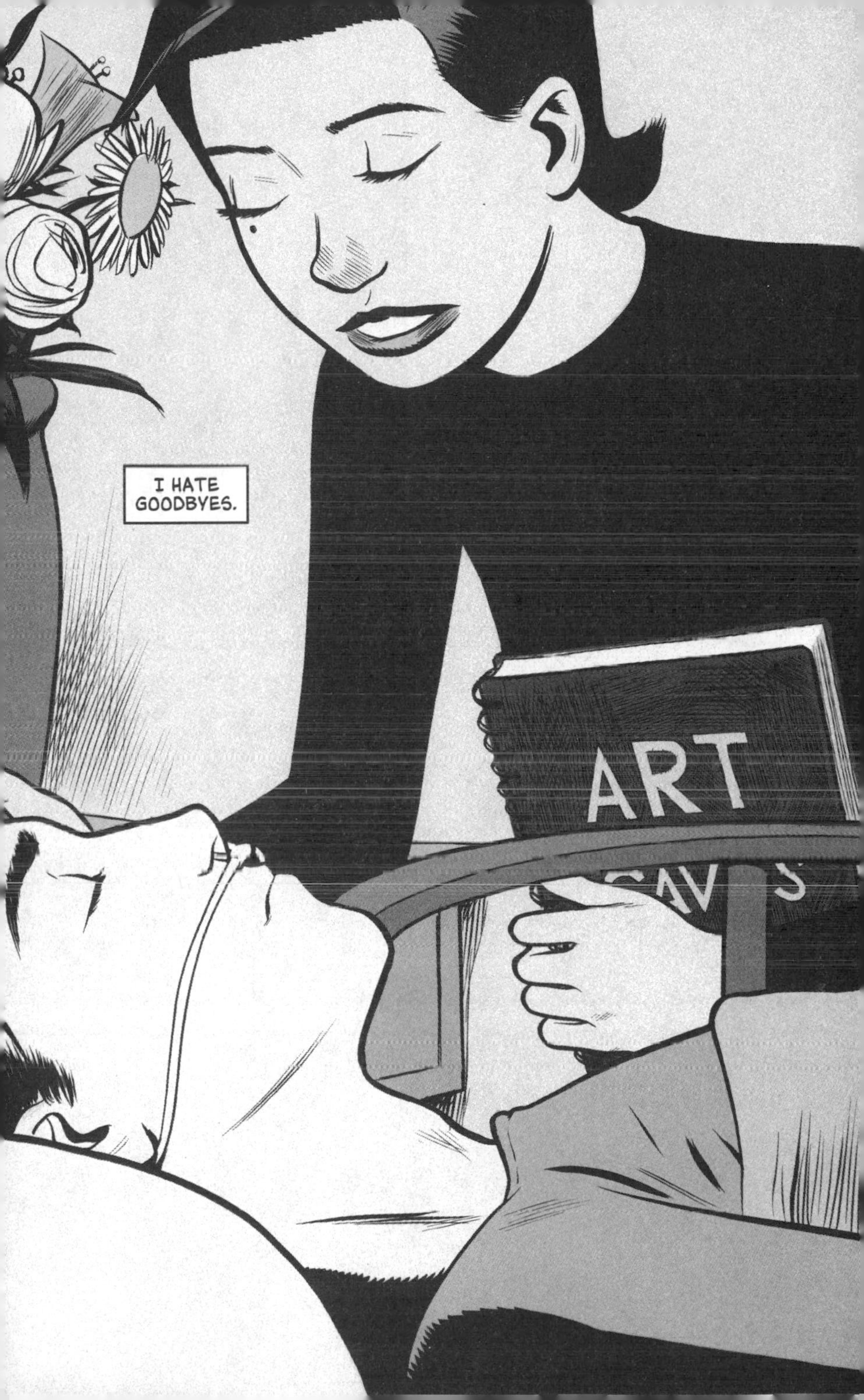
I HATE GOODBYES.
ART

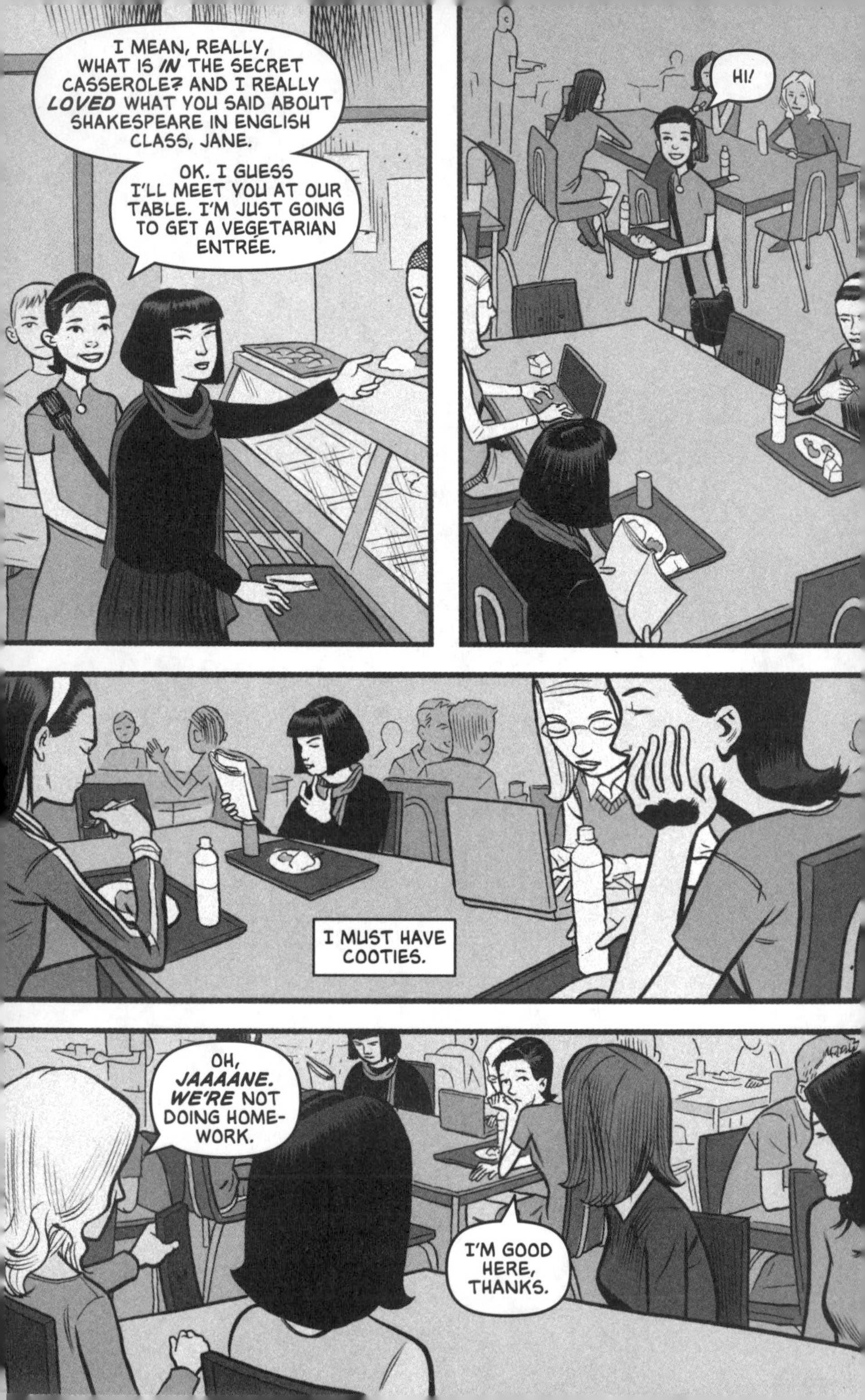

I MEAN, REALLY, WHAT IS *IN* THE SECRET CASSEROLE? AND I REALLY *LOVED* WHAT YOU SAID ABOUT SHAKESPEARE IN ENGLISH CLASS, JANE.
OK. I GUESS I'LL MEET YOU AT OUR TABLE. I'M JUST GOING TO GET A VEGETARIAN ENTRÉE.
HI!
I MUST HAVE COOTIES.
OH, *JAAAANE. WE'RE* NOT DOING HOME-WORK.
I'M GOOD HERE, THANKS.

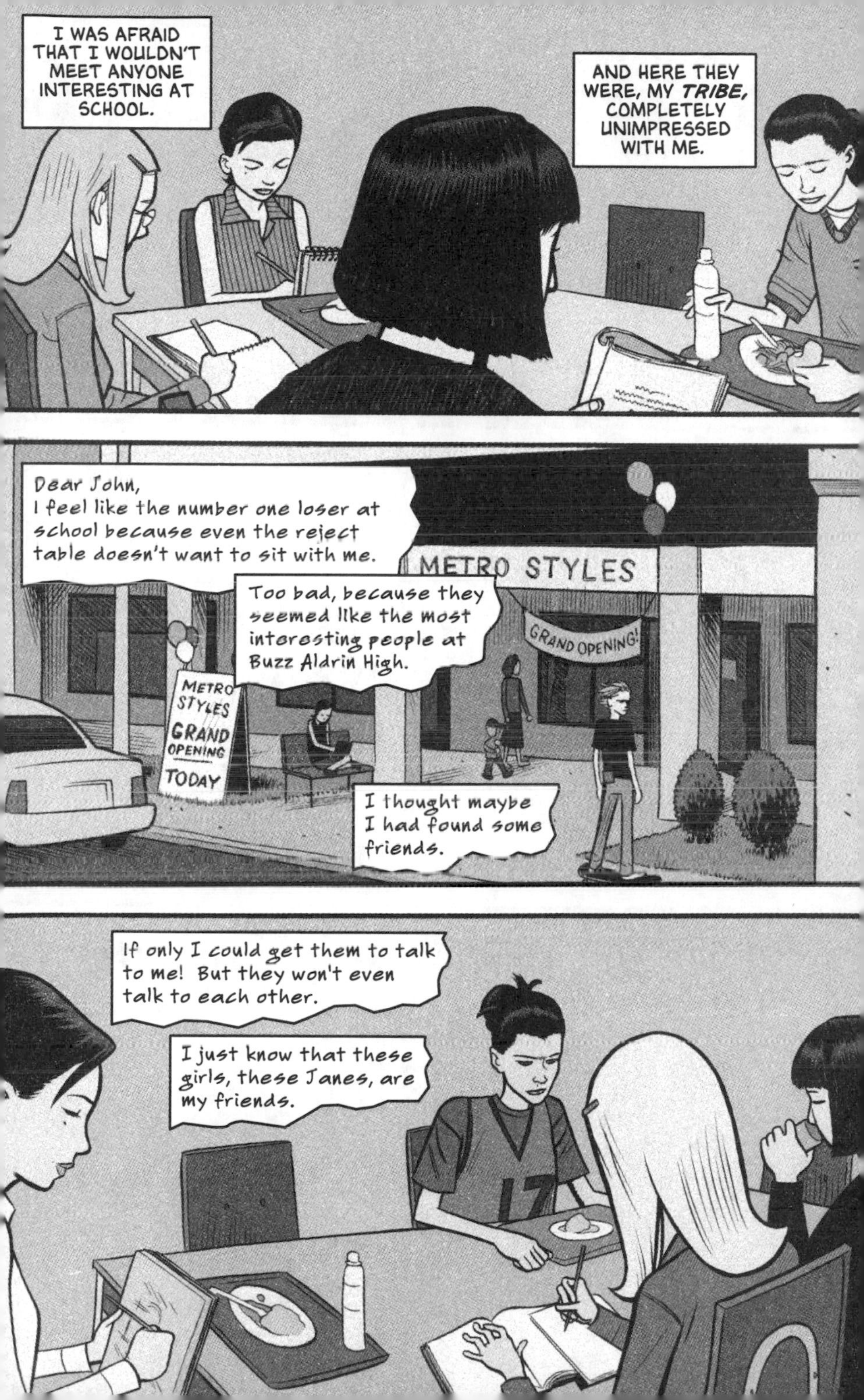
I WAS AFRAID THAT I WOULDN'T MEET ANYONE INTERESTING AT SCHOOL.
AND HERE THEY WERE, MY *TRIBE,* COMPLETELY UNIMPRESSED WITH ME.
Dear John,
I feel like the number one loser at school because even the reject table doesn't want to sit with me.
METRO STYLES
Too bad, because they seemed like the most interesting people at Buzz Aldrin High.
GRAND OPENING!
METRO STYLES GRAND OPENING TODAY
I thought maybe I had found some friends.
If only I could get them to talk to me! But they won't even talk to each other.
I just know that these girls, these Janes, are my friends.
17

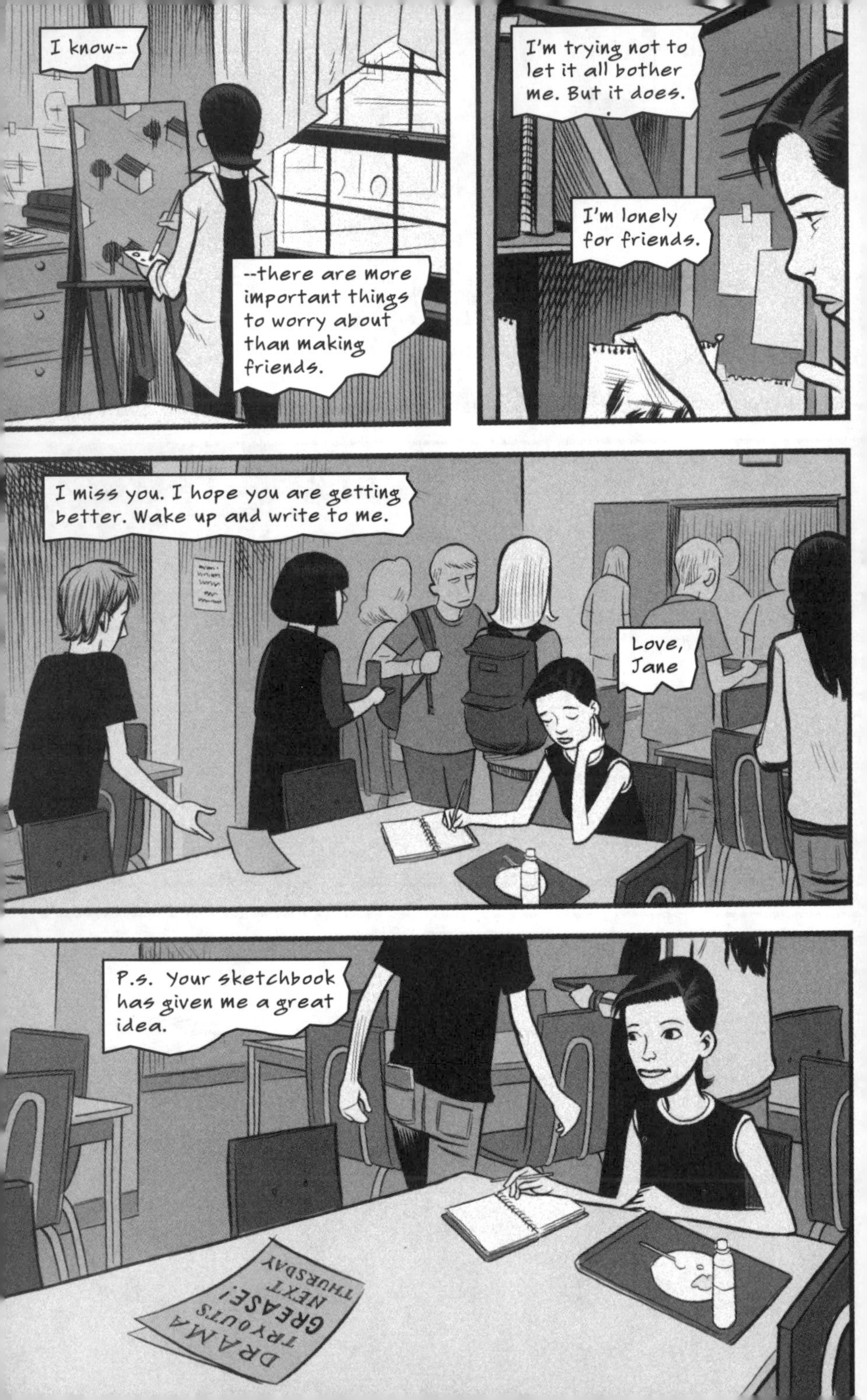
I know--
--there are more important things to worry about than making friends.
I'm trying not to let it all bother me. But it does.
I'm lonely for friends.
I miss you. I hope you are getting better. Wake up and write to me.
Love, Jane
P.S. Your sketchbook has given me a great idea.
DRAMA
TRYOUTS
GREASE!
NEXT
THURSDAY

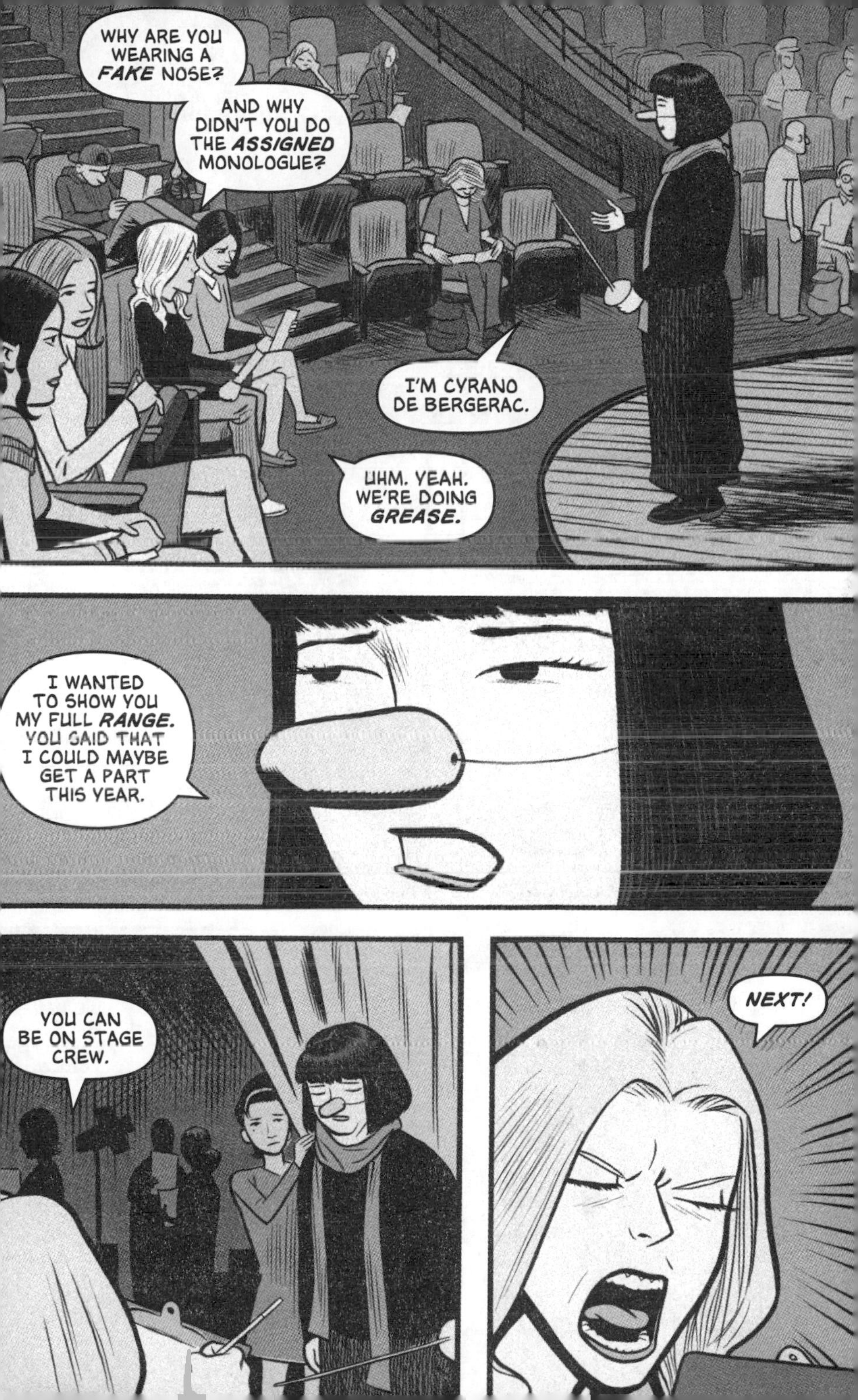
WHY ARE YOU WEARING A FAKE NOSE?
AND WHY DIDN'T YOU DO THE ASSIGNED MONOLOGUE?
I'M CYRANO DE BERGERAC.
UHM. YEAH. WE'RE DOING GREASE.
I WANTED TO SHOW YOU MY FULL RANGE. YOU SAID THAT I COULD MAYBE GET A PART THIS YEAR.
YOU CAN BE ON STAGE CREW.
NEXT!

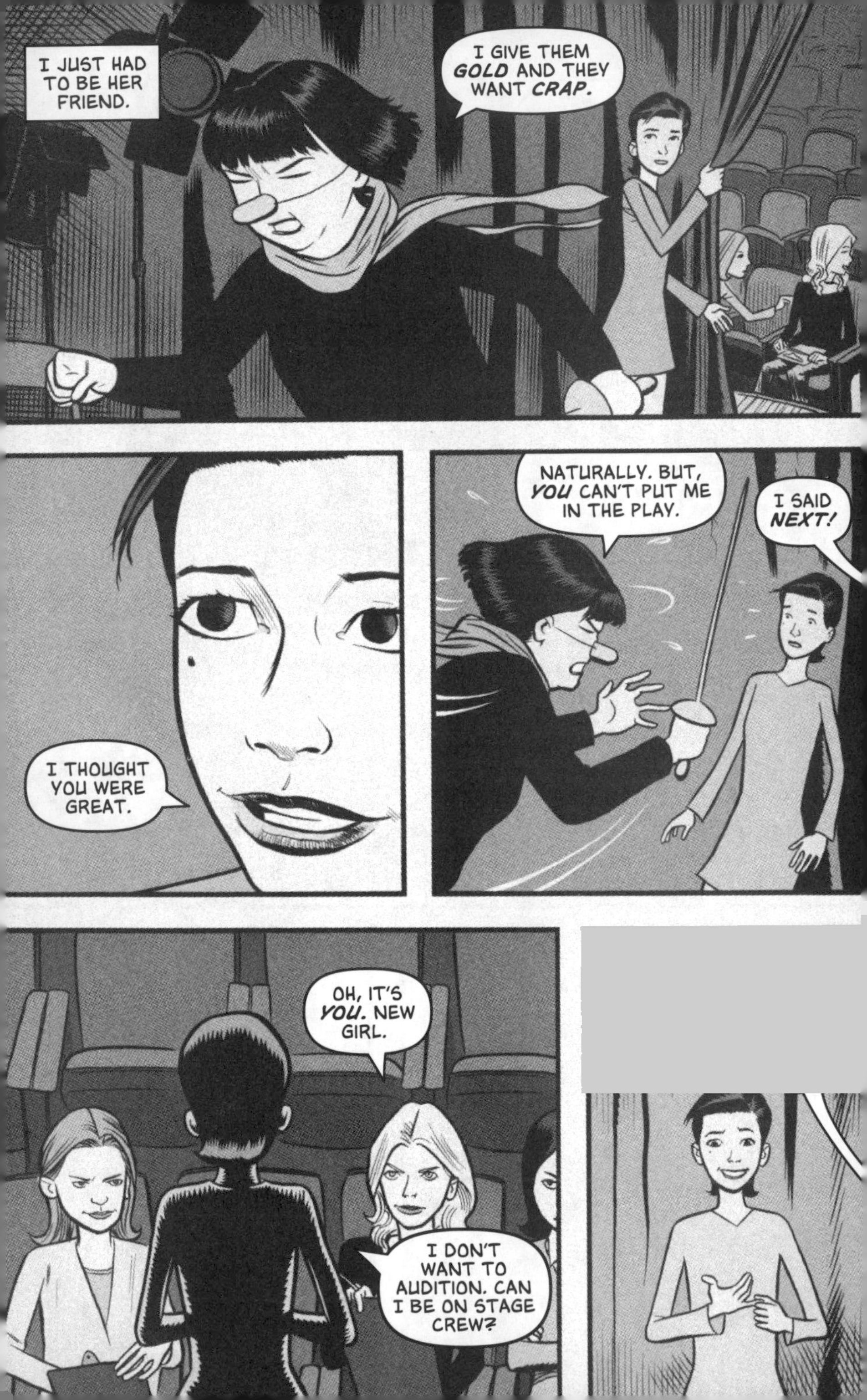
I JUST HAD TO BE HER FRIEND.
I GIVE THEM GOLD AND THEY WANT CRAP.
I THOUGHT YOU WERE GREAT.
NATURALLY. BUT, YOU CAN'T PUT ME IN THE PLAY.
I SAID NEXT!
OH, IT'S YOU. NEW GIRL.
I DON'T WANT TO AUDITION. CAN I BE ON STAGE CREW?

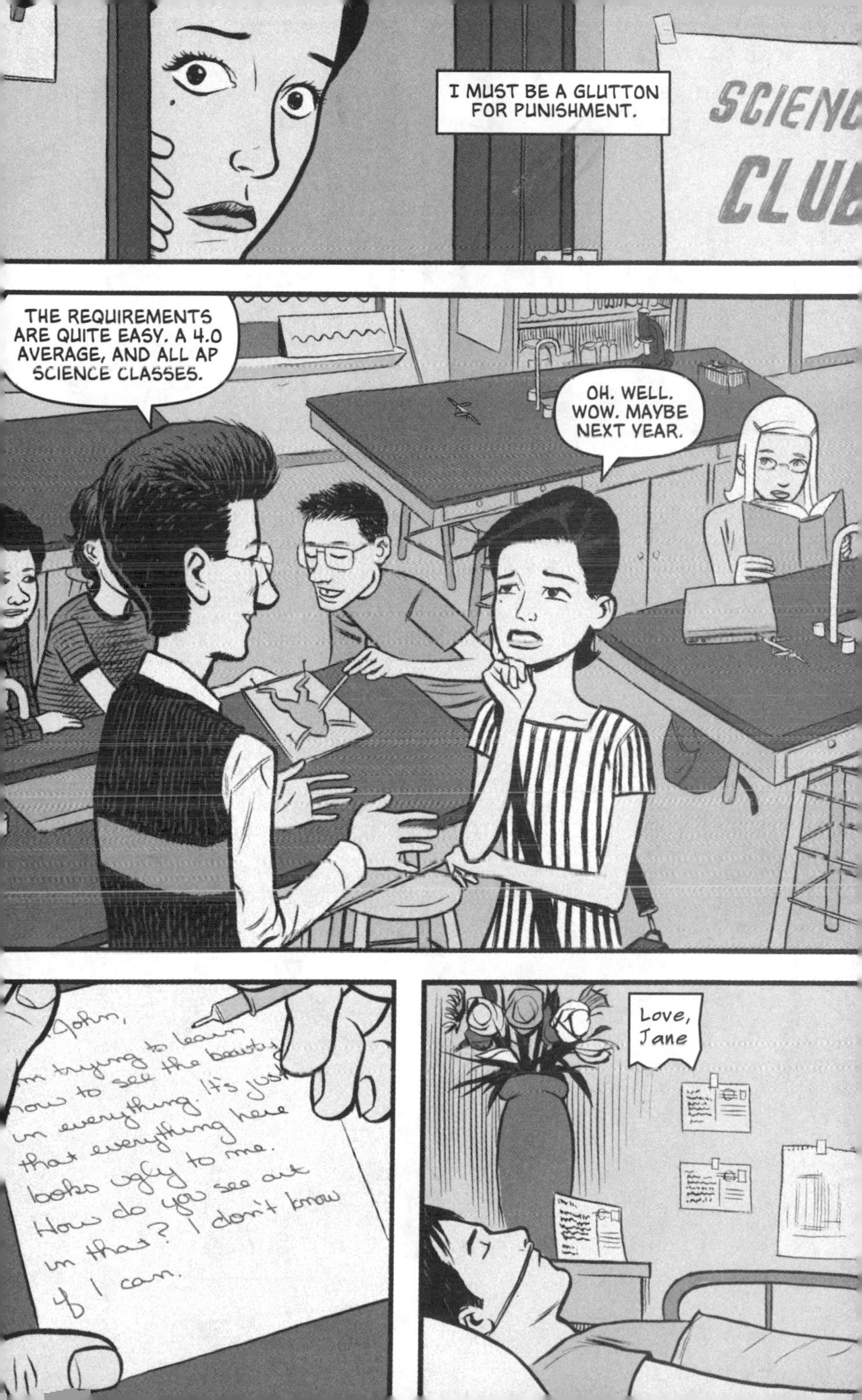
I MUST BE A GLUTTON FOR PUNISHMENT.
SCIENC
CLUB
THE REQUIREMENTS ARE QUITE EASY. A 4.0 AVERAGE, AND ALL AP SCIENCE CLASSES.
OH. WELL. WOW. MAYBE NEXT YEAR.
John,
m trying to learn
ow to see the beaut
in everything. It's just
that everything here
looks ugly to me.
How do you see art
in that? I don't know
if I can.
Love, Jane

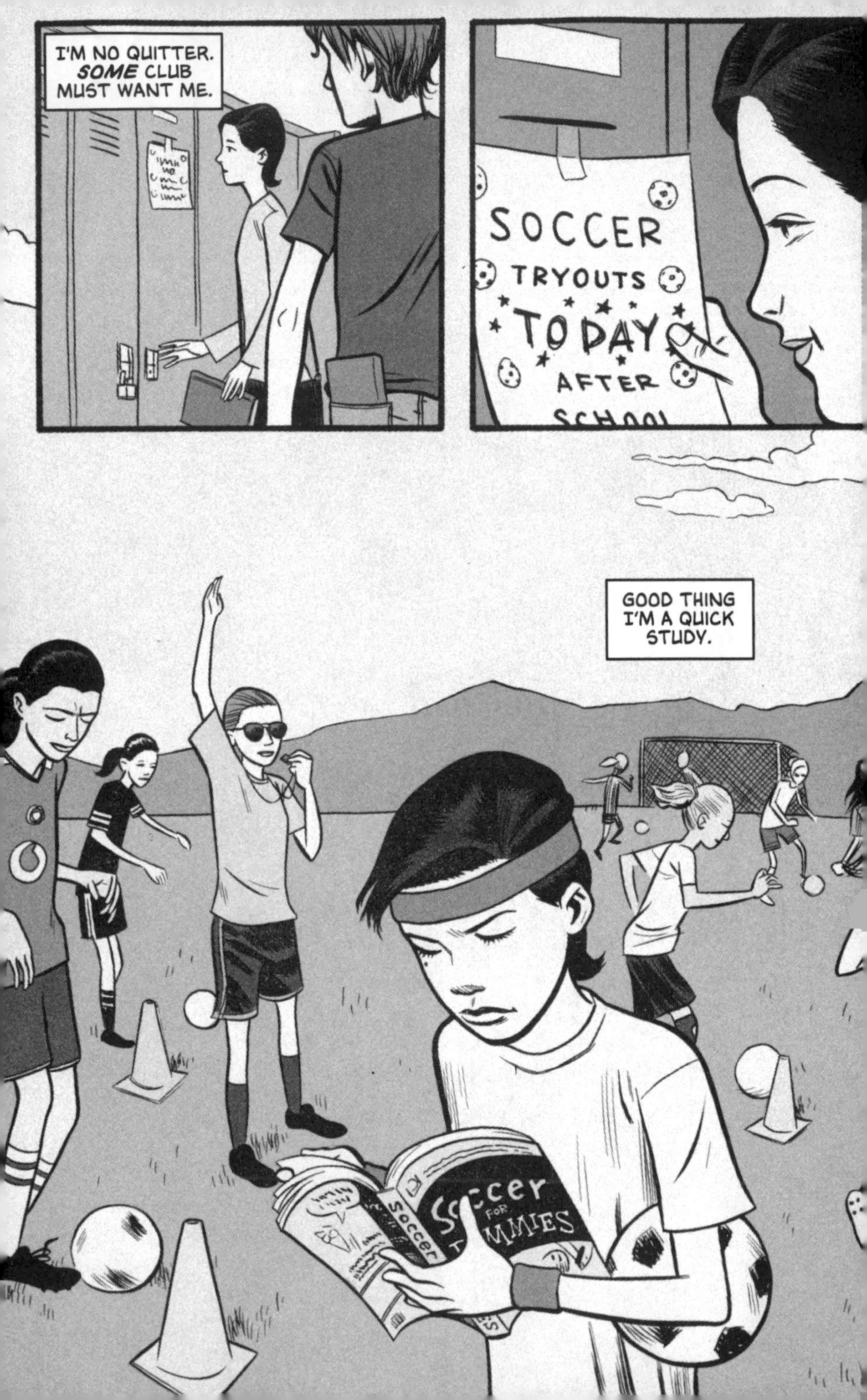
I'M NO QUITTER. SOME CLUB MUST WANT ME.
SOCCER TRYOUTS TODAY AFTER SCHOOL
GOOD THING I'M A QUICK STUDY.
Soccer FOR DUMMIES

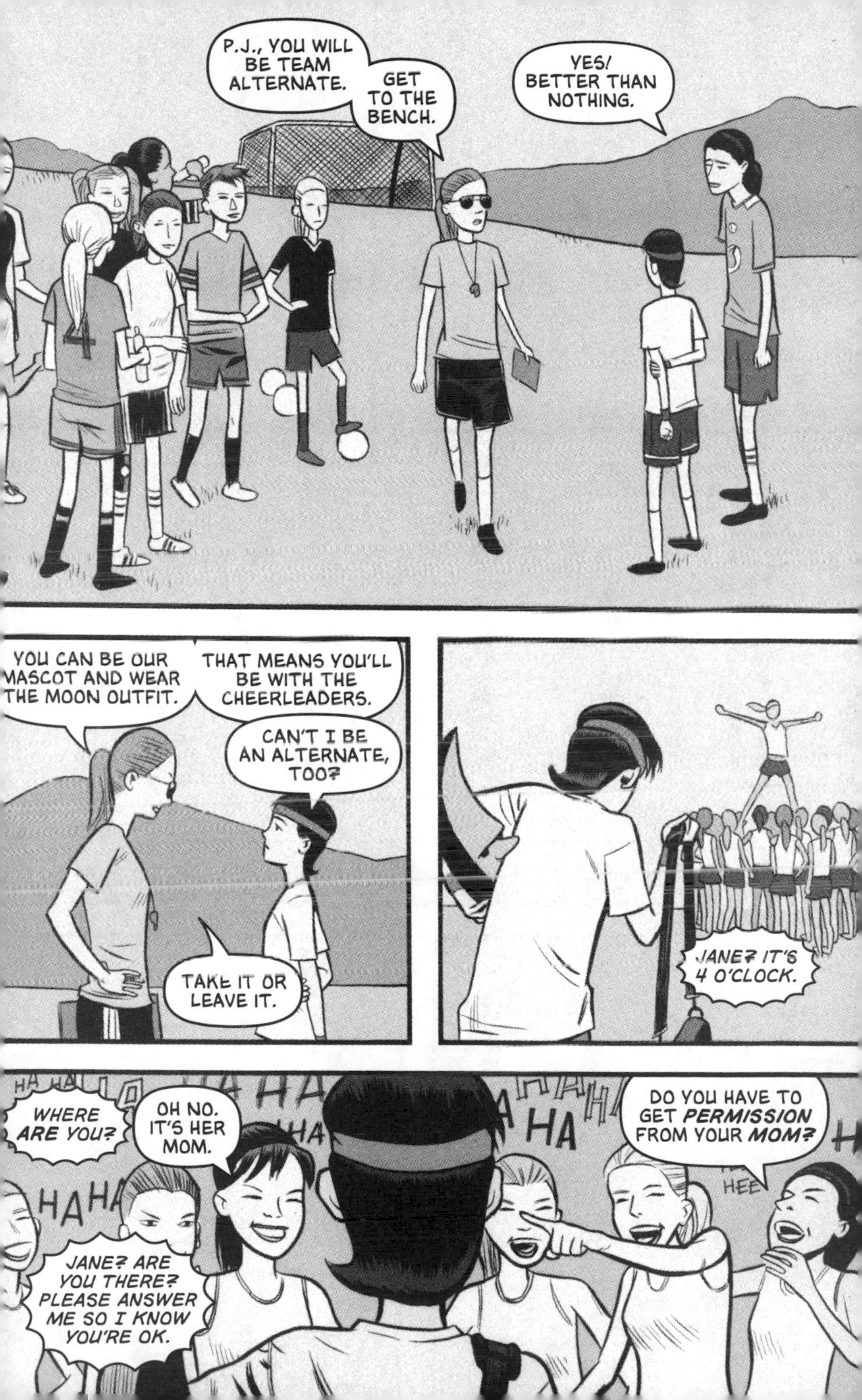
P.J., YOU WILL BE TEAM ALTERNATE.
GET TO THE BENCH.
YES! BETTER THAN NOTHING.
YOU CAN BE OUR MASCOT AND WEAR THE MOON OUTFIT.
THAT MEANS YOU'LL BE WITH THE CHEERLEADERS.
CAN'T I BE AN ALTERNATE, TOO?
TAKE IT OR LEAVE IT.
JANE? IT'S 4 O'CLOCK.
WHERE ARE YOU?
OH NO. IT'S HER MOM.
DO YOU HAVE TO GET PERMISSION FROM YOUR MOM?
HA HA HA HA HA HA
HEE
JANE? ARE YOU THERE? PLEASE ANSWER ME SO I KNOW YOU'RE OK.

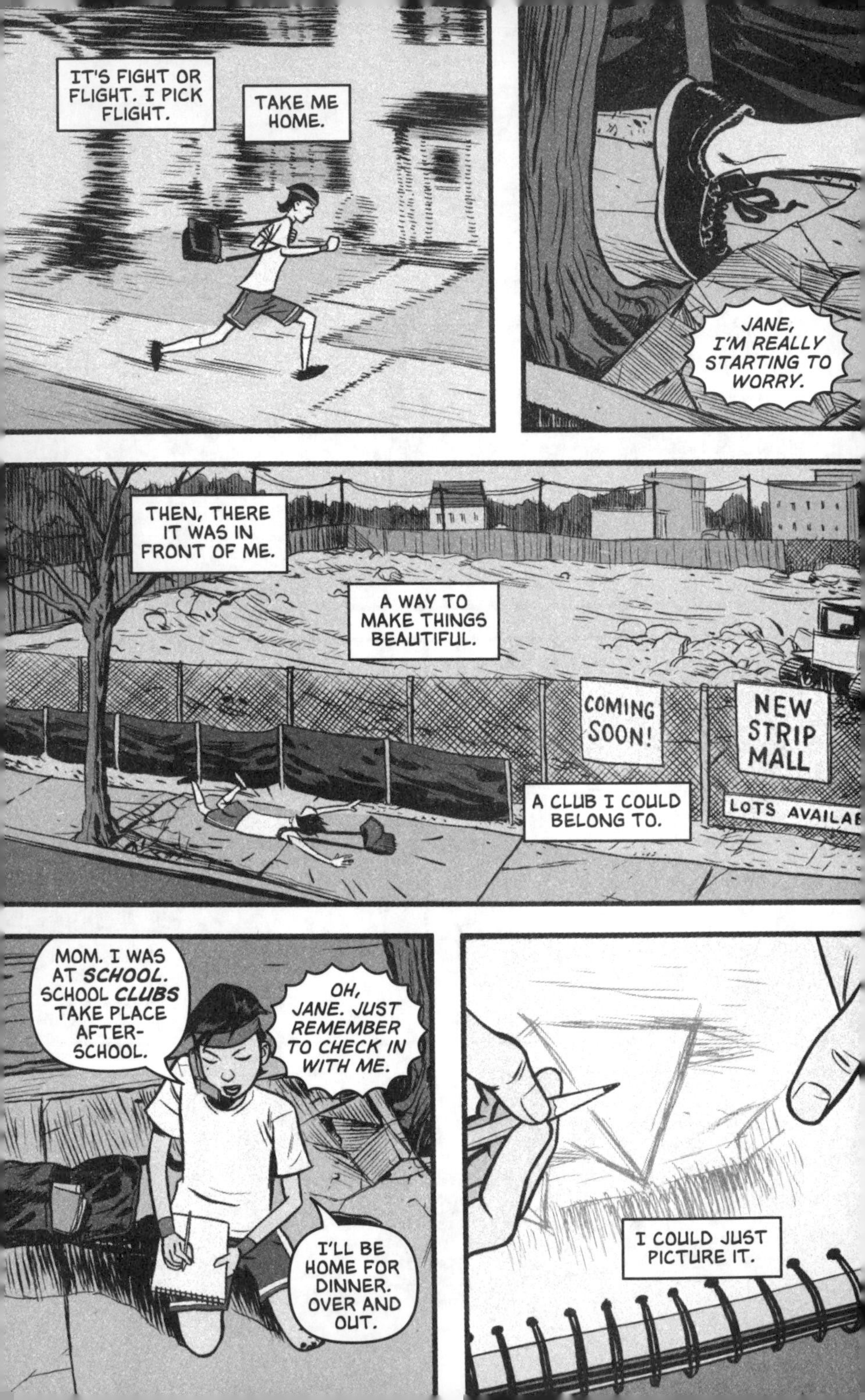
IT'S FIGHT OR FLIGHT. I PICK FLIGHT.
TAKE ME HOME.
JANE, I'M REALLY STARTING TO WORRY.
THEN, THERE IT WAS IN FRONT OF ME.
A WAY TO MAKE THINGS BEAUTIFUL.
COMING SOON!
NEW STRIP MALL
A CLUB I COULD BELONG TO.
LOTS AVAILA
MOM. I WAS AT *SCHOOL*. SCHOOL *CLUBS* TAKE PLACE AFTER-SCHOOL.
OH, JANE. JUST *REMEMBER* TO CHECK IN WITH ME.
I'LL BE HOME FOR DINNER. OVER AND OUT.
I COULD JUST PICTURE IT.

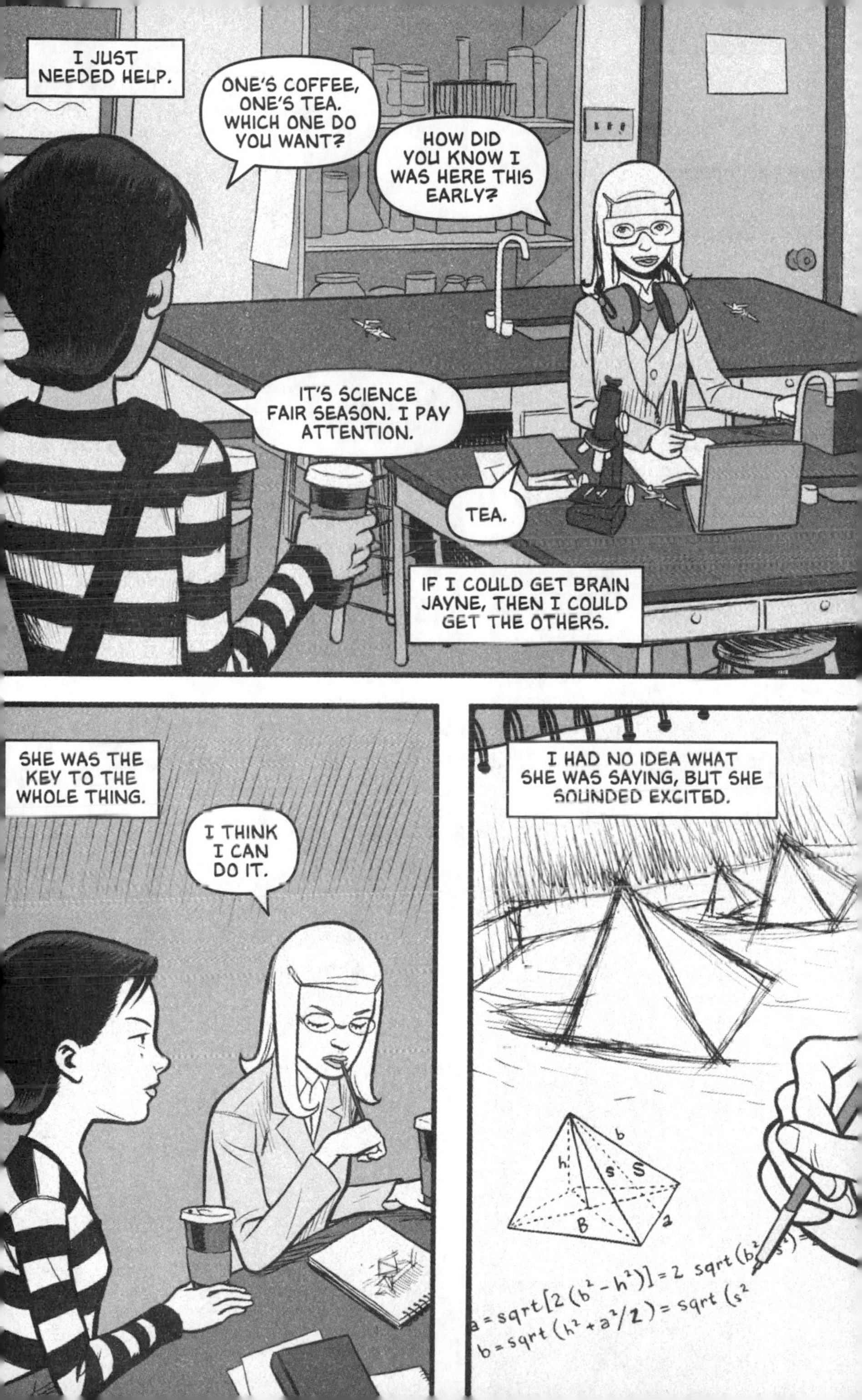
I JUST NEEDED HELP.
ONE'S COFFEE, ONE'S TEA. WHICH ONE DO YOU WANT?
HOW DID YOU KNOW I WAS HERE THIS EARLY?
IT'S SCIENCE FAIR SEASON. I PAY ATTENTION.
TEA.
IF I COULD GET BRAIN JAYNE, THEN I COULD GET THE OTHERS.
SHE WAS THE KEY TO THE WHOLE THING.
I THINK I CAN DO IT.
I HAD NO IDEA WHAT SHE WAS SAYING, BUT SHE SOUNDED EXCITED.
b
h
s
S
B
a
a = sqrt[2(b² - h²)] = 2 sqrt(b²
b = sqrt(h² + a²/2) = sqrt(s²

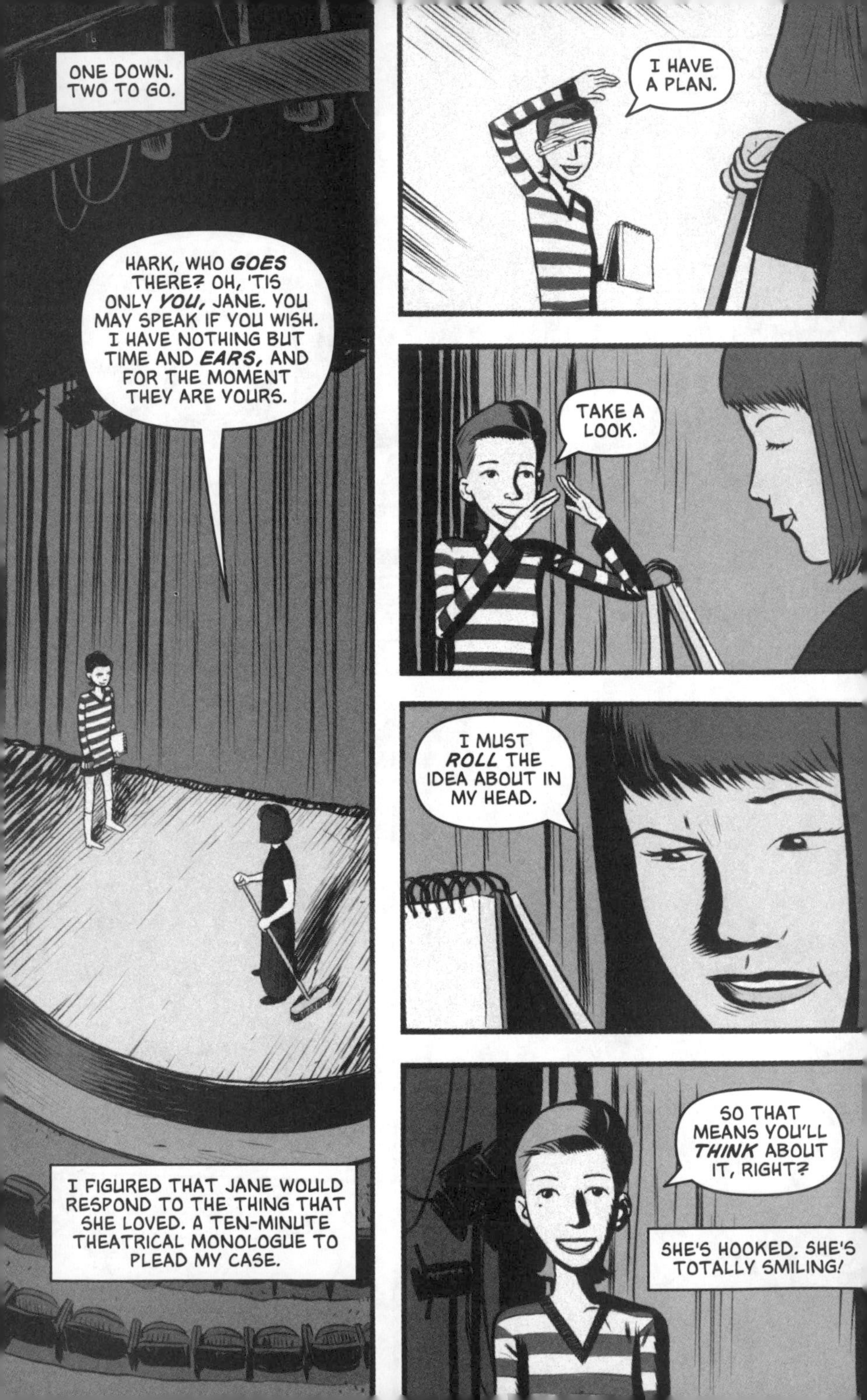
ONE DOWN. TWO TO GO.
HARK, WHO GOES THERE? OH, 'TIS ONLY YOU, JANE. YOU MAY SPEAK IF YOU WISH. I HAVE NOTHING BUT TIME AND EARS, AND FOR THE MOMENT THEY ARE YOURS.
I FIGURED THAT JANE WOULD RESPOND TO THE THING THAT SHE LOVED. A TEN-MINUTE THEATRICAL MONOLOGUE TO PLEAD MY CASE.
I HAVE A PLAN.
TAKE A LOOK.
I MUST ROLL THE IDEA ABOUT IN MY HEAD.
SO THAT MEANS YOU'LL THINK ABOUT IT, RIGHT?
SHE'S HOOKED. SHE'S TOTALLY SMILING!

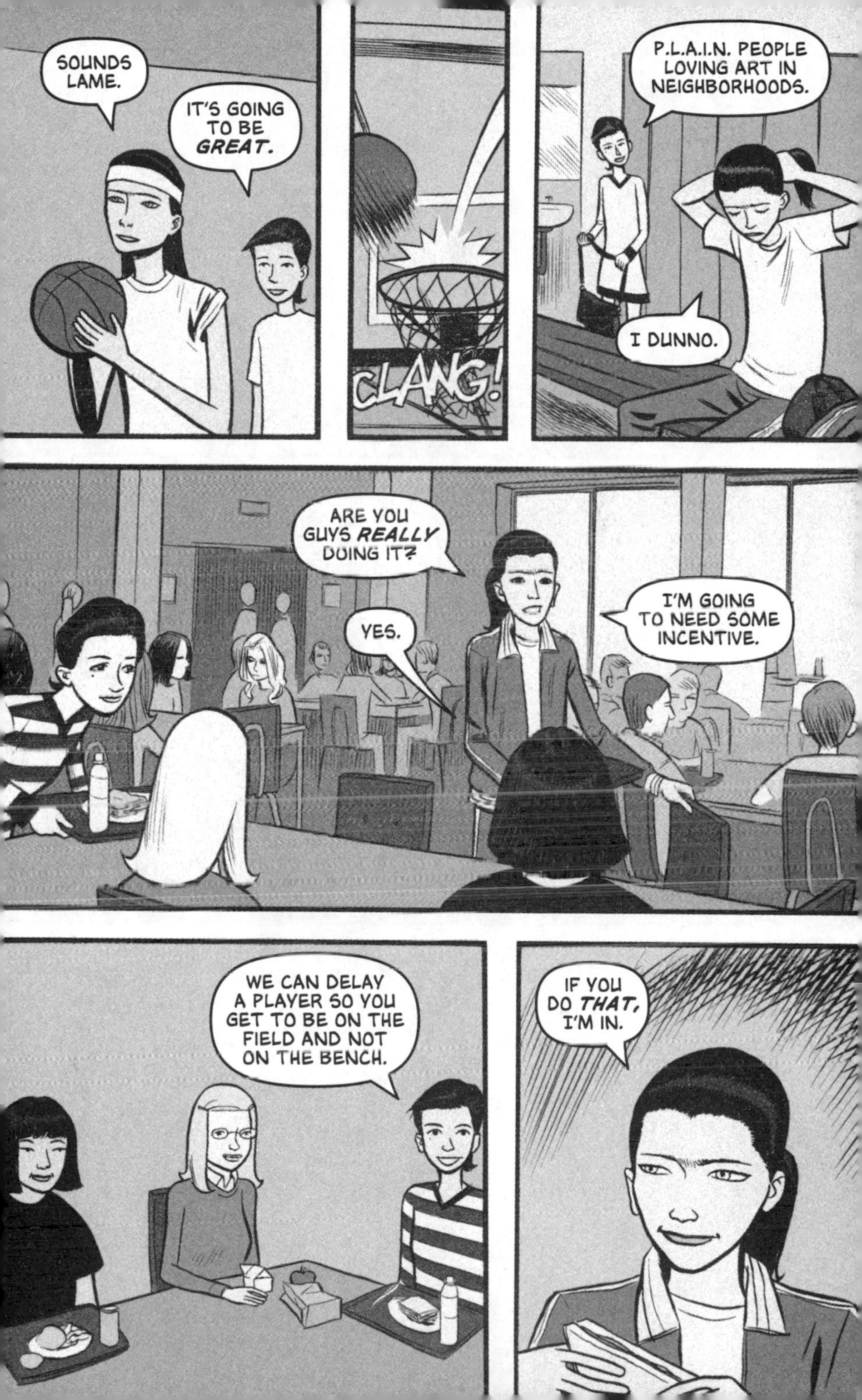
SOUNDS LAME.
IT'S GOING TO BE *GREAT*.
CLANG!
P.L.A.I.N. PEOPLE LOVING ART IN NEIGHBORHOODS.
I DUNNO.
ARE YOU GUYS *REALLY* DOING IT?
YES.
I'M GOING TO NEED SOME INCENTIVE.
WE CAN DELAY A PLAYER SO YOU GET TO BE ON THE FIELD AND NOT ON THE BENCH.
IF YOU DO *THAT*, I'M IN.

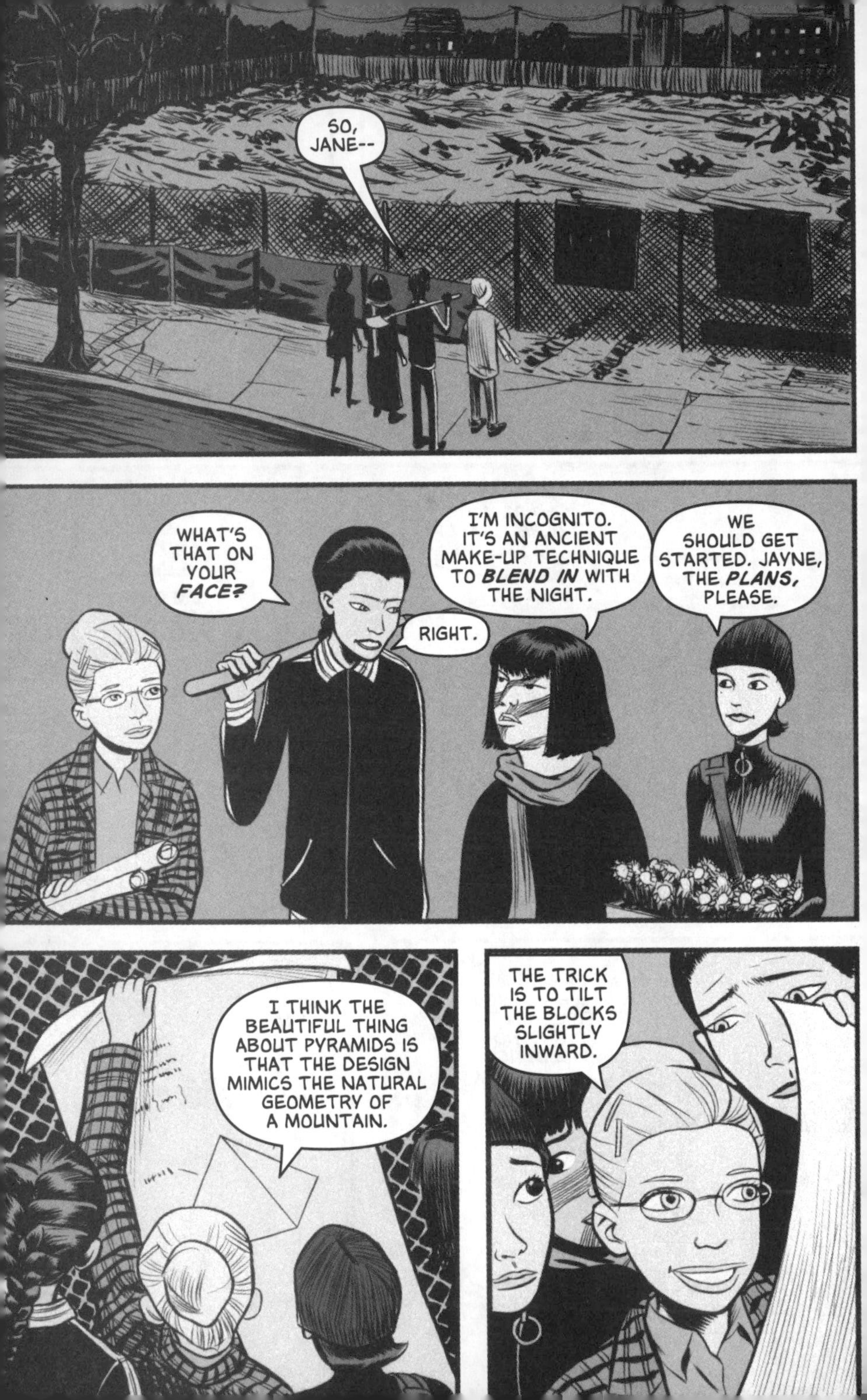
SO, JANE--
WHAT'S THAT ON YOUR FACE?
RIGHT.
I'M INCOGNITO. IT'S AN ANCIENT MAKE-UP TECHNIQUE TO BLEND IN WITH THE NIGHT.
WE SHOULD GET STARTED. JAYNE, THE PLANS, PLEASE.
I THINK THE BEAUTIFUL THING ABOUT PYRAMIDS IS THAT THE DESIGN MIMICS THE NATURAL GEOMETRY OF A MOUNTAIN.
THE TRICK IS TO TILT THE BLOCKS SLIGHTLY INWARD.

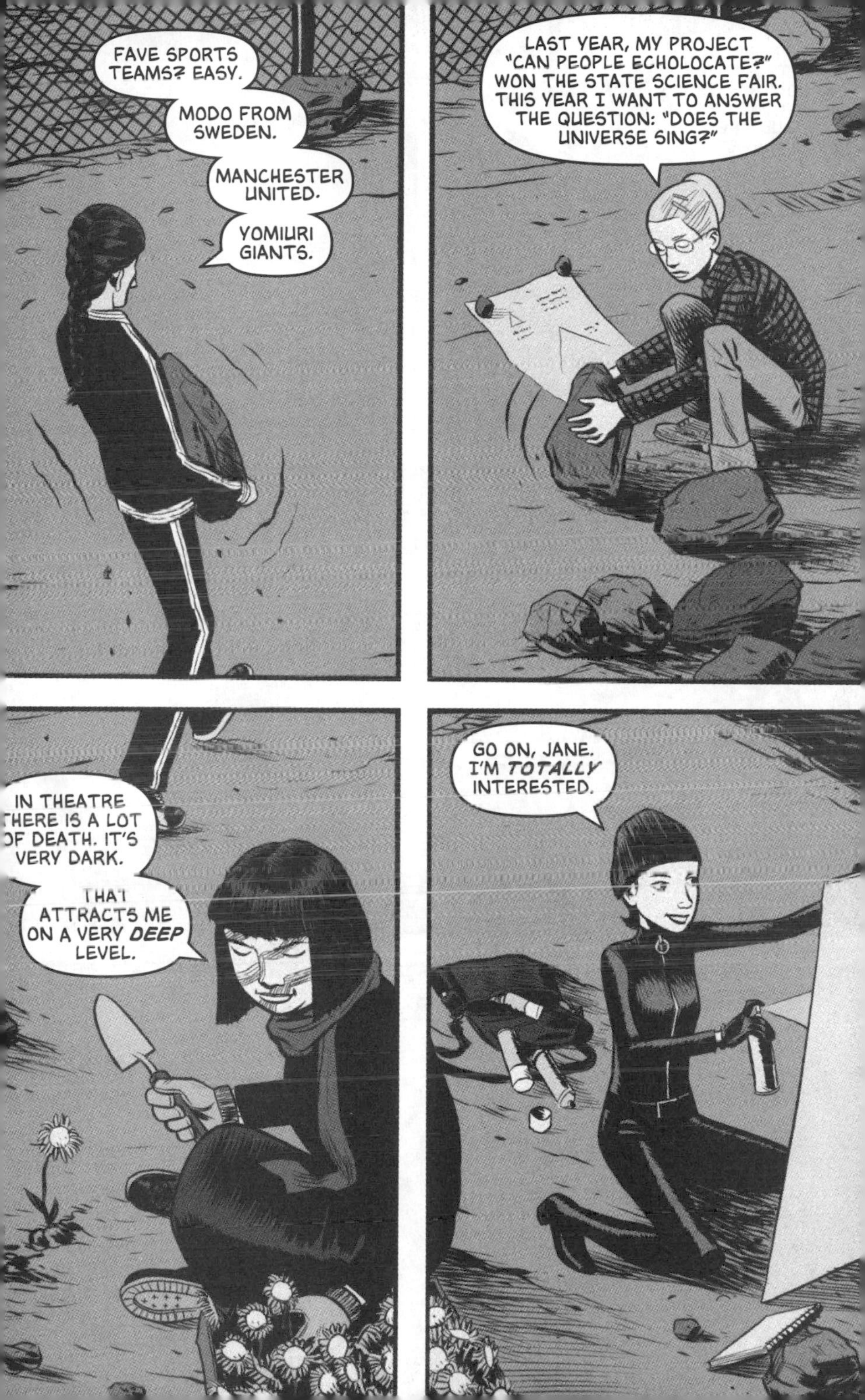
FAVE SPORTS TEAMS? EASY.
MODO FROM SWEDEN.
MANCHESTER UNITED.
YOMIURI GIANTS.
LAST YEAR, MY PROJECT "CAN PEOPLE ECHOLOCATE?" WON THE STATE SCIENCE FAIR. THIS YEAR I WANT TO ANSWER THE QUESTION: "DOES THE UNIVERSE SING?"
IN THEATRE THERE IS A LOT OF DEATH. IT'S VERY DARK.
THAT ATTRACTS ME ON A VERY *DEEP* LEVEL.
GO ON, JANE. I'M *TOTALLY* INTERESTED.

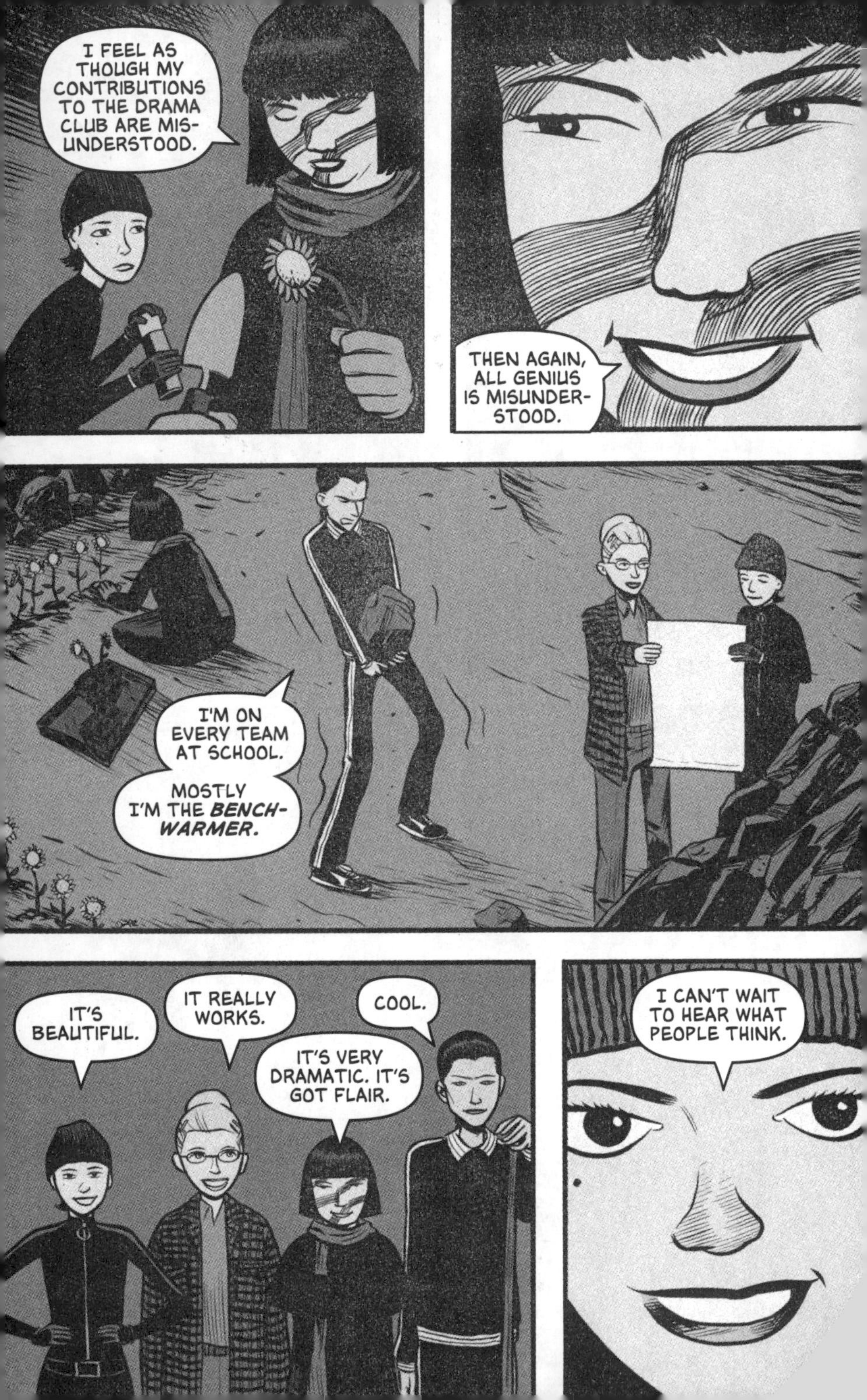
I FEEL AS THOUGH MY CONTRIBUTIONS TO THE DRAMA CLUB ARE MIS-UNDERSTOOD.
THEN AGAIN, ALL GENIUS IS MISUNDER-STOOD.
I'M ON EVERY TEAM AT SCHOOL.
MOSTLY I'M THE *BENCH-WARMER*.
IT'S BEAUTIFUL.
IT REALLY WORKS.
COOL.
IT'S VERY DRAMATIC. IT'S GOT FLAIR.
I CAN'T WAIT TO HEAR WHAT PEOPLE THINK.

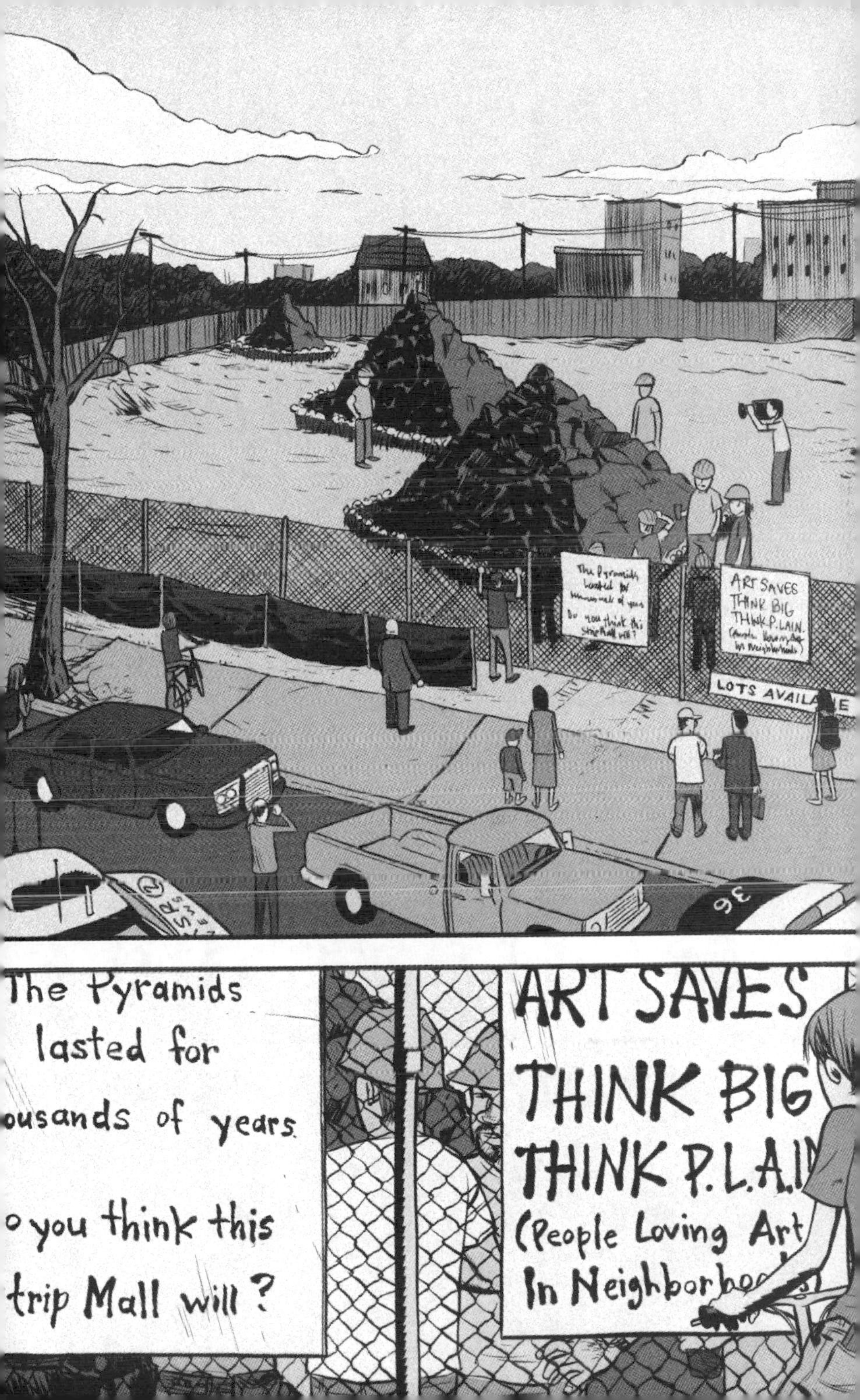
ART SAVES
THINK BIG
THINK P.LAIN.
LOTS AVAILA
The Pyramids
lasted for
ousands of years
o you think this
trip Mall will ?
ART SAVES
THINK BIG
THINK P.L.A.I
(People Loving Art
In Neighborbo

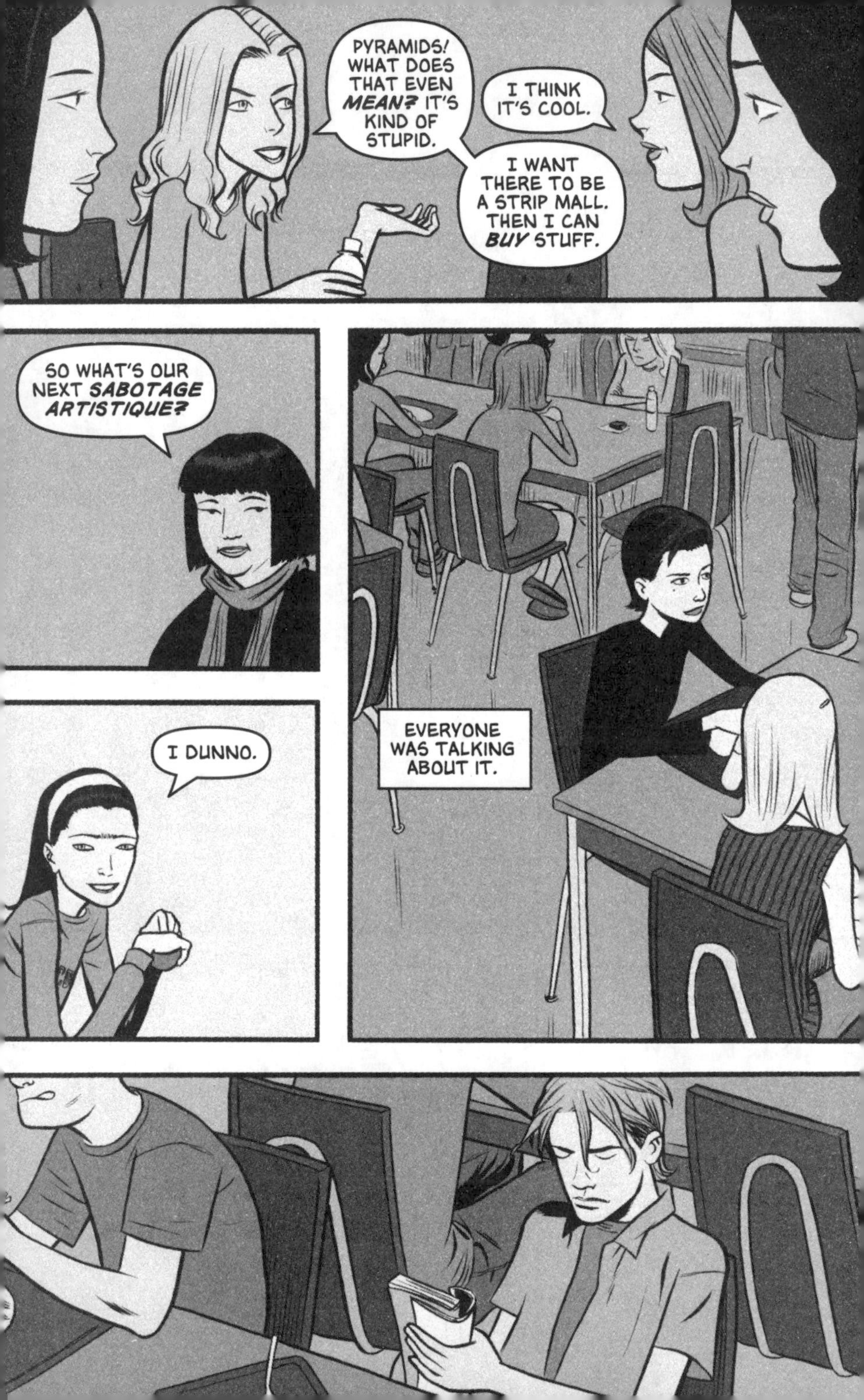
PYRAMIDS! WHAT DOES THAT EVEN MEAN? IT'S KIND OF STUPID.
I THINK IT'S COOL.
I WANT THERE TO BE A STRIP MALL. THEN I CAN BUY STUFF.
SO WHAT'S OUR NEXT SABOTAGE ARTISTIQUE?
I DUNNO.
EVERYONE WAS TALKING ABOUT IT.

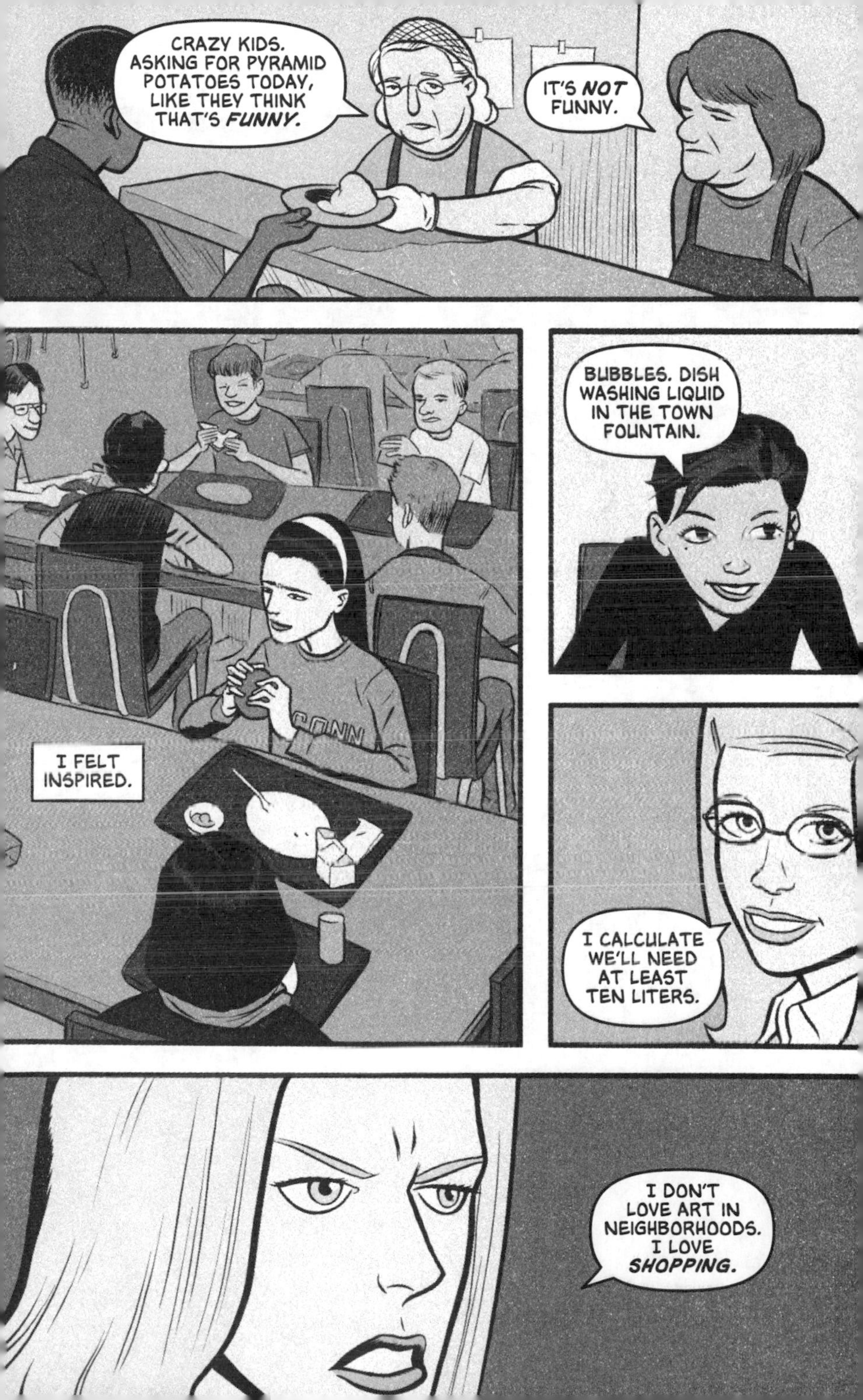
CRAZY KIDS. ASKING FOR PYRAMID POTATOES TODAY, LIKE THEY THINK THAT'S *FUNNY.*
IT'S *NOT* FUNNY.
I FELT INSPIRED.
BUBBLES. DISH WASHING LIQUID IN THE TOWN FOUNTAIN.
I CALCULATE WE'LL NEED AT LEAST TEN LITERS.
I DON'T LOVE ART IN NEIGHBORHOODS. I LOVE *SHOPPING.*

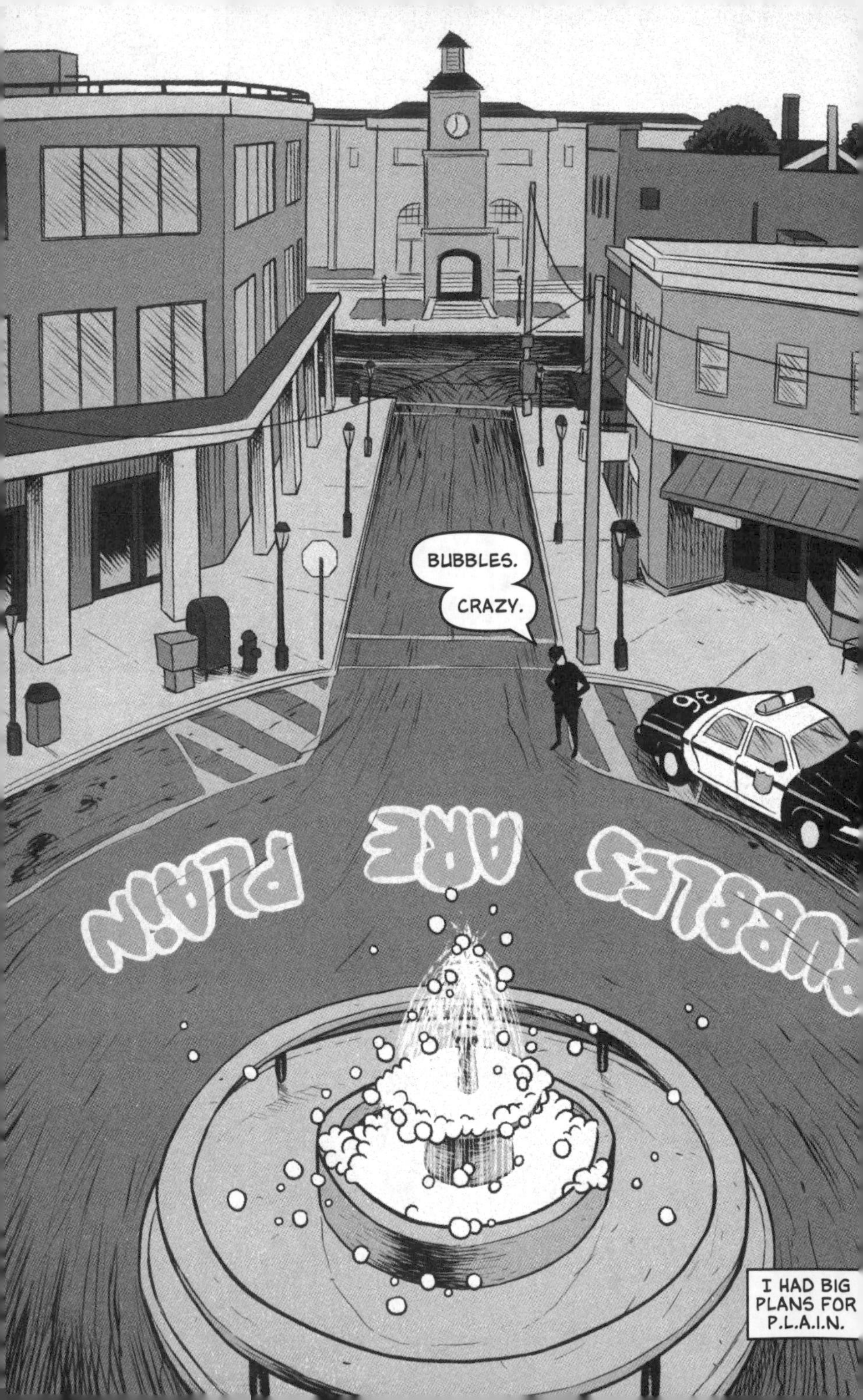
BUBBLES.
CRAZY.
I HAD BIG PLANS FOR P.L.A.I.N.

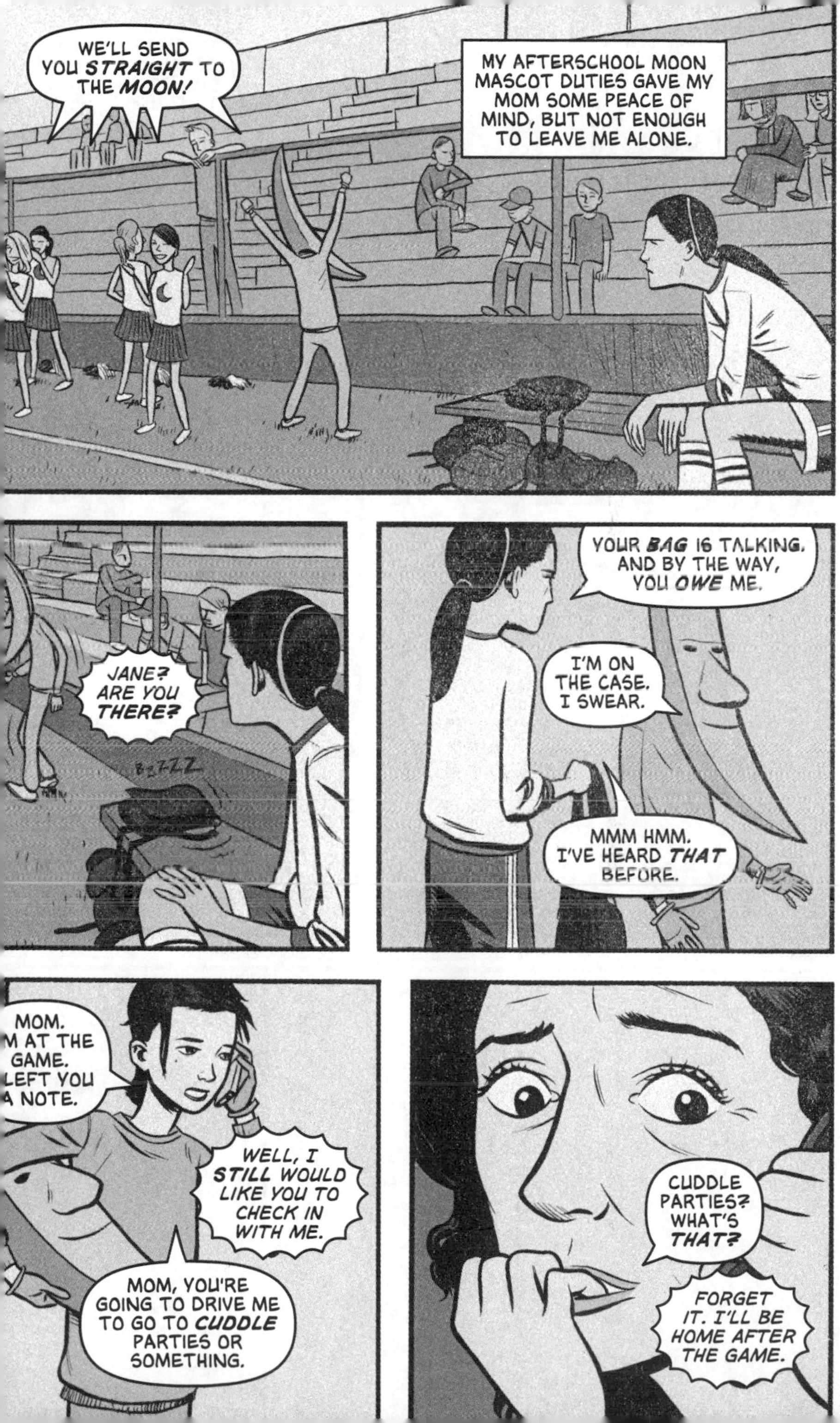
WE'LL SEND YOU STRAIGHT TO THE MOON!
MY AFTERSCHOOL MOON MASCOT DUTIES GAVE MY MOM SOME PEACE OF MIND, BUT NOT ENOUGH TO LEAVE ME ALONE.
JANE? ARE YOU THERE?
B-Z-Z-Z
YOUR BAG IS TALKING. AND BY THE WAY, YOU OWE ME.
I'M ON THE CASE. I SWEAR.
MMM HMM. I'VE HEARD THAT BEFORE.
MOM. M AT THE GAME. LEFT YOU A NOTE.
WELL, I STILL WOULD LIKE YOU TO CHECK IN WITH ME.
MOM, YOU'RE GOING TO DRIVE ME TO GO TO CUDDLE PARTIES OR SOMETHING.
CUDDLE PARTIES? WHAT'S THAT?
FORGET IT. I'LL BE HOME AFTER THE GAME.

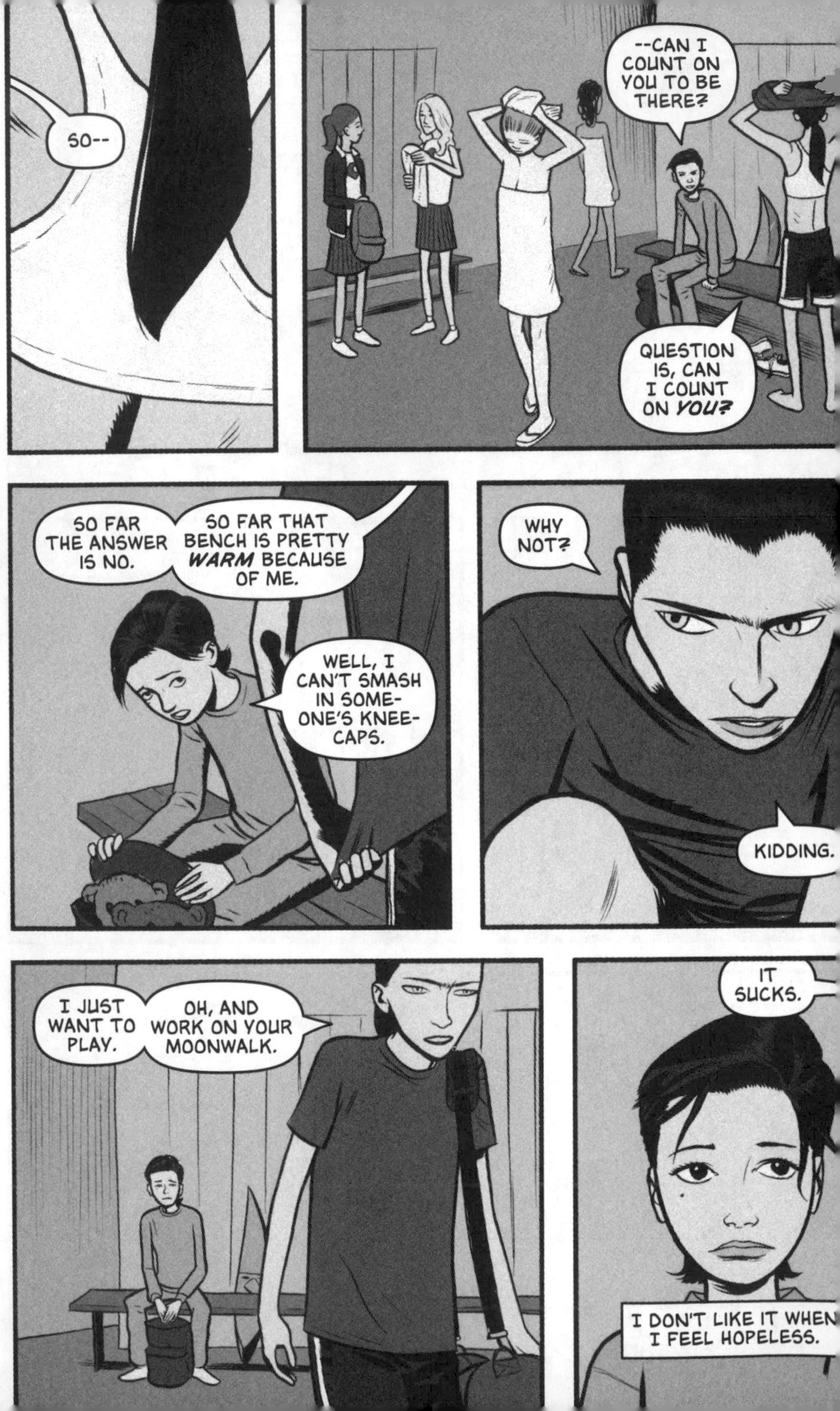
SO--
--CAN I COUNT ON YOU TO BE THERE?
QUESTION IS, CAN I COUNT ON *YOU?*
SO FAR THE ANSWER IS NO.
SO FAR THAT BENCH IS PRETTY *WARM* BECAUSE OF ME.
WELL, I CAN'T SMASH IN SOME-ONE'S KNEE-CAPS.
WHY NOT?
KIDDING.
I JUST WANT TO PLAY.
OH, AND WORK ON YOUR MOONWALK.
IT SUCKS.
I DON'T LIKE IT WHEN I FEEL HOPELESS.

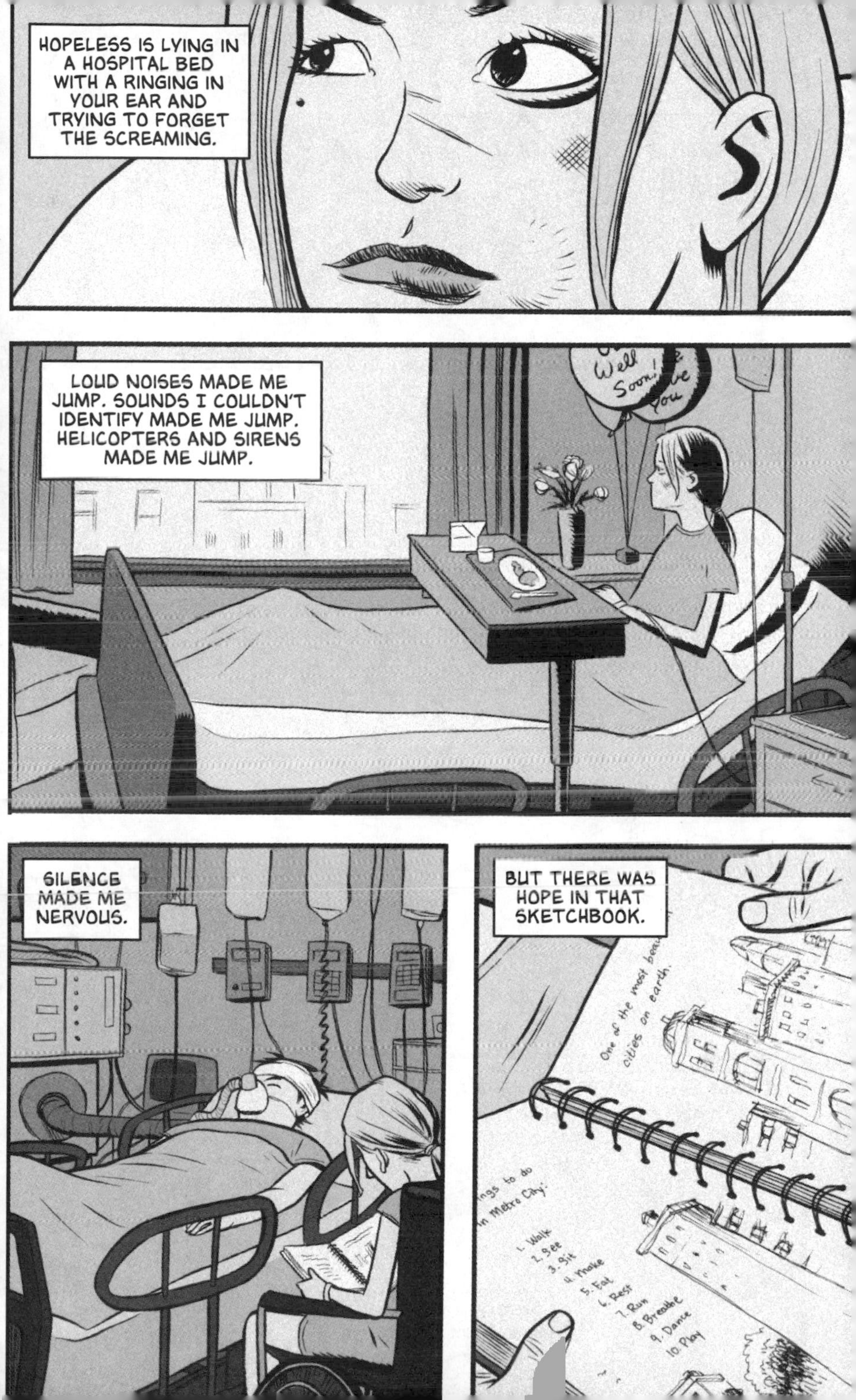
HOPELESS IS LYING IN A HOSPITAL BED WITH A RINGING IN YOUR EAR AND TRYING TO FORGET THE SCREAMING.
LOUD NOISES MADE ME JUMP. SOUNDS I COULDN'T IDENTIFY MADE ME JUMP. HELICOPTERS AND SIRENS MADE ME JUMP.
Well Soon!
SILENCE MADE ME NERVOUS.
BUT THERE WAS HOPE IN THAT SKETCHBOOK.
cities on earth.
1. Walk
2. See
3. Sit
4. Make
5. Eat
6. Rest
7. Run
8. Breathe
9. Dance
10. Play

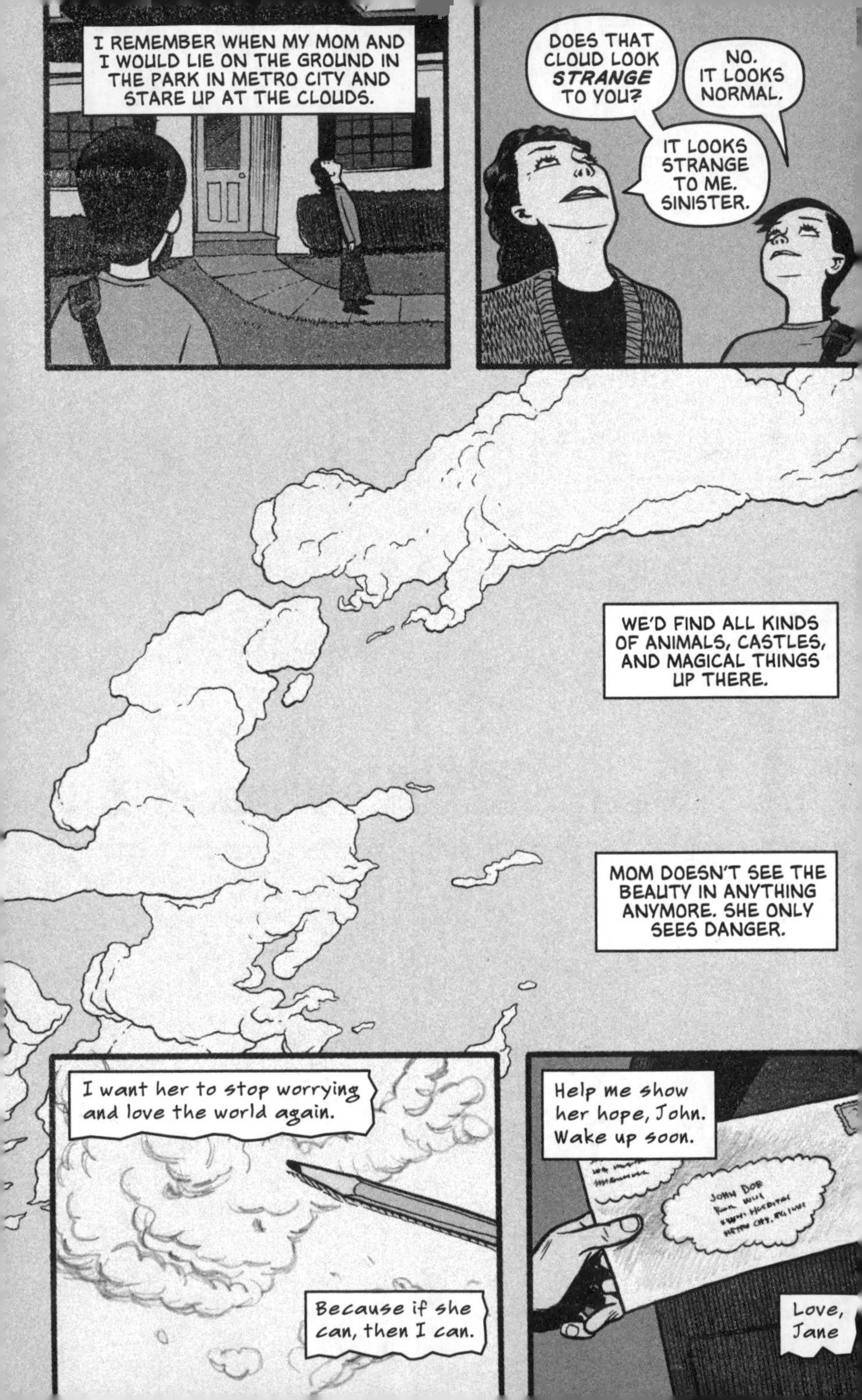
I REMEMBER WHEN MY MOM AND I WOULD LIE ON THE GROUND IN THE PARK IN METRO CITY AND STARE UP AT THE CLOUDS.
DOES THAT CLOUD LOOK *STRANGE* TO YOU?
NO. IT LOOKS NORMAL.
IT LOOKS STRANGE TO ME. SINISTER.
WE'D FIND ALL KINDS OF ANIMALS, CASTLES, AND MAGICAL THINGS UP THERE.
MOM DOESN'T SEE THE BEAUTY IN ANYTHING ANYMORE. SHE ONLY SEES DANGER.
I want her to stop worrying and love the world again.
Because if she can, then I can.
Help me show her hope, John. Wake up soon.
JOHN DOE
Love, Jane

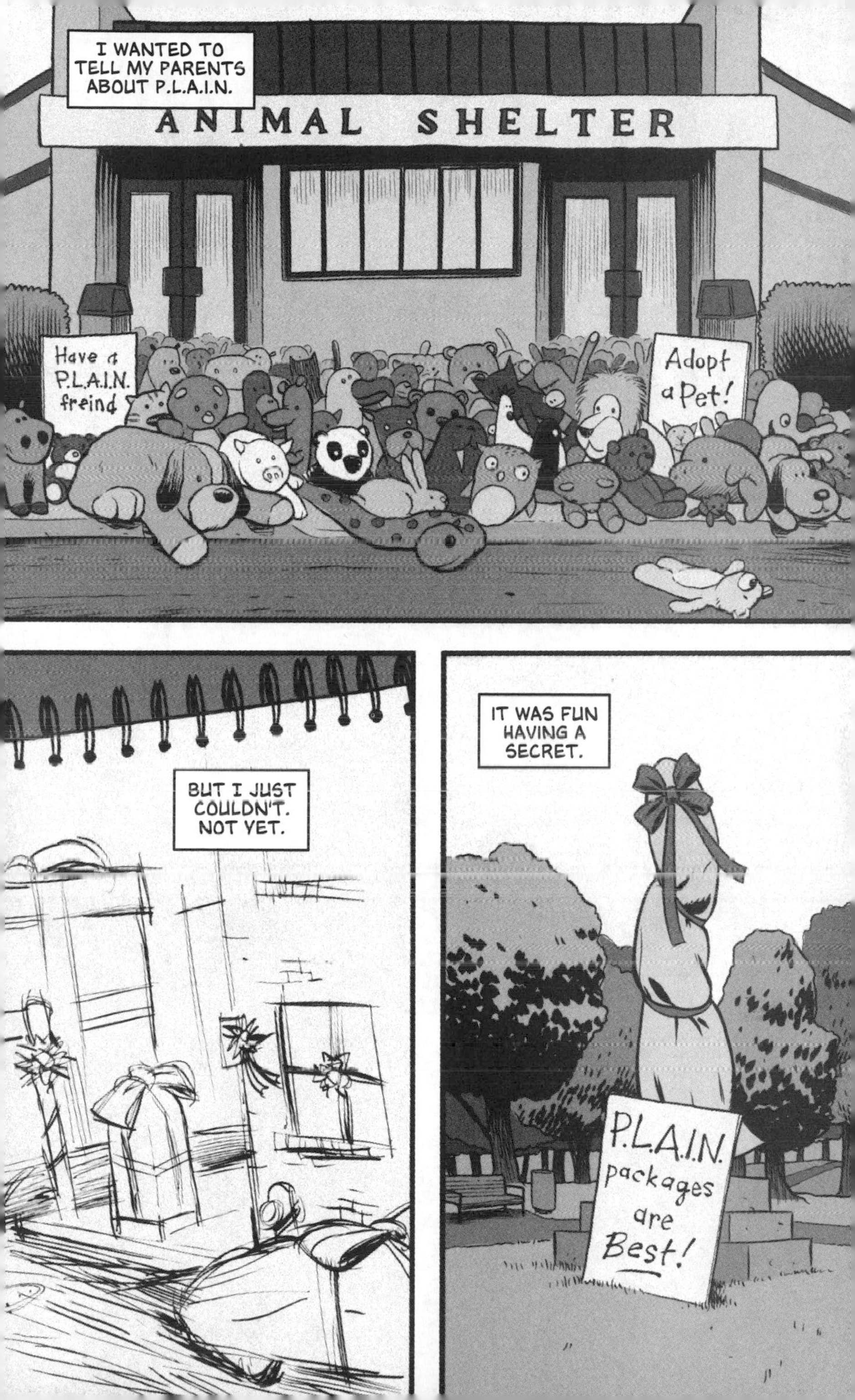
I WANTED TO TELL MY PARENTS ABOUT P.L.A.I.N.
ANIMAL SHELTER
Have a P.L.A.I.N. freind
Adopt a Pet!
BUT I JUST COULDN'T. NOT YET.
IT WAS FUN HAVING A SECRET.
P.L.A.I.N. packages are Best!

Attacks in plain view!!!

Yet another art attack, this time hitting Main and Elm, where various objects were wrapped up like a present.

Who are these artists and what do they want?

"The scariest part of this whole incident, is that they could be anyone."

Chilling words from the Chief of Police offers little hope that attacks can ...happy ending.

THE WHOLE TOWN WAS TALKING ABOUT P.L.A.I.N. EVERYONE HAD AN OPINION ABOUT WHAT WE WERE DOING.

EXTRA CREDIT

$$s(\omega t + \phi) - A_1 \cos(\omega t + \phi_1) + A_2 \cos(\omega t + \phi_2)$$

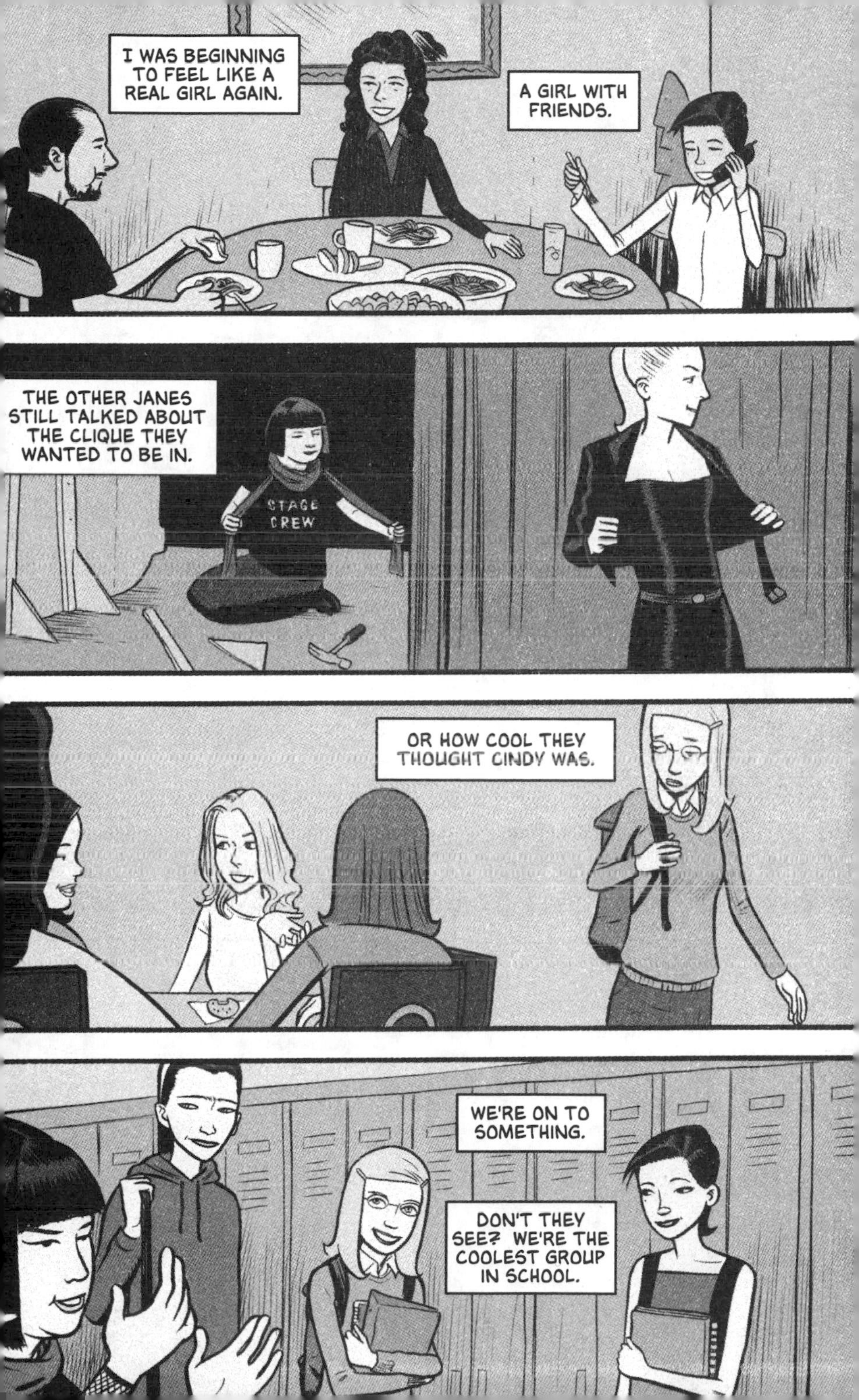
I WAS BEGINNING TO FEEL LIKE A REAL GIRL AGAIN.
A GIRL WITH FRIENDS.
THE OTHER JANES STILL TALKED ABOUT THE CLIQUE THEY WANTED TO BE IN.
STAGE CREW
OR HOW COOL THEY THOUGHT CINDY WAS.
WE'RE ON TO SOMETHING.
DON'T THEY SEE? WE'RE THE COOLEST GROUP IN SCHOOL.

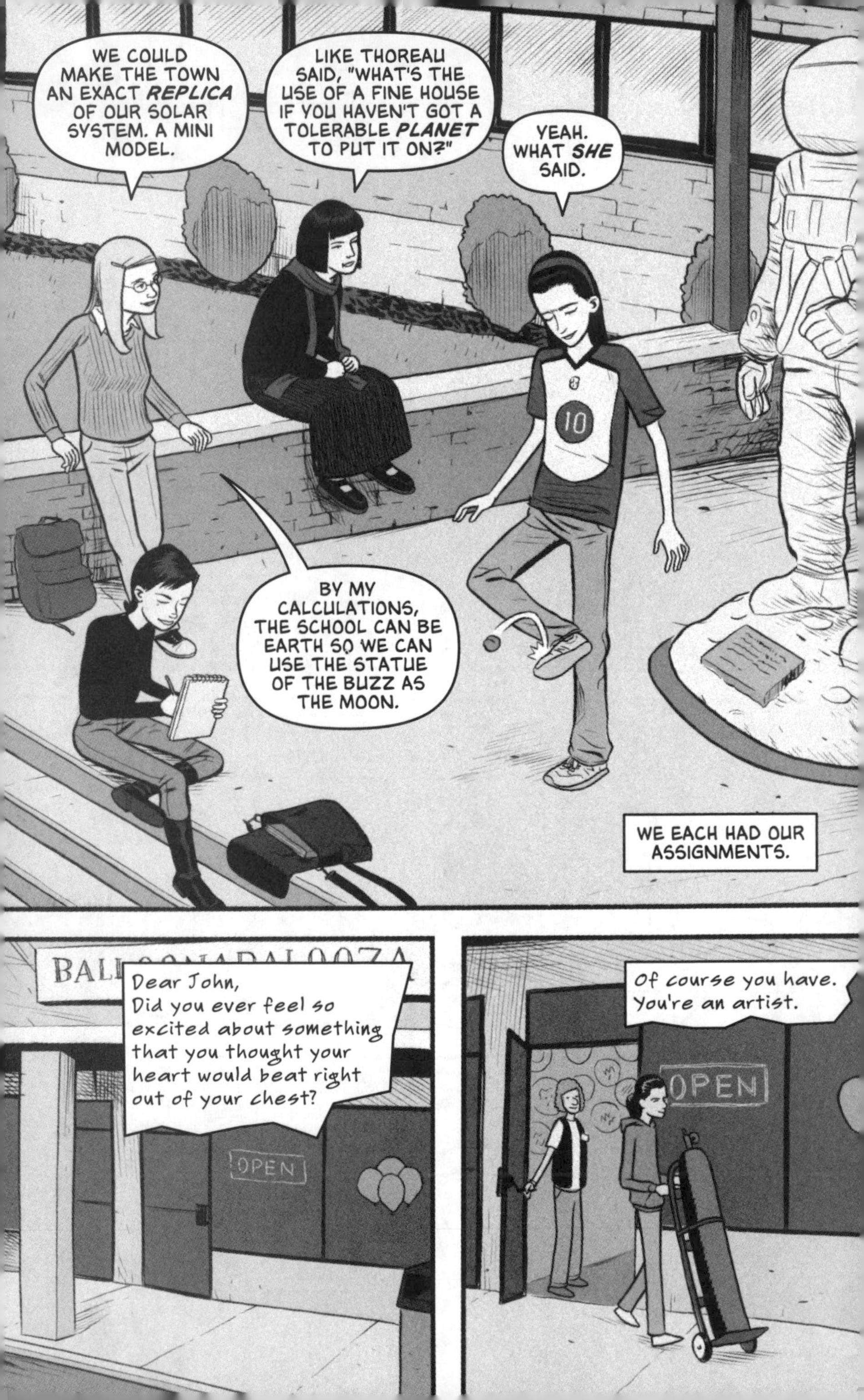
WE COULD MAKE THE TOWN AN EXACT *REPLICA* OF OUR SOLAR SYSTEM. A MINI MODEL.
LIKE THOREAU SAID, "WHAT'S THE USE OF A FINE HOUSE IF YOU HAVEN'T GOT A TOLERABLE *PLANET* TO PUT IT ON?"
YEAH. WHAT *SHE* SAID.
10
BY MY CALCULATIONS, THE SCHOOL CAN BE EARTH SO WE CAN USE THE STATUE OF THE BUZZ AS THE MOON.
WE EACH HAD OUR ASSIGNMENTS.
Dear John,
Did you ever feel so excited about something that you thought your heart would beat right out of your chest?
OPEN
Of course you have. You're an artist.
OPEN

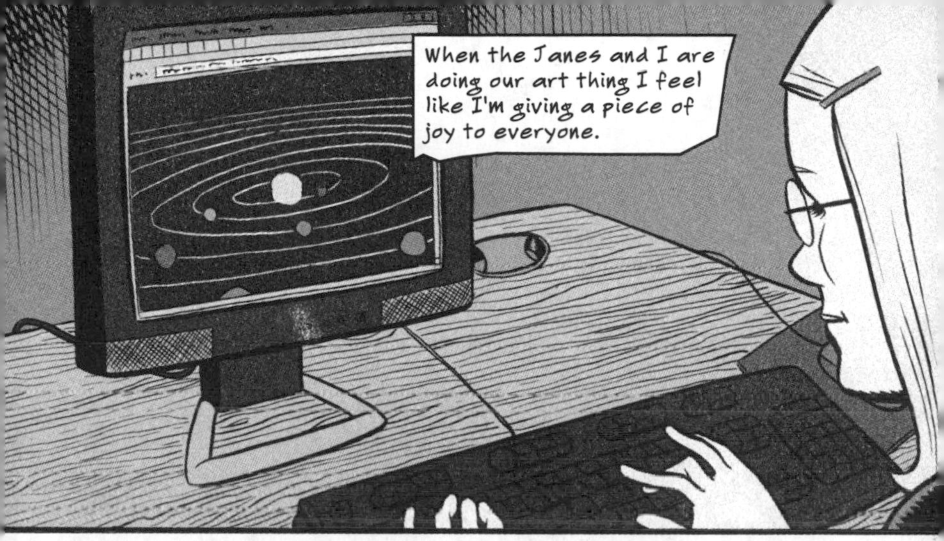
When the Janes and I are doing our art thing I feel like I'm giving a piece of joy to everyone.

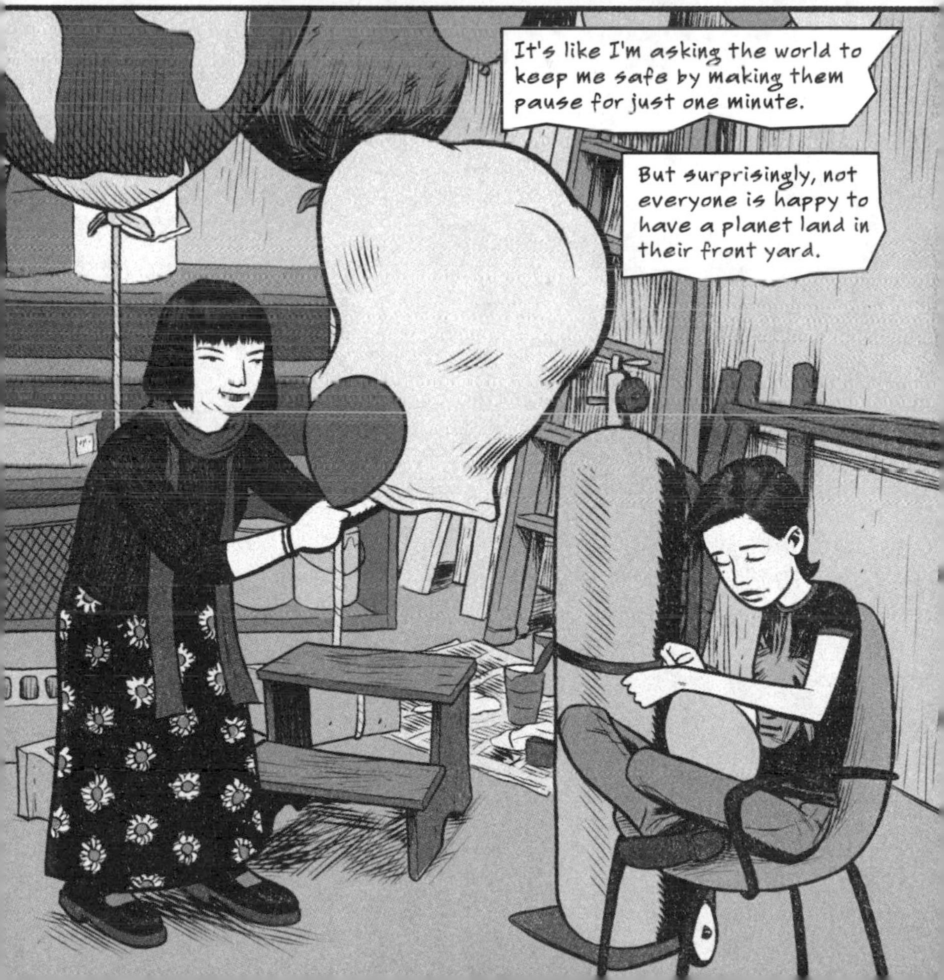
It's like I'm asking the world to keep me safe by making them pause for just one minute.
But surprisingly, not everyone is happy to have a planet land in their front yard.

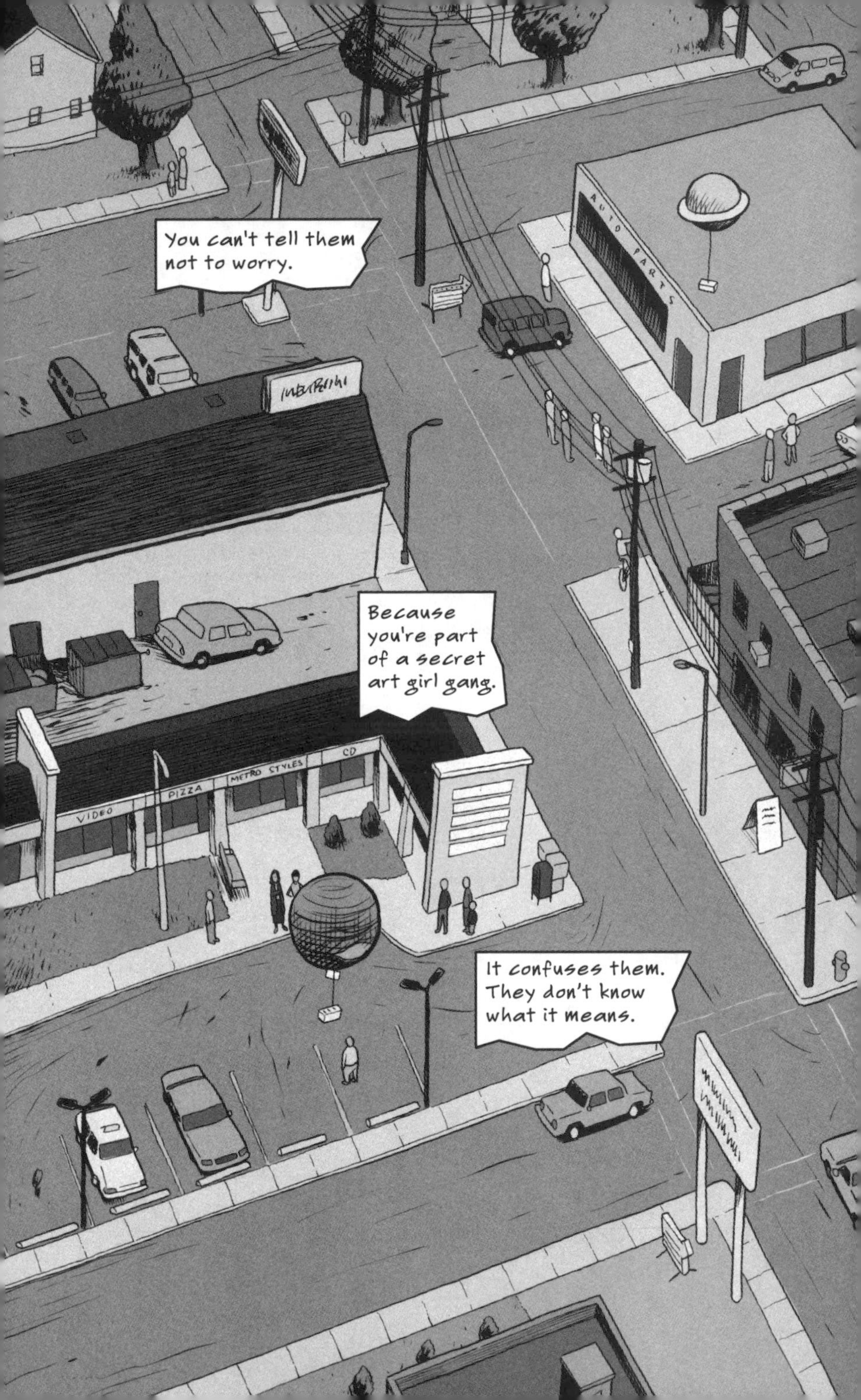
You can't tell them not to worry.
AUTO PARTS
Because you're part of a secret art girl gang.
VIDEO
PIZZA
METRO STYLES
CD
It confuses them. They don't know what it means.

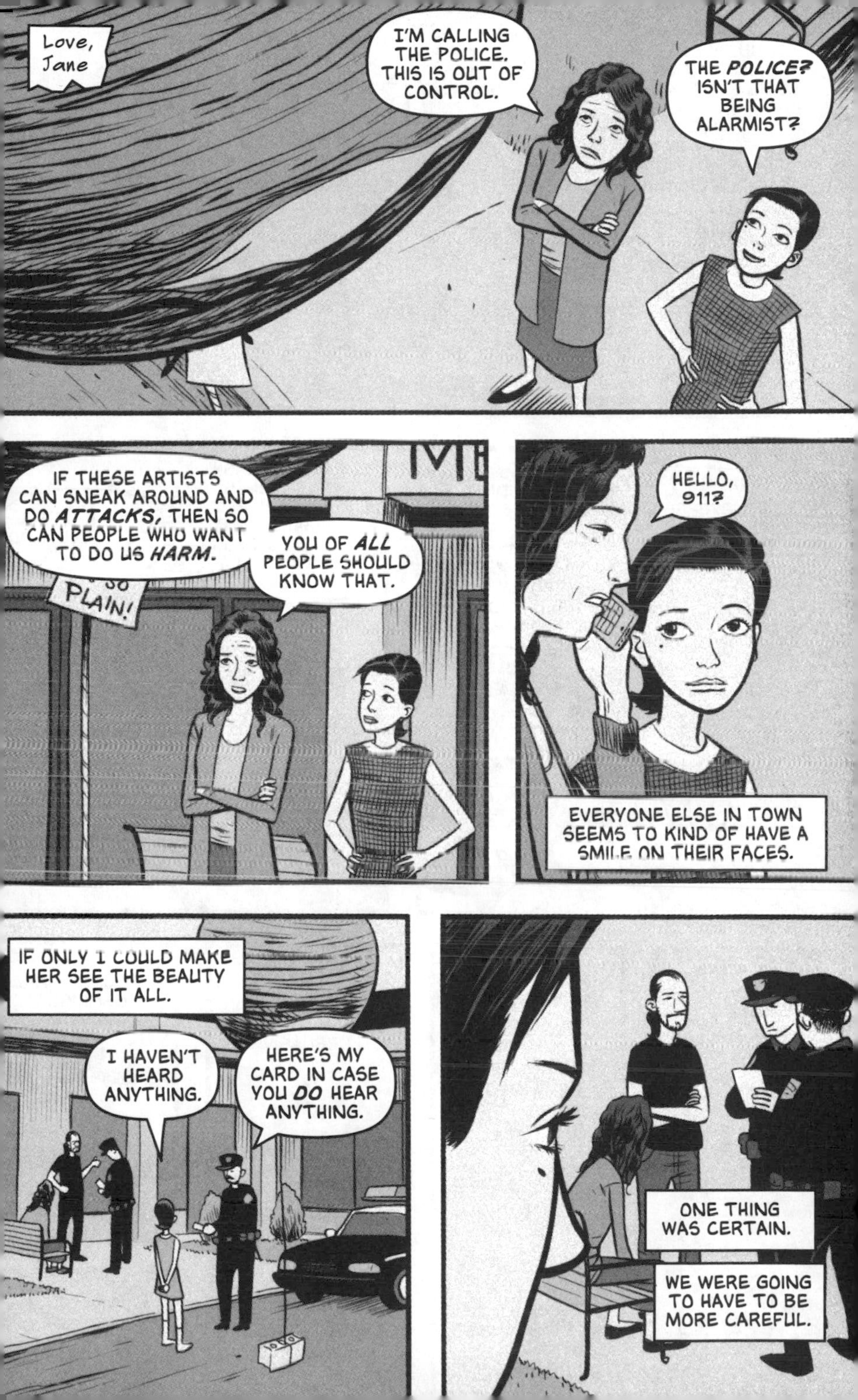
Love, Jane
I'M CALLING THE POLICE. THIS IS OUT OF CONTROL.
THE POLICE? ISN'T THAT BEING ALARMIST?
IF THESE ARTISTS CAN SNEAK AROUND AND DO ATTACKS, THEN SO CAN PEOPLE WHO WANT TO DO US HARM.
YOU OF ALL PEOPLE SHOULD KNOW THAT.
PLAIN!
HELLO, 911?
EVERYONE ELSE IN TOWN SEEMS TO KIND OF HAVE A SMILE ON THEIR FACES.
IF ONLY I COULD MAKE HER SEE THE BEAUTY OF IT ALL.
I HAVEN'T HEARD ANYTHING.
HERE'S MY CARD IN CASE YOU DO HEAR ANYTHING.
ONE THING WAS CERTAIN.
WE WERE GOING TO HAVE TO BE MORE CAREFUL.

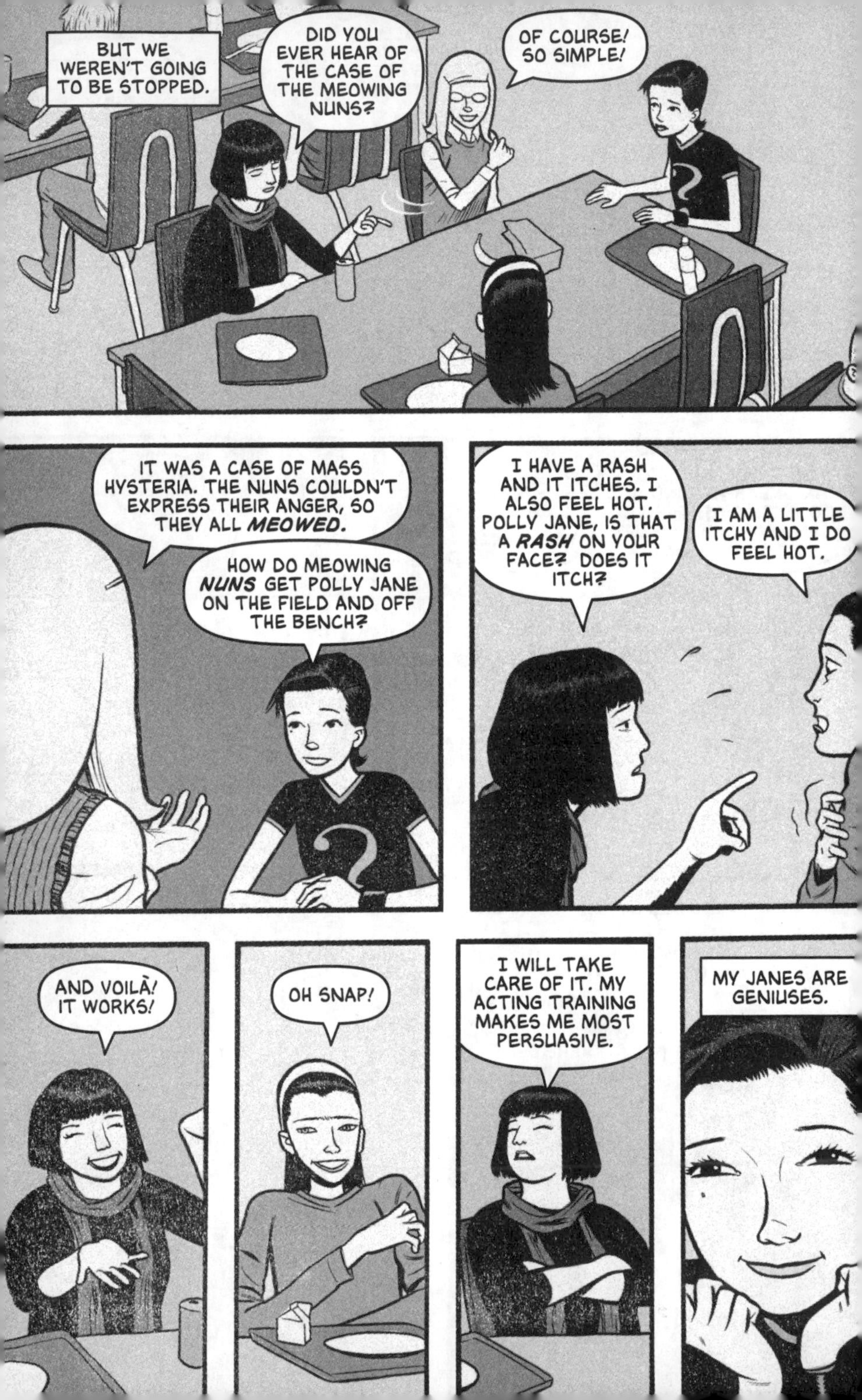

BUT WE WEREN'T GOING TO BE STOPPED.
DID YOU EVER HEAR OF THE CASE OF THE MEOWING NUNS?
OF COURSE! SO SIMPLE!
IT WAS A CASE OF MASS HYSTERIA. THE NUNS COULDN'T EXPRESS THEIR ANGER, SO THEY ALL *MEOWED.*
HOW DO MEOWING *NUNS* GET POLLY JANE ON THE FIELD AND OFF THE BENCH?
I HAVE A RASH AND IT ITCHES. I ALSO FEEL HOT. POLLY JANE, IS THAT A *RASH* ON YOUR FACE? DOES IT ITCH?
I AM A LITTLE ITCHY AND I DO FEEL HOT.
AND VOILÀ! IT WORKS!
OH SNAP!
I WILL TAKE CARE OF IT. MY ACTING TRAINING MAKES ME MOST PERSUASIVE.
MY JANES ARE GENIUSES.

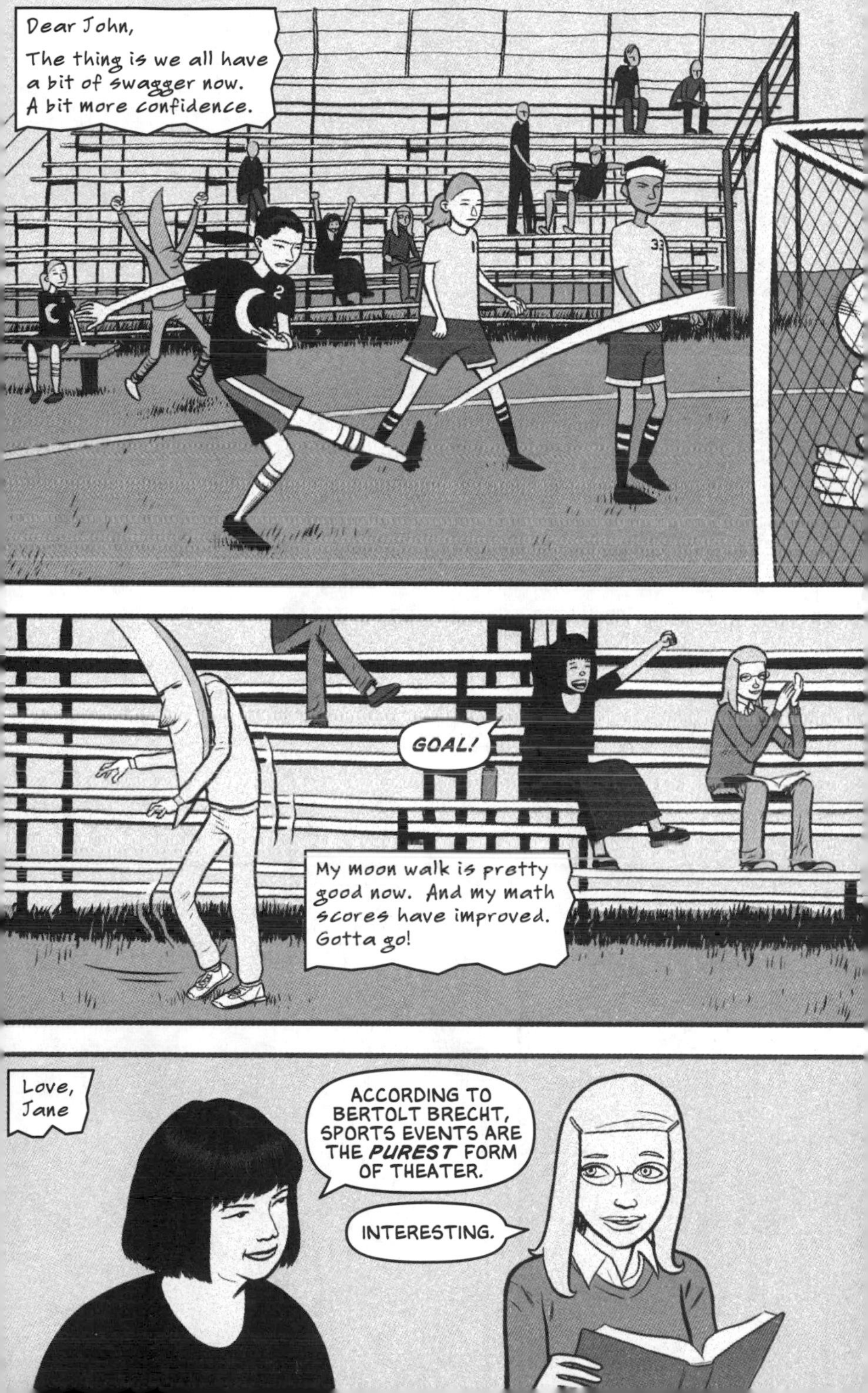
Dear John,
The thing is we all have a bit of swagger now. A bit more confidence.
GOAL!
My moon walk is pretty good now. And my math scores have improved. Gotta go!
Love, Jane
ACCORDING TO BERTOLT BRECHT, SPORTS EVENTS ARE THE *PUREST* FORM OF THEATER.
INTERESTING.

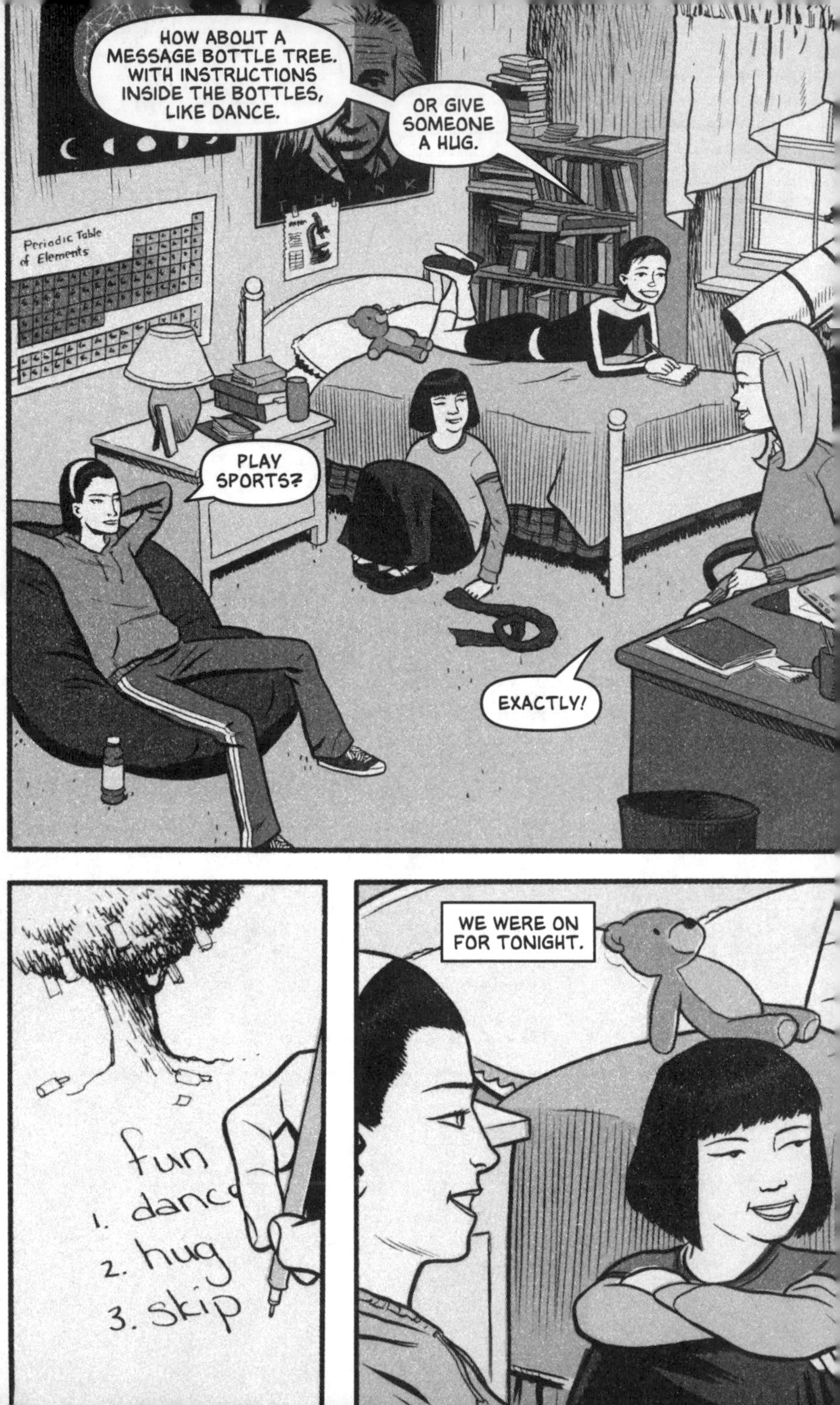
HOW ABOUT A MESSAGE BOTTLE TREE. WITH INSTRUCTIONS INSIDE THE BOTTLES, LIKE DANCE.
OR GIVE SOMEONE A HUG.
Periodic Table of Elements
PLAY SPORTS?
EXACTLY!
fun
1. danc
2. hug
3. skip
WE WERE ON FOR TONIGHT.

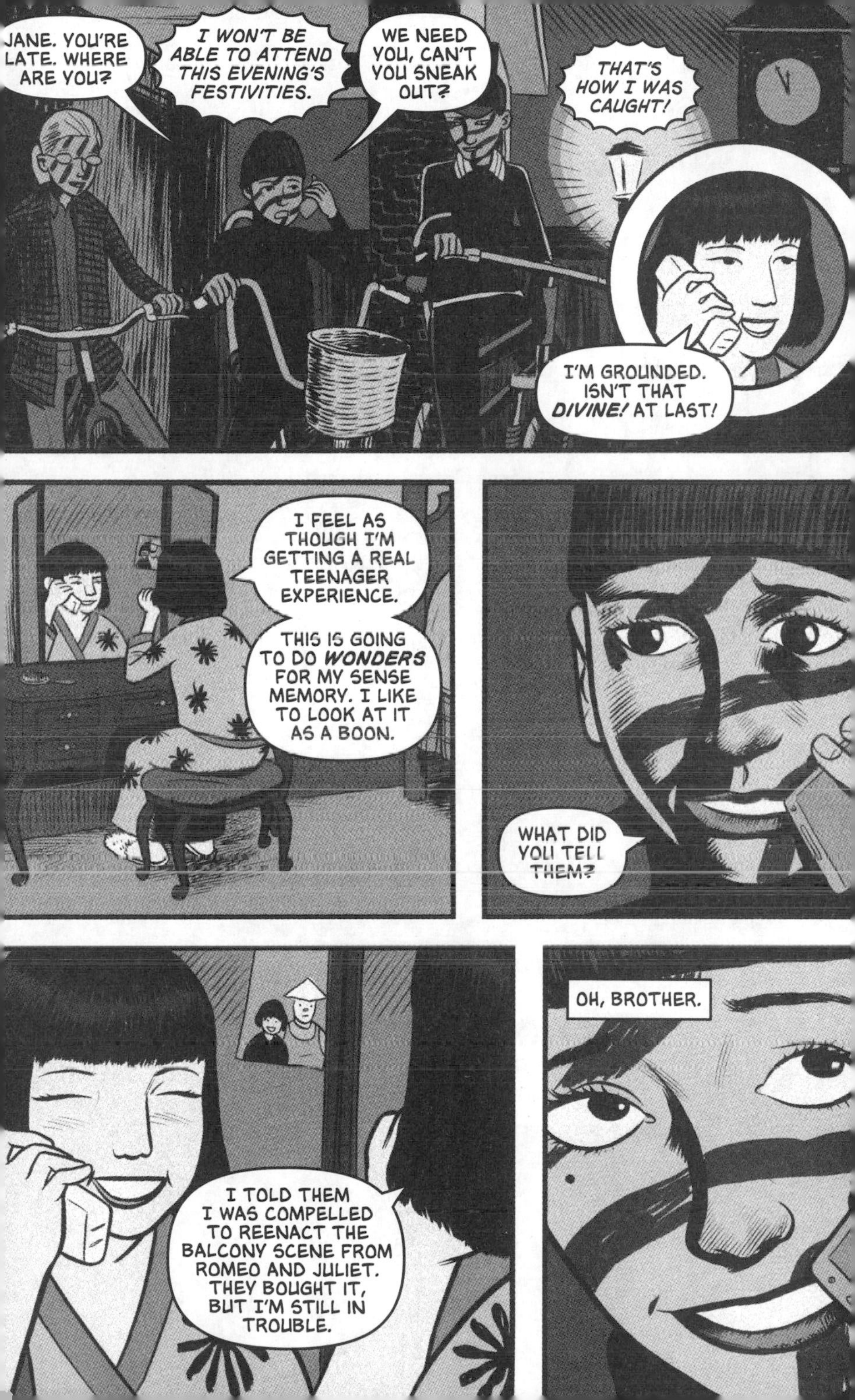
JANE. YOU'RE LATE. WHERE ARE YOU?
I WON'T BE ABLE TO ATTEND THIS EVENING'S FESTIVITIES.
WE NEED YOU, CAN'T YOU SNEAK OUT?
THAT'S HOW I WAS CAUGHT!
I'M GROUNDED. ISN'T THAT DIVINE! AT LAST!
I FEEL AS THOUGH I'M GETTING A REAL TEENAGER EXPERIENCE.
THIS IS GOING TO DO WONDERS FOR MY SENSE MEMORY. I LIKE TO LOOK AT IT AS A BOON.
WHAT DID YOU TELL THEM?
I TOLD THEM I WAS COMPELLED TO REENACT THE BALCONY SCENE FROM ROMEO AND JULIET. THEY BOUGHT IT, BUT I'M STILL IN TROUBLE.
OH, BROTHER.

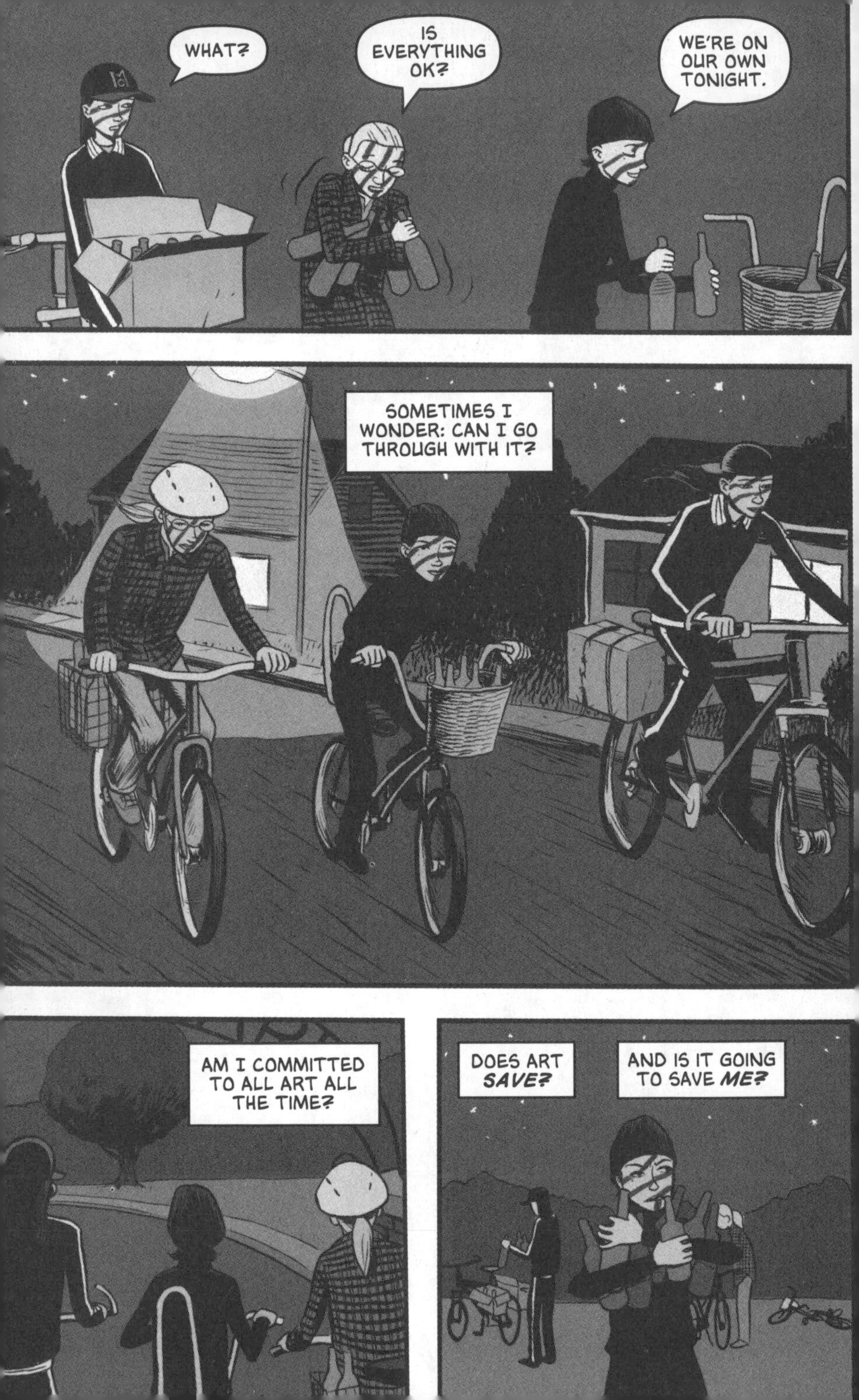
WHAT?
IS EVERYTHING OK?
WE'RE ON OUR OWN TONIGHT.
SOMETIMES I WONDER: CAN I GO THROUGH WITH IT?
AM I COMMITTED TO ALL ART ALL THE TIME?
DOES ART *SAVE*?
AND IS IT GOING TO SAVE *ME*?

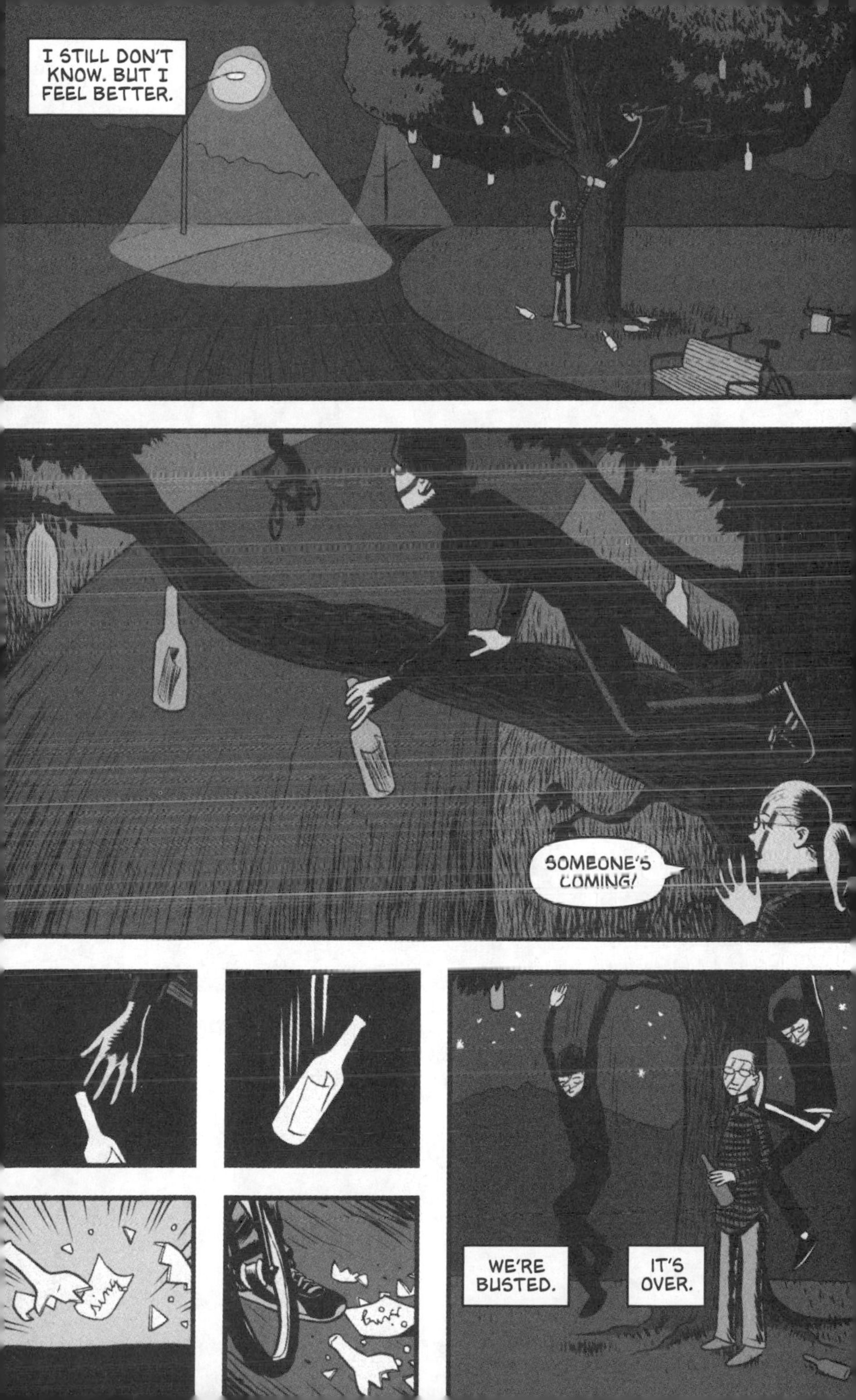
I STILL DON'T KNOW. BUT I FEEL BETTER.
SOMEONE'S COMING!
WE'RE BUSTED.
IT'S OVER.

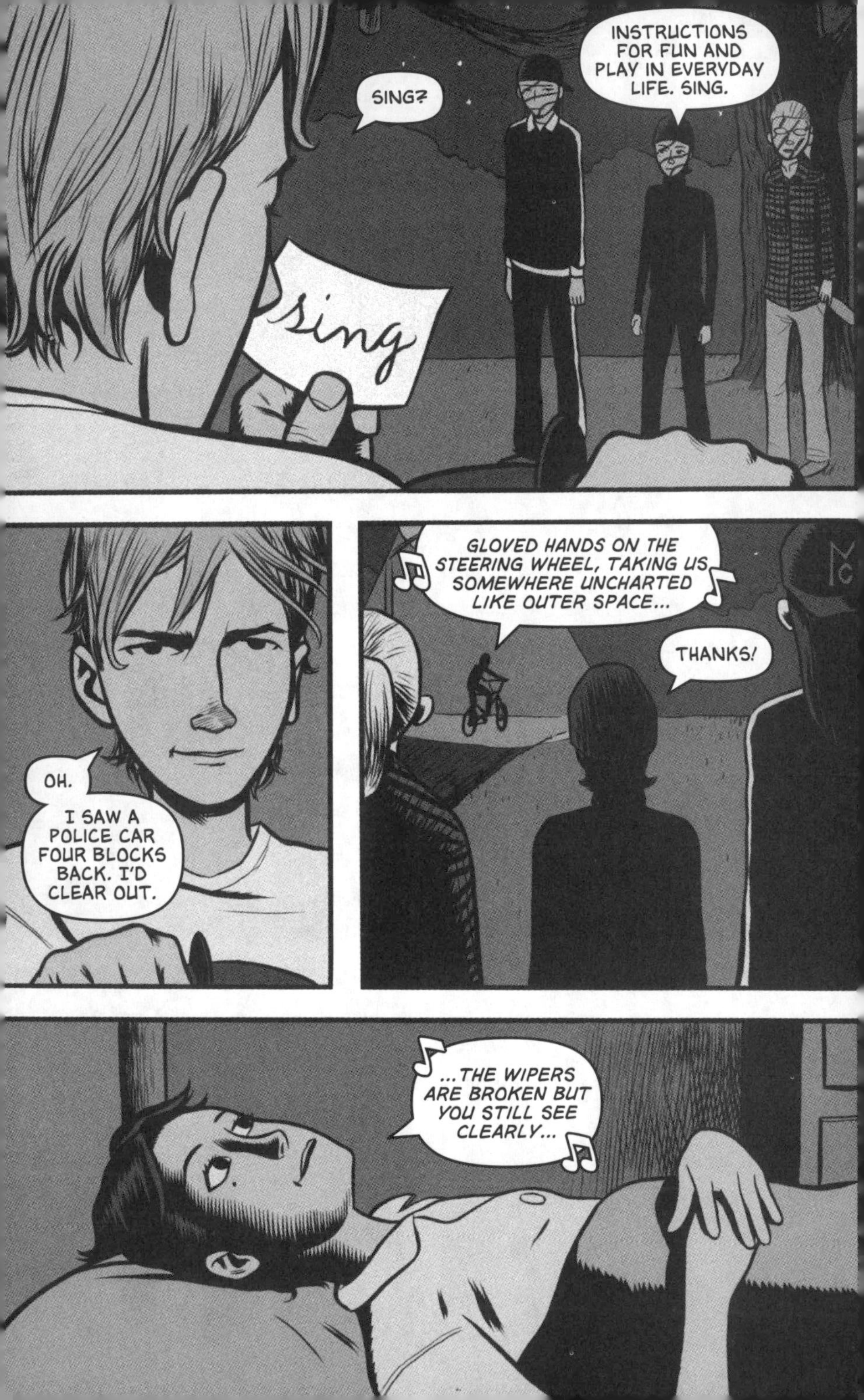
sing
SING?
INSTRUCTIONS FOR FUN AND PLAY IN EVERYDAY LIFE. SING.
OH.
I SAW A POLICE CAR FOUR BLOCKS BACK. I'D CLEAR OUT.
GLOVED HANDS ON THE STEERING WHEEL, TAKING US SOMEWHERE UNCHARTED LIKE OUTER SPACE...
THANKS!
...THE WIPERS ARE BROKEN BUT YOU STILL SEE CLEARLY...

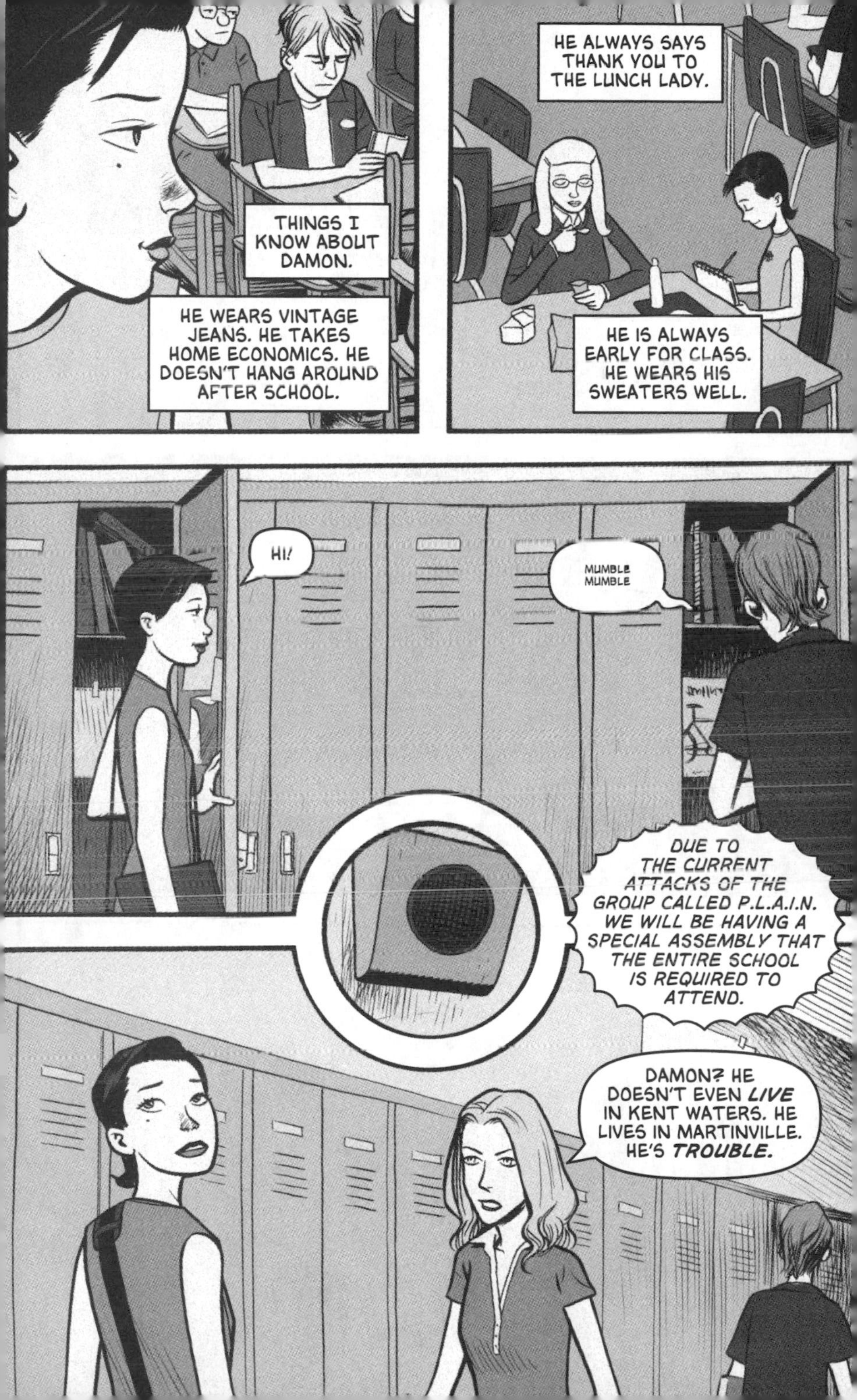
THINGS I KNOW ABOUT DAMON.
HE WEARS VINTAGE JEANS. HE TAKES HOME ECONOMICS. HE DOESN'T HANG AROUND AFTER SCHOOL.
HE ALWAYS SAYS THANK YOU TO THE LUNCH LADY.
HE IS ALWAYS EARLY FOR CLASS. HE WEARS HIS SWEATERS WELL.
HI!
MUMBLE MUMBLE
DUE TO THE CURRENT ATTACKS OF THE GROUP CALLED P.L.A.I.N. WE WILL BE HAVING A SPECIAL ASSEMBLY THAT THE ENTIRE SCHOOL IS REQUIRED TO ATTEND.
DAMON? HE DOESN'T EVEN LIVE IN KENT WATERS. HE LIVES IN MARTINVILLE. HE'S TROUBLE.

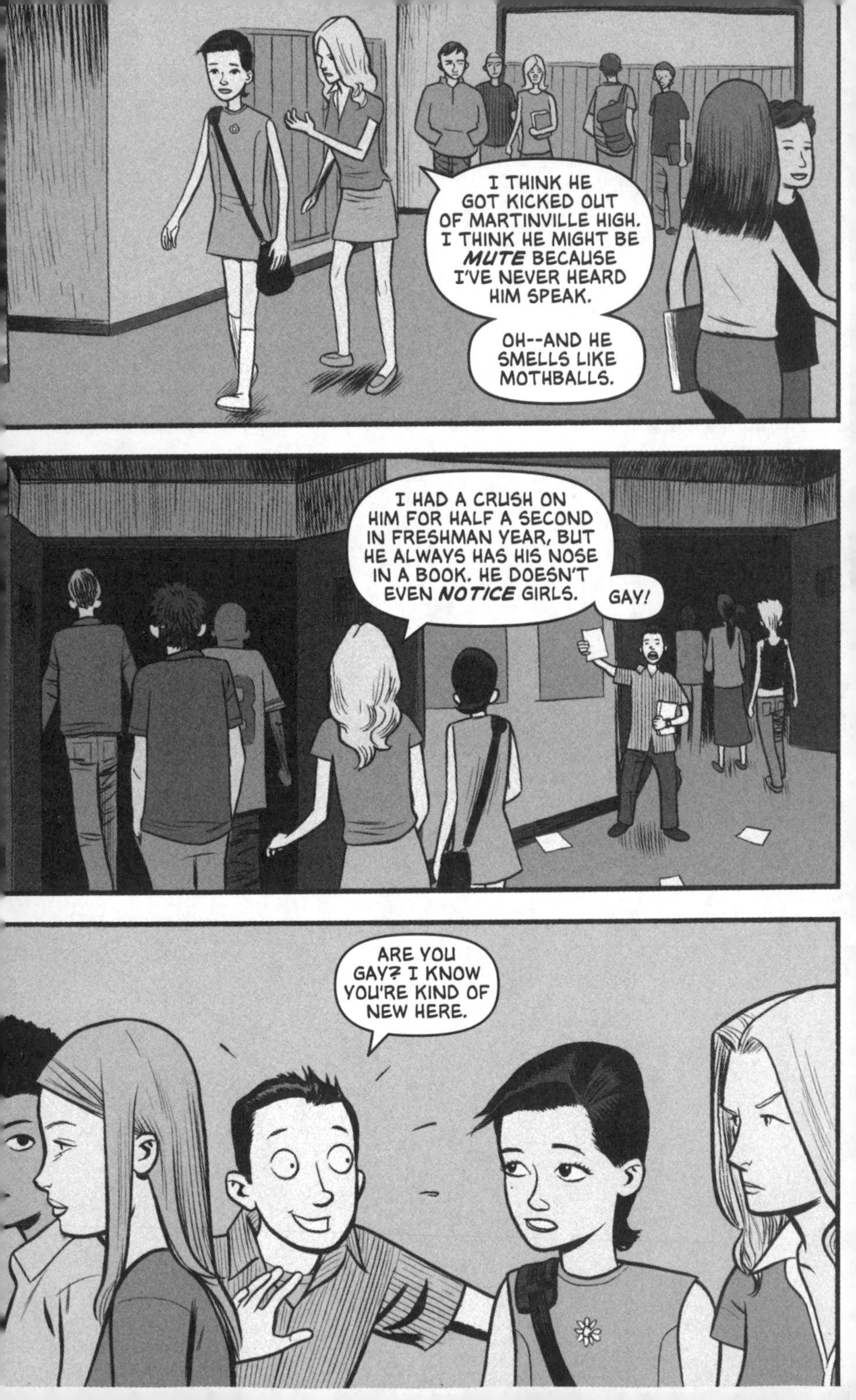
I THINK HE GOT KICKED OUT OF MARTINVILLE HIGH. I THINK HE MIGHT BE *MUTE* BECAUSE I'VE NEVER HEARD HIM SPEAK.
OH--AND HE SMELLS LIKE MOTHBALLS.
I HAD A CRUSH ON HIM FOR HALF A SECOND IN FRESHMAN YEAR, BUT HE ALWAYS HAS HIS NOSE IN A BOOK. HE DOESN'T EVEN *NOTICE* GIRLS.
GAY!
ARE YOU GAY? I KNOW YOU'RE KIND OF NEW HERE.

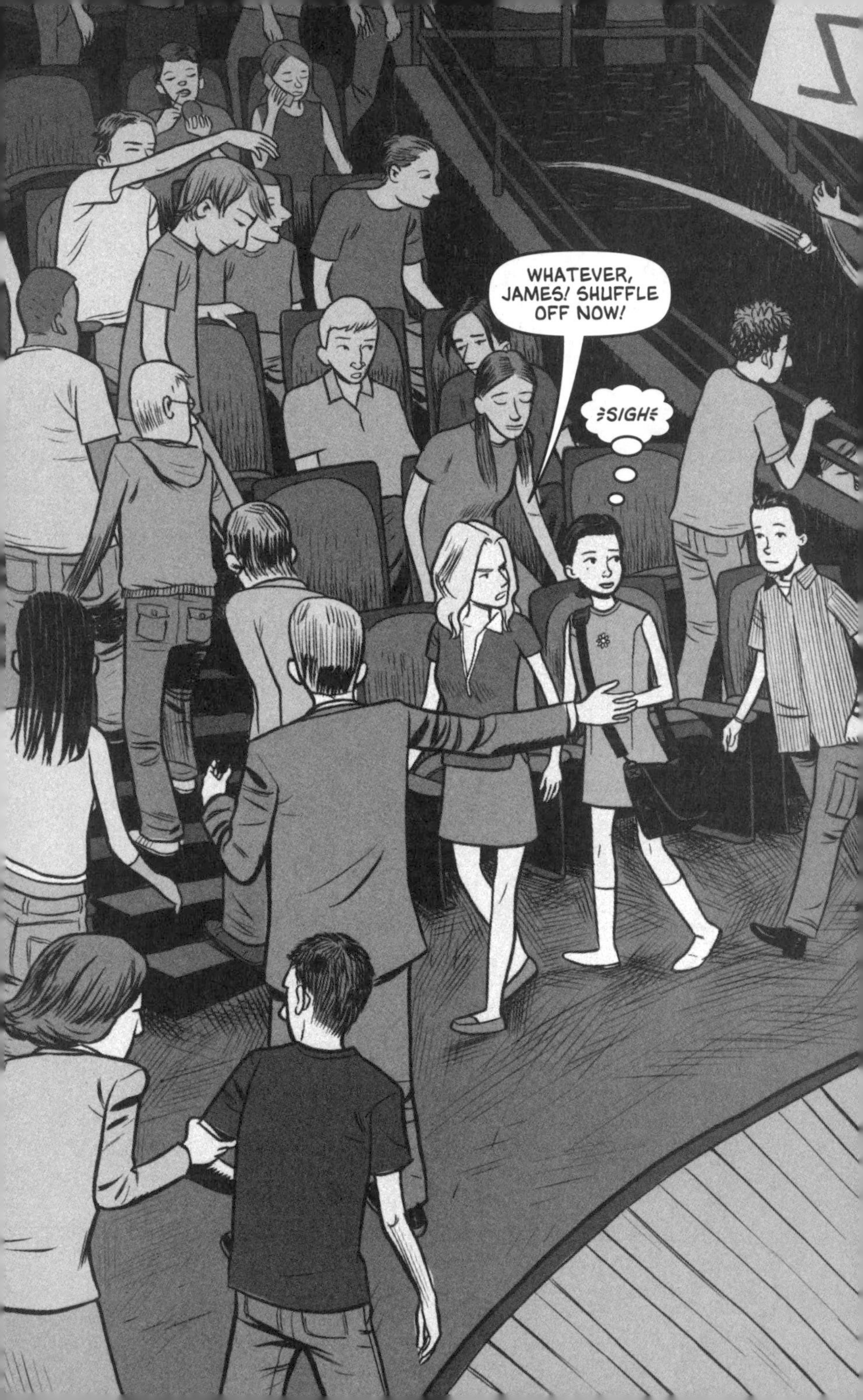
WHATEVER, JAMES! SHUFFLE OFF NOW!
SIGH

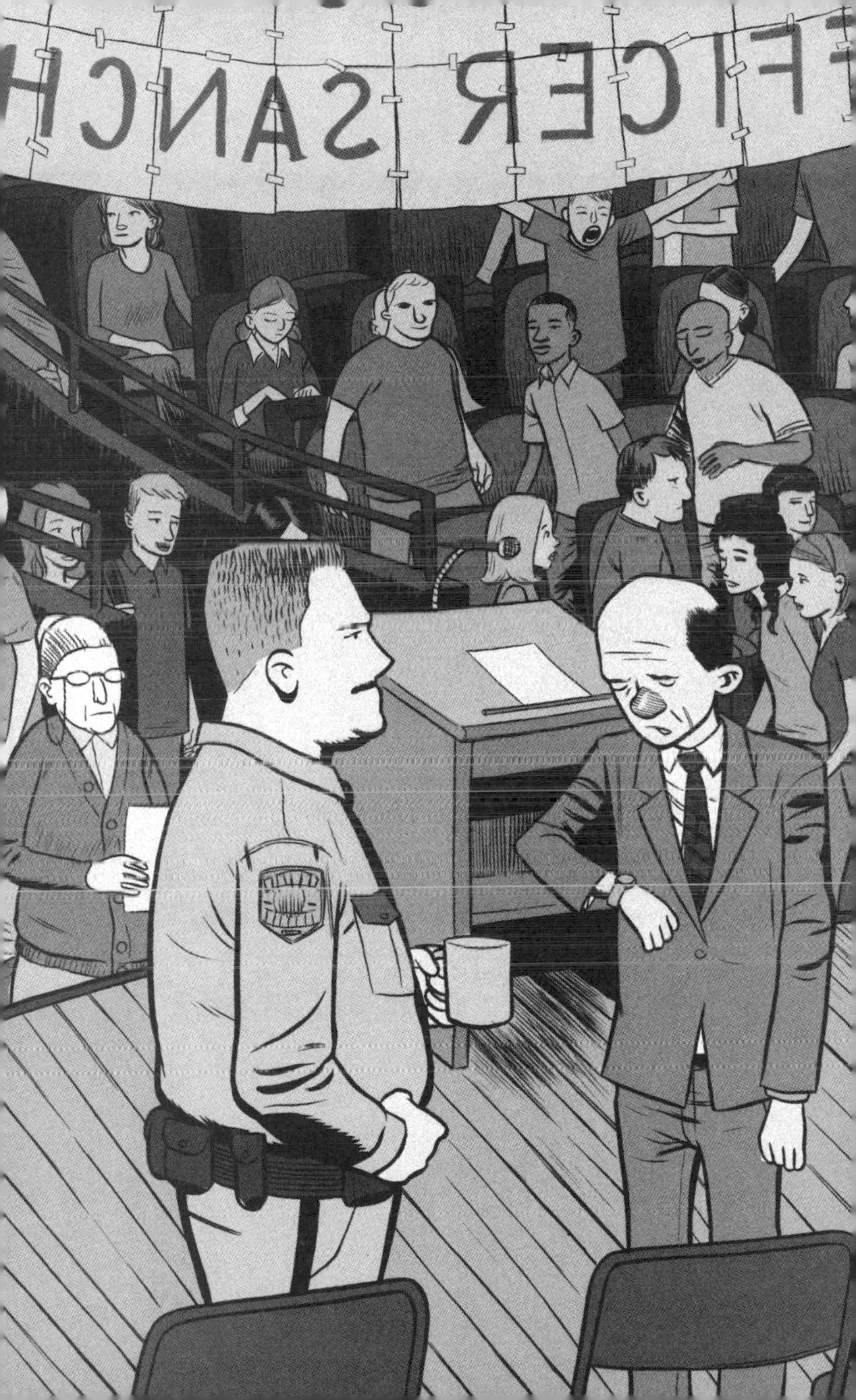
FICER SANCH

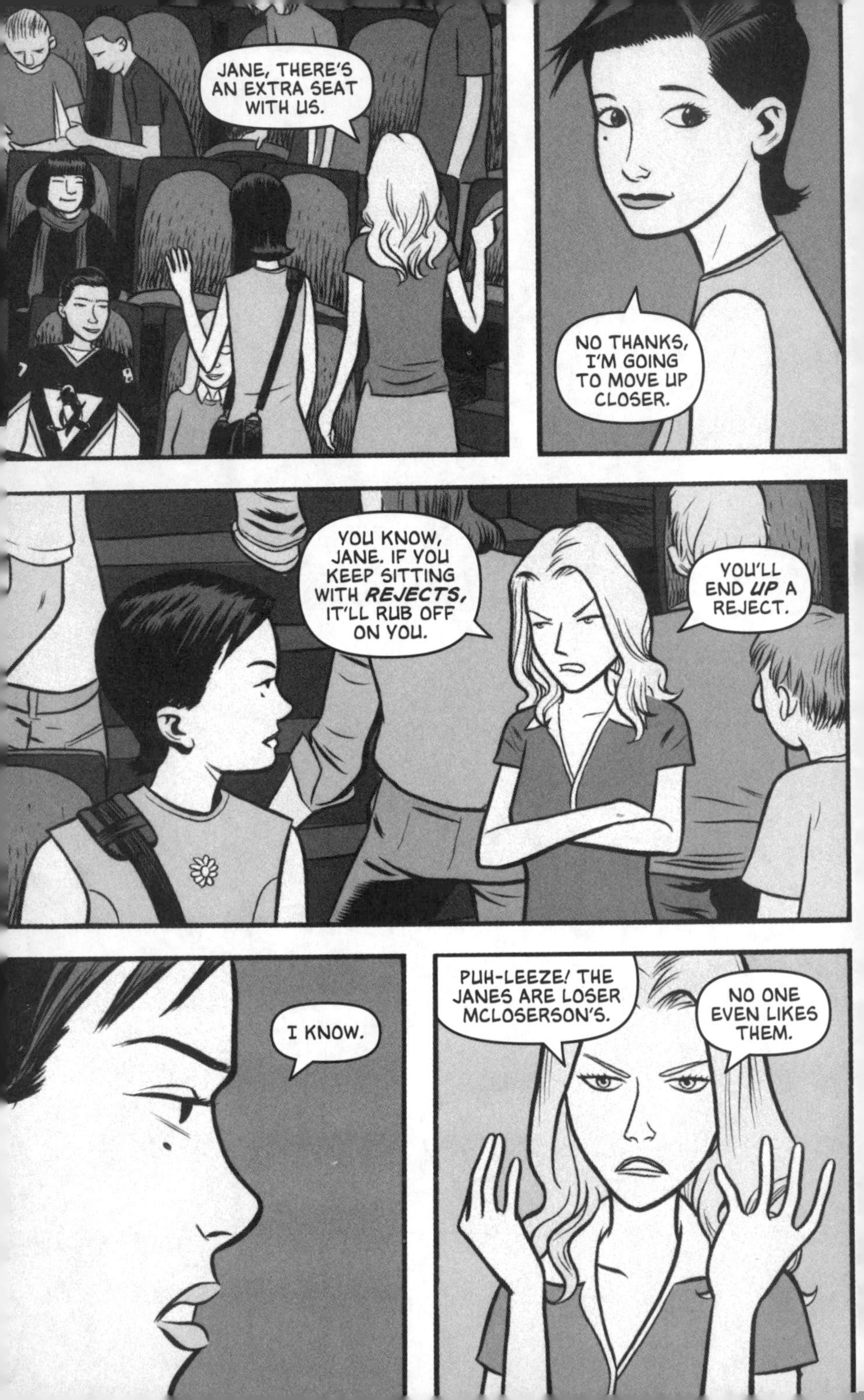
JANE, THERE'S AN EXTRA SEAT WITH US.
NO THANKS, I'M GOING TO MOVE UP CLOSER.
YOU KNOW, JANE. IF YOU KEEP SITTING WITH *REJECTS,* IT'LL RUB OFF ON YOU.
YOU'LL END *UP* A REJECT.
I KNOW.
PUH-LEEZE! THE JANES ARE LOSER MCLOSERSON'S.
NO ONE EVEN LIKES THEM.

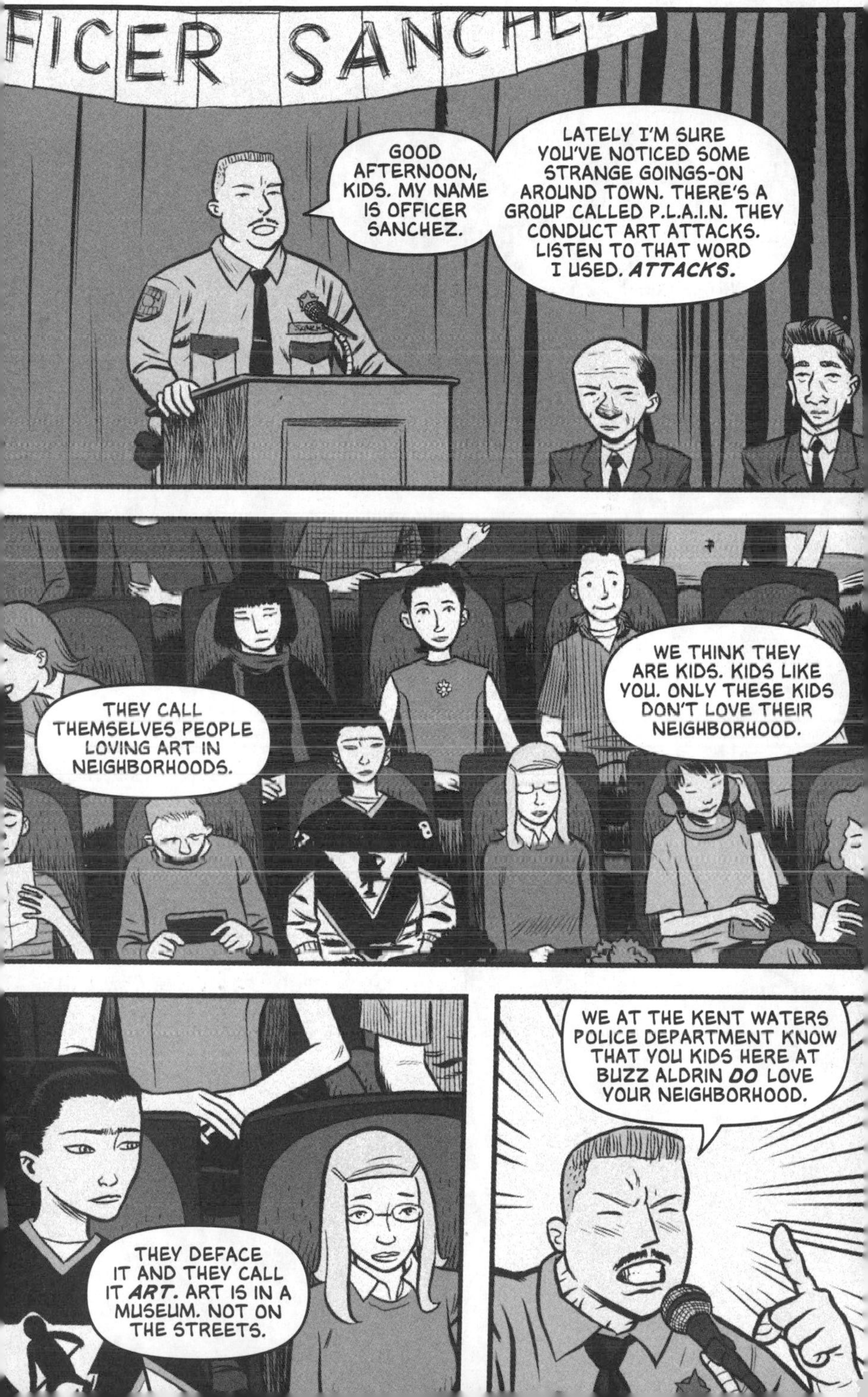
FICER SANCHE
GOOD AFTERNOON, KIDS. MY NAME IS OFFICER SANCHEZ.
LATELY I'M SURE YOU'VE NOTICED SOME STRANGE GOINGS-ON AROUND TOWN. THERE'S A GROUP CALLED P.L.A.I.N. THEY CONDUCT ART ATTACKS. LISTEN TO THAT WORD I USED. *ATTACKS.*
THEY CALL THEMSELVES PEOPLE LOVING ART IN NEIGHBORHOODS.
WE THINK THEY ARE KIDS. KIDS LIKE YOU. ONLY THESE KIDS DON'T LOVE THEIR NEIGHBORHOOD.
THEY DEFACE IT AND THEY CALL IT *ART.* ART IS IN A MUSEUM. NOT ON THE STREETS.
WE AT THE KENT WATERS POLICE DEPARTMENT KNOW THAT YOU KIDS HERE AT BUZZ ALDRIN *DO* LOVE YOUR NEIGHBORHOOD.

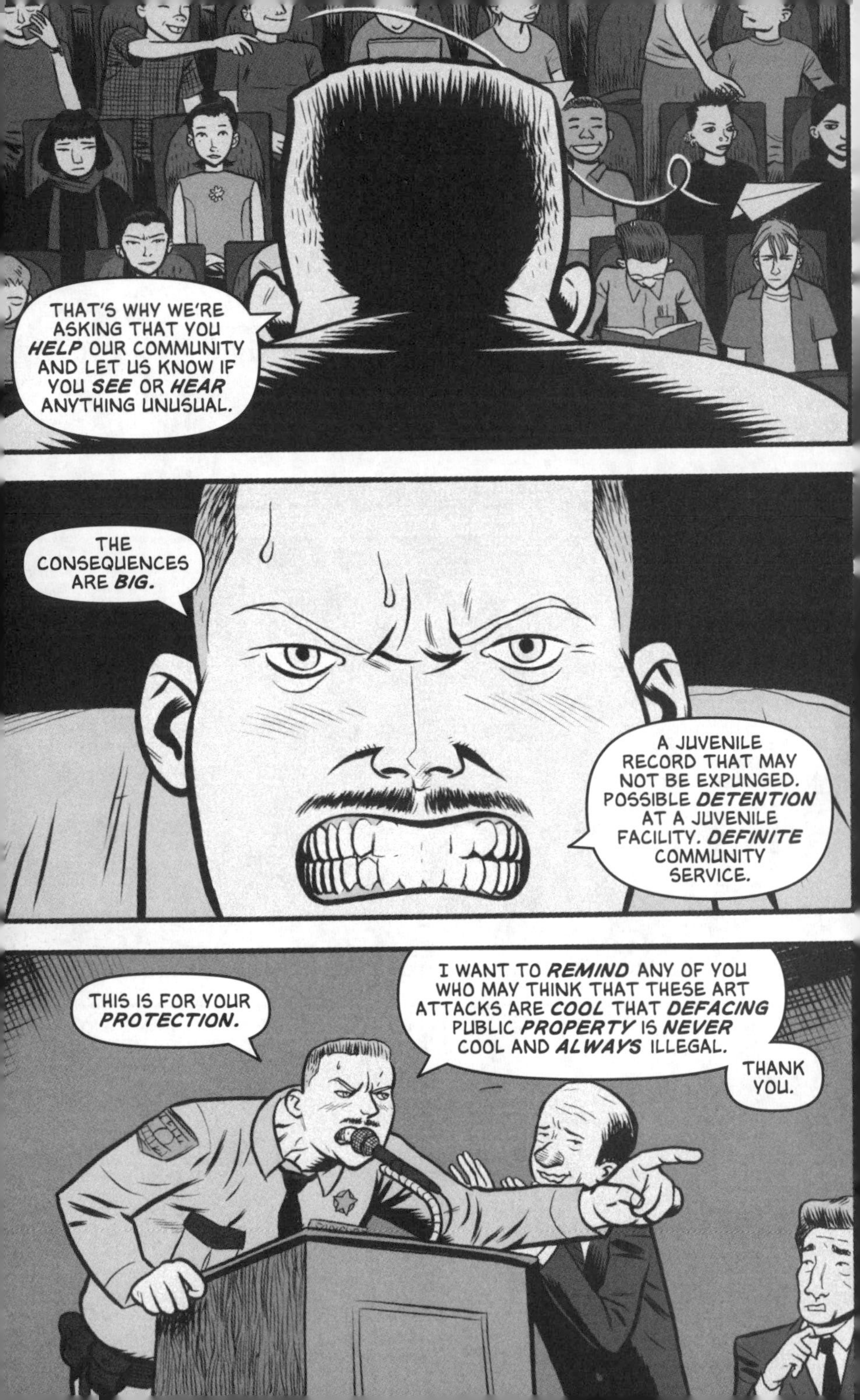
THAT'S WHY WE'RE ASKING THAT YOU HELP OUR COMMUNITY AND LET US KNOW IF YOU SEE OR HEAR ANYTHING UNUSUAL.
THE CONSEQUENCES ARE BIG.
A JUVENILE RECORD THAT MAY NOT BE EXPUNGED. POSSIBLE DETENTION AT A JUVENILE FACILITY. DEFINITE COMMUNITY SERVICE.
THIS IS FOR YOUR PROTECTION.
I WANT TO REMIND ANY OF YOU WHO MAY THINK THAT THESE ART ATTACKS ARE COOL THAT DEFACING PUBLIC PROPERTY IS NEVER COOL AND ALWAYS ILLEGAL.
THANK YOU.

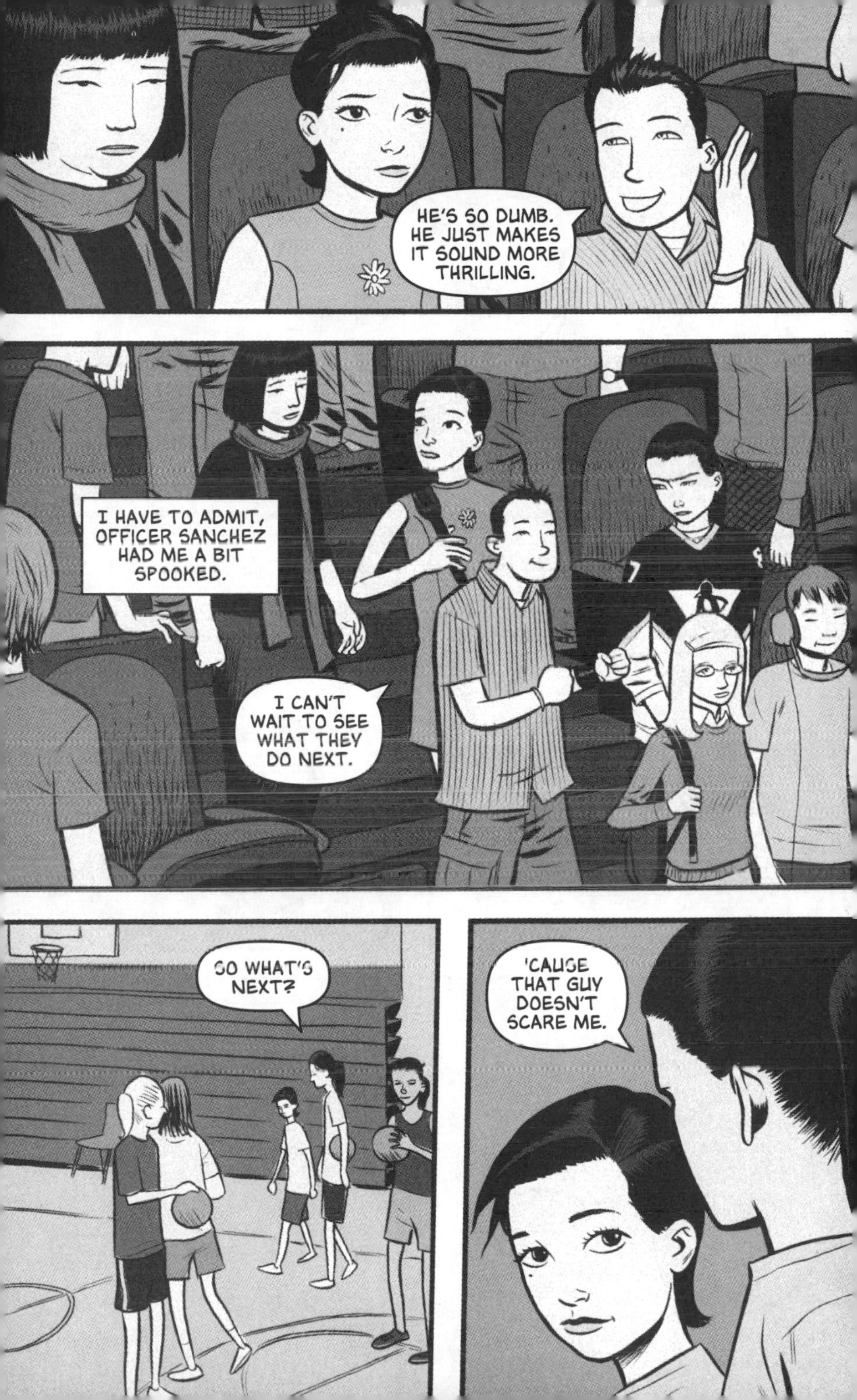
HE'S SO DUMB. HE JUST MAKES IT SOUND MORE THRILLING.
I HAVE TO ADMIT, OFFICER SANCHEZ HAD ME A BIT SPOOKED.
I CAN'T WAIT TO SEE WHAT THEY DO NEXT.
SO WHAT'S NEXT?
'CAUSE THAT GUY DOESN'T SCARE ME.

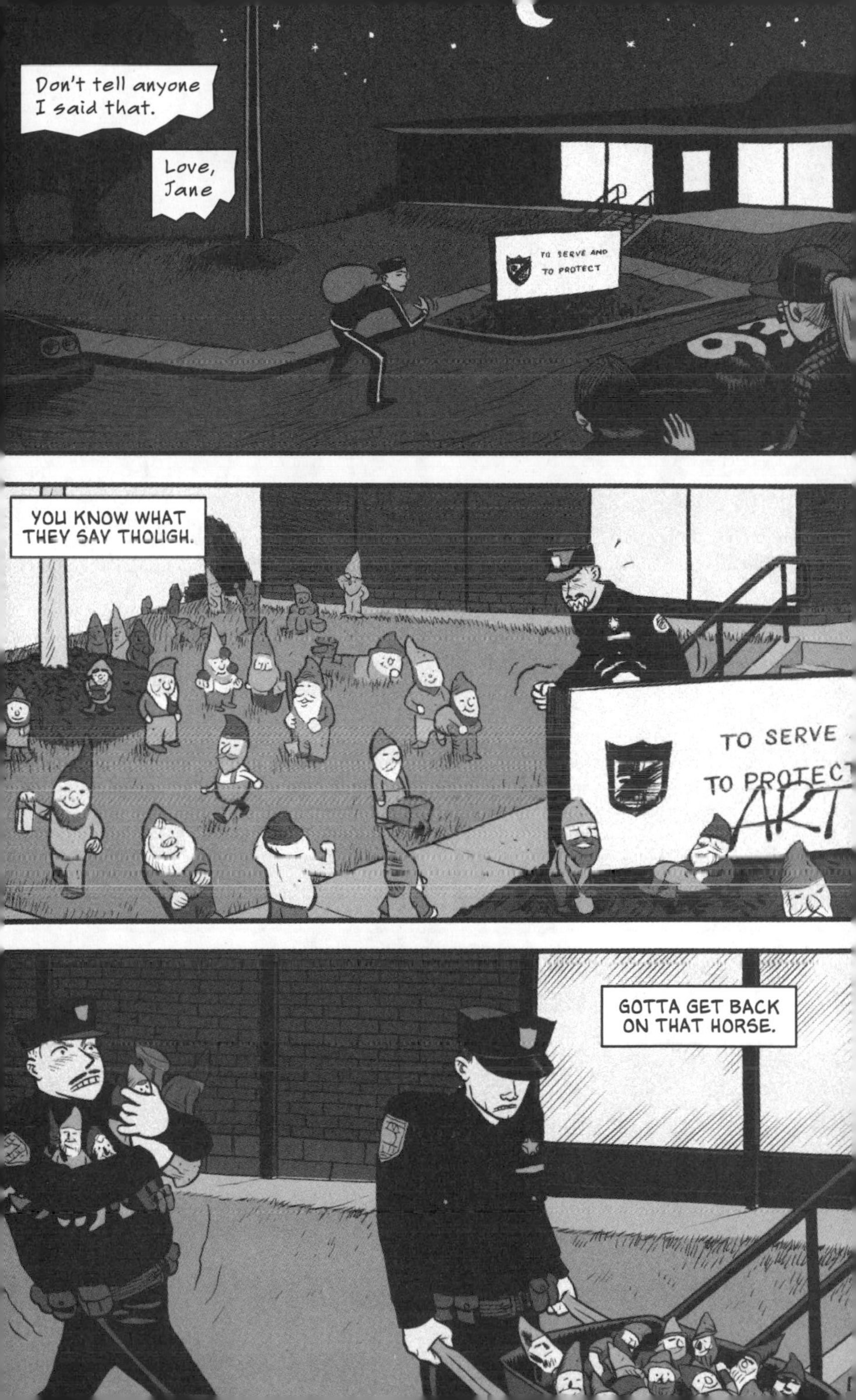

Don't tell anyone I said that.
Love, Jane
TO SERVE AND TO PROTECT
YOU KNOW WHAT THEY SAY THOUGH.
TO SERVE
TO PROTECT
ART
GOTTA GET BACK ON THAT HORSE.

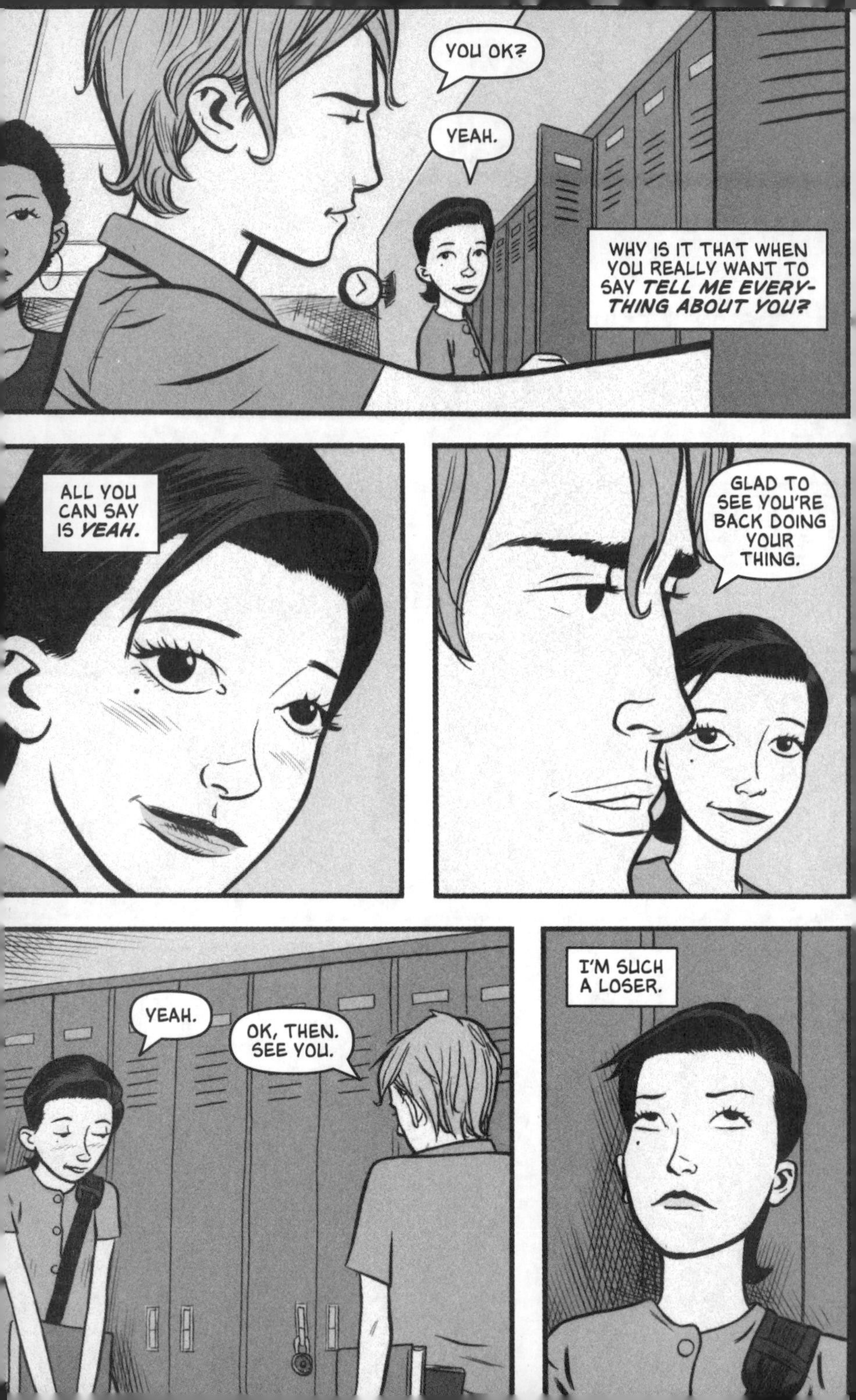
YOU OK?
YEAH.
WHY IS IT THAT WHEN YOU REALLY WANT TO SAY *TELL ME EVERY-THING ABOUT YOU?*
ALL YOU CAN SAY IS *YEAH.*
GLAD TO SEE YOU'RE BACK DOING YOUR THING.
YEAH.
OK, THEN. SEE YOU.
I'M SUCH A LOSER.

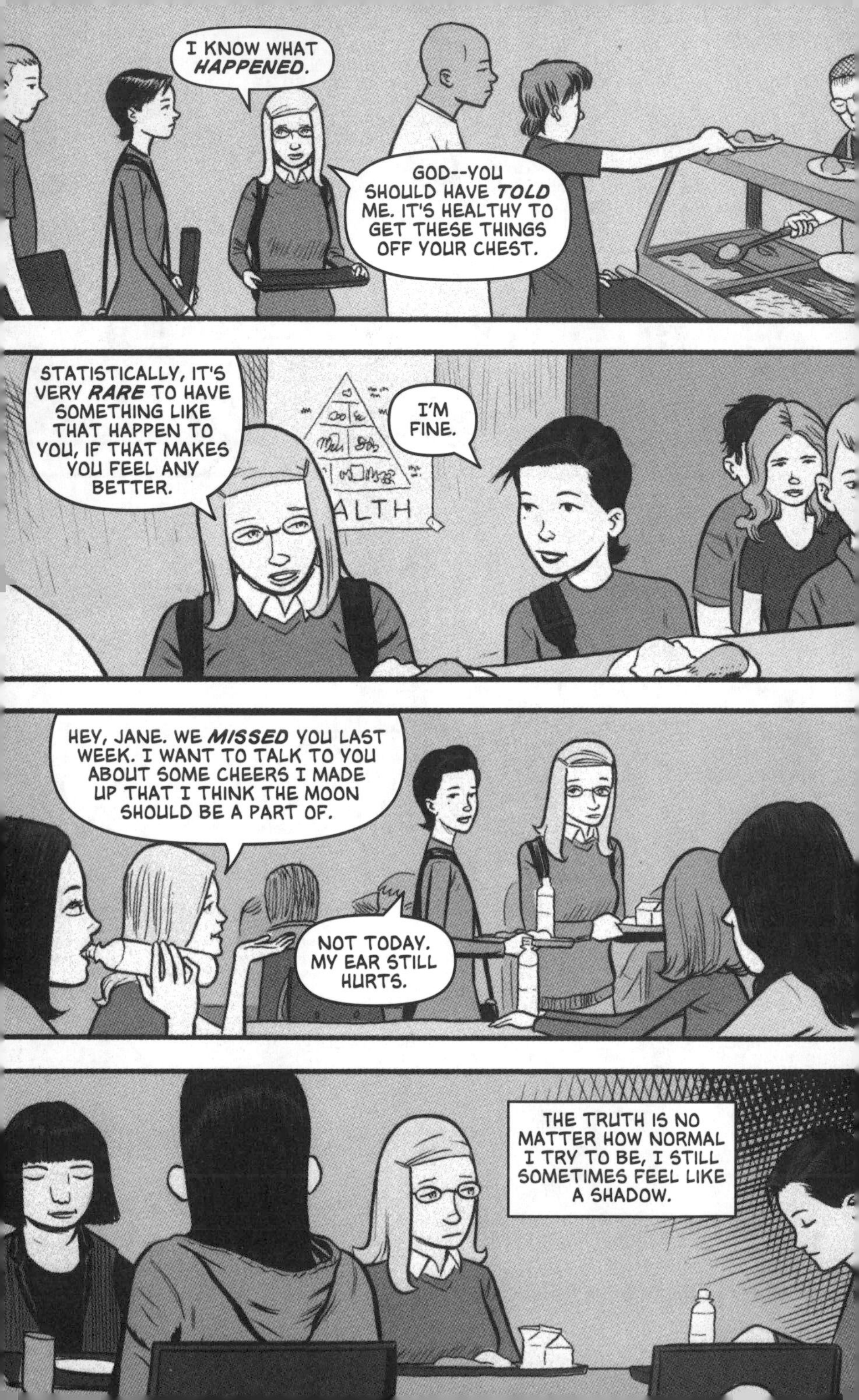
I KNOW WHAT *HAPPENED.*
GOD--YOU SHOULD HAVE *TOLD* ME. IT'S HEALTHY TO GET THESE THINGS OFF YOUR CHEST.
STATISTICALLY, IT'S VERY *RARE* TO HAVE SOMETHING LIKE THAT HAPPEN TO YOU, IF THAT MAKES YOU FEEL ANY BETTER.
I'M FINE.
ALTH
HEY, JANE. WE *MISSED* YOU LAST WEEK. I WANT TO TALK TO YOU ABOUT SOME CHEERS I MADE UP THAT I THINK THE MOON SHOULD BE A PART OF.
NOT TODAY. MY EAR STILL HURTS.
THE TRUTH IS NO MATTER HOW NORMAL I TRY TO BE, I STILL SOMETIMES FEEL LIKE A SHADOW.

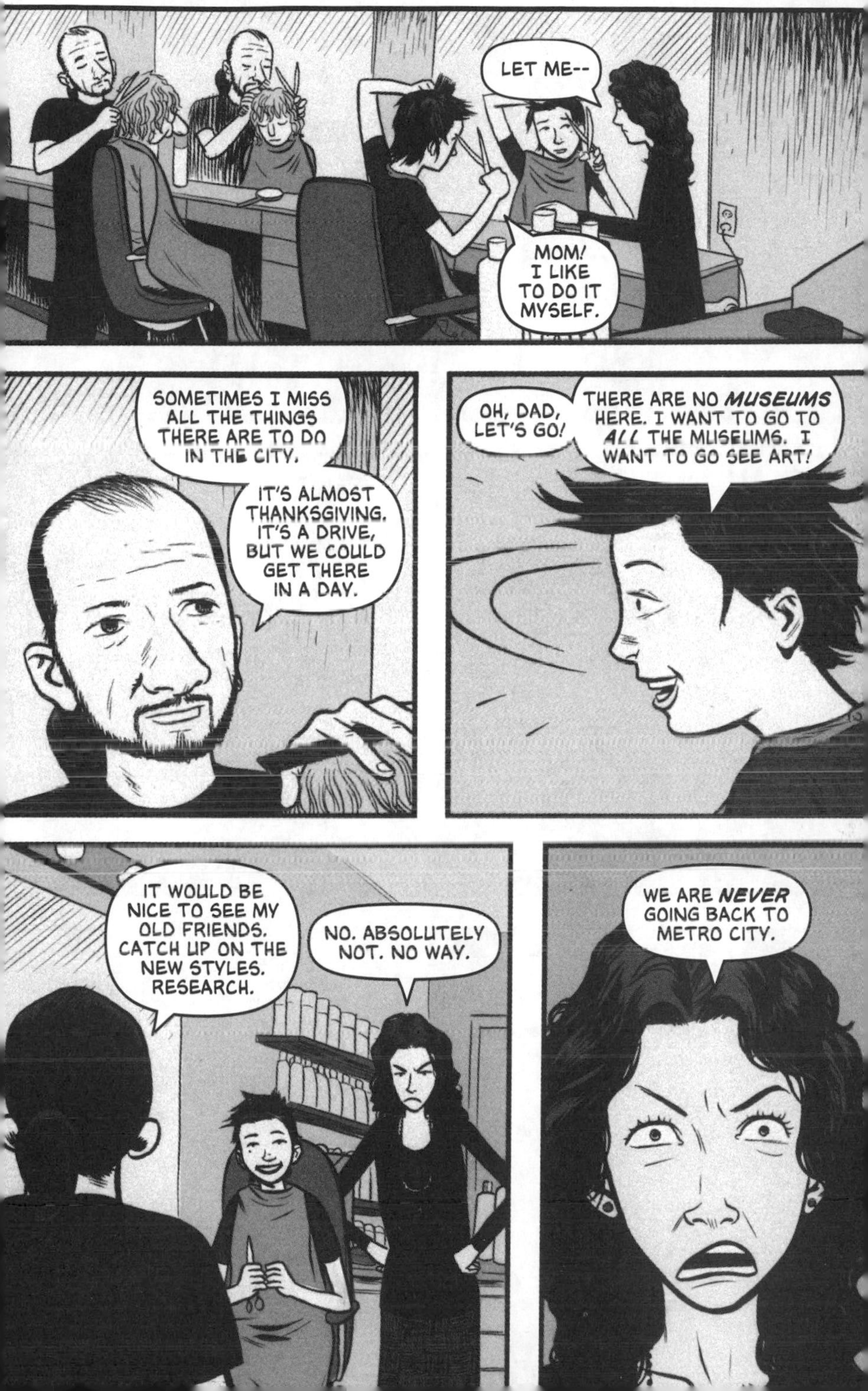
LET ME--
MOM! I LIKE TO DO IT MYSELF.
SOMETIMES I MISS ALL THE THINGS THERE ARE TO DO IN THE CITY.
IT'S ALMOST THANKSGIVING. IT'S A DRIVE, BUT WE COULD GET THERE IN A DAY.
OH, DAD, LET'S GO!
THERE ARE NO *MUSEUMS* HERE. I WANT TO GO TO *ALL* THE MUSEUMS. I WANT TO GO SEE ART!
IT WOULD BE NICE TO SEE MY OLD FRIENDS. CATCH UP ON THE NEW STYLES. RESEARCH.
NO. ABSOLUTELY NOT. NO WAY.
WE ARE ***NEVER*** GOING BACK TO METRO CITY.

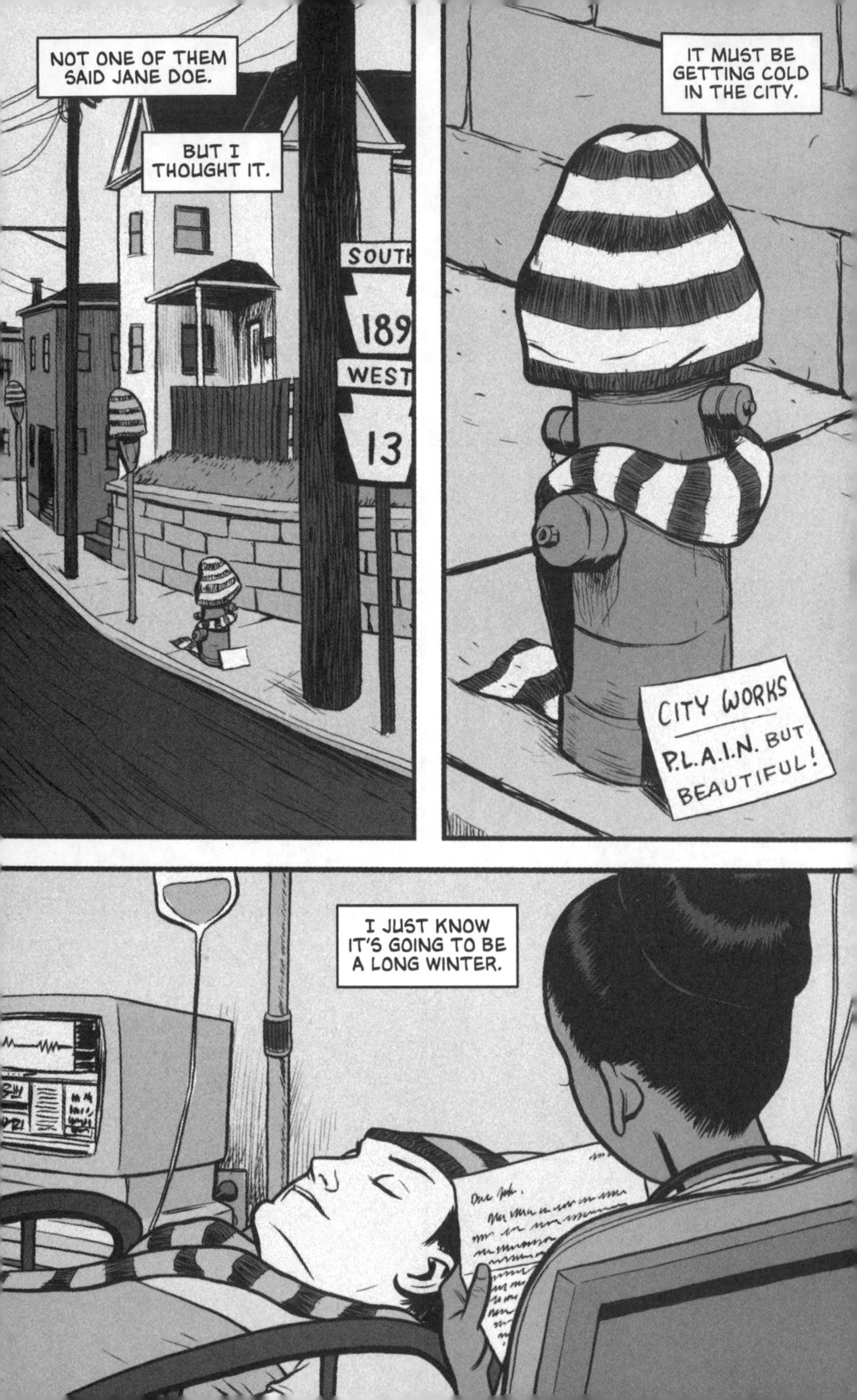
NOT ONE OF THEM SAID JANE DOE.
BUT I THOUGHT IT.
SOUTH
189
WEST
13
IT MUST BE GETTING COLD IN THE CITY.
CITY WORKS
P.L.A.I.N. BUT BEAUTIFUL!
I JUST KNOW IT'S GOING TO BE A LONG WINTER.

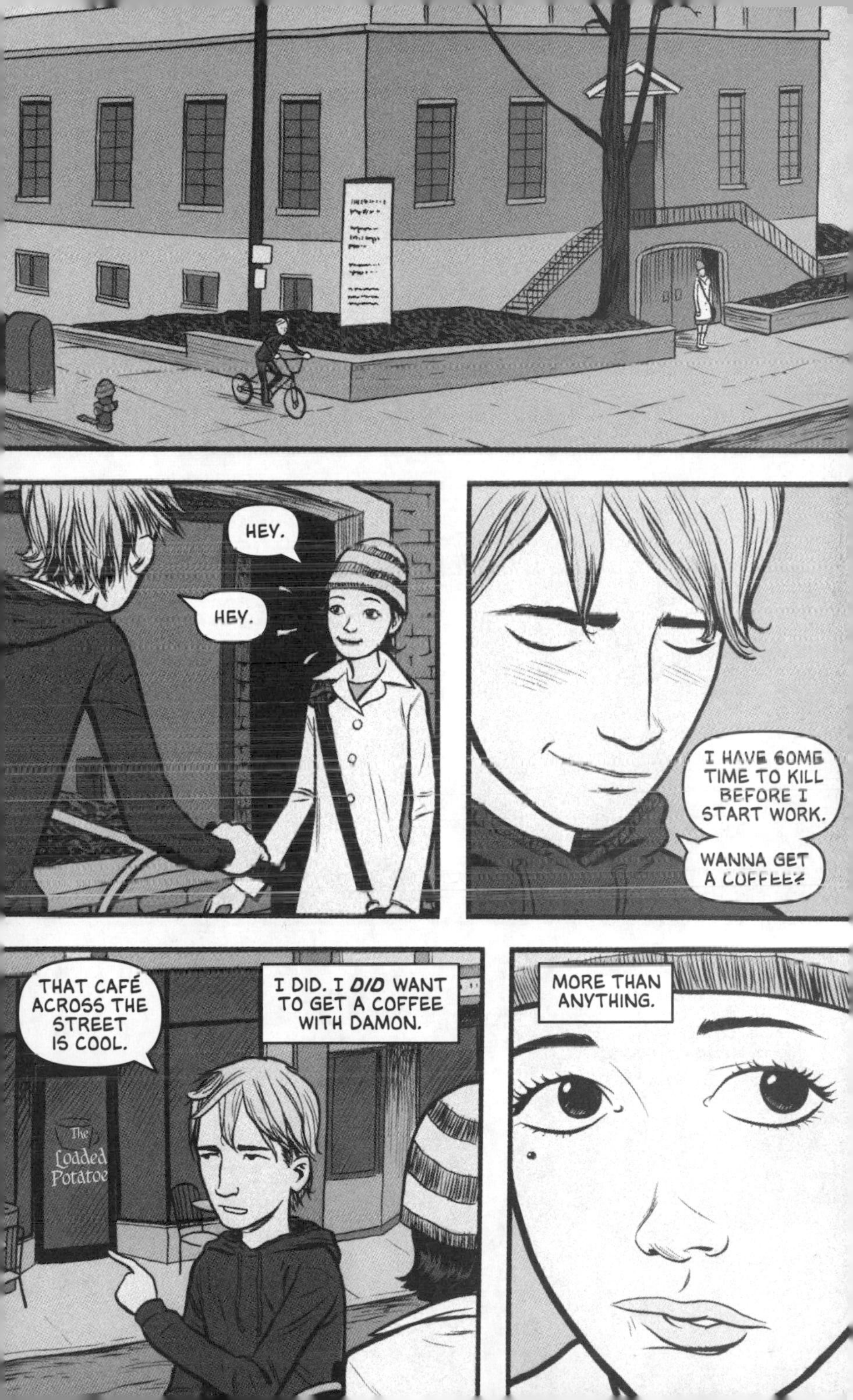

HEY.
HEY.
I HAVE SOME TIME TO KILL BEFORE I START WORK.
WANNA GET A COFFEE?
THAT CAFÉ ACROSS THE STREET IS COOL.
I DID. I *DID* WANT TO GET A COFFEE WITH DAMON.
The Loaded Potatoe
MORE THAN ANYTHING.

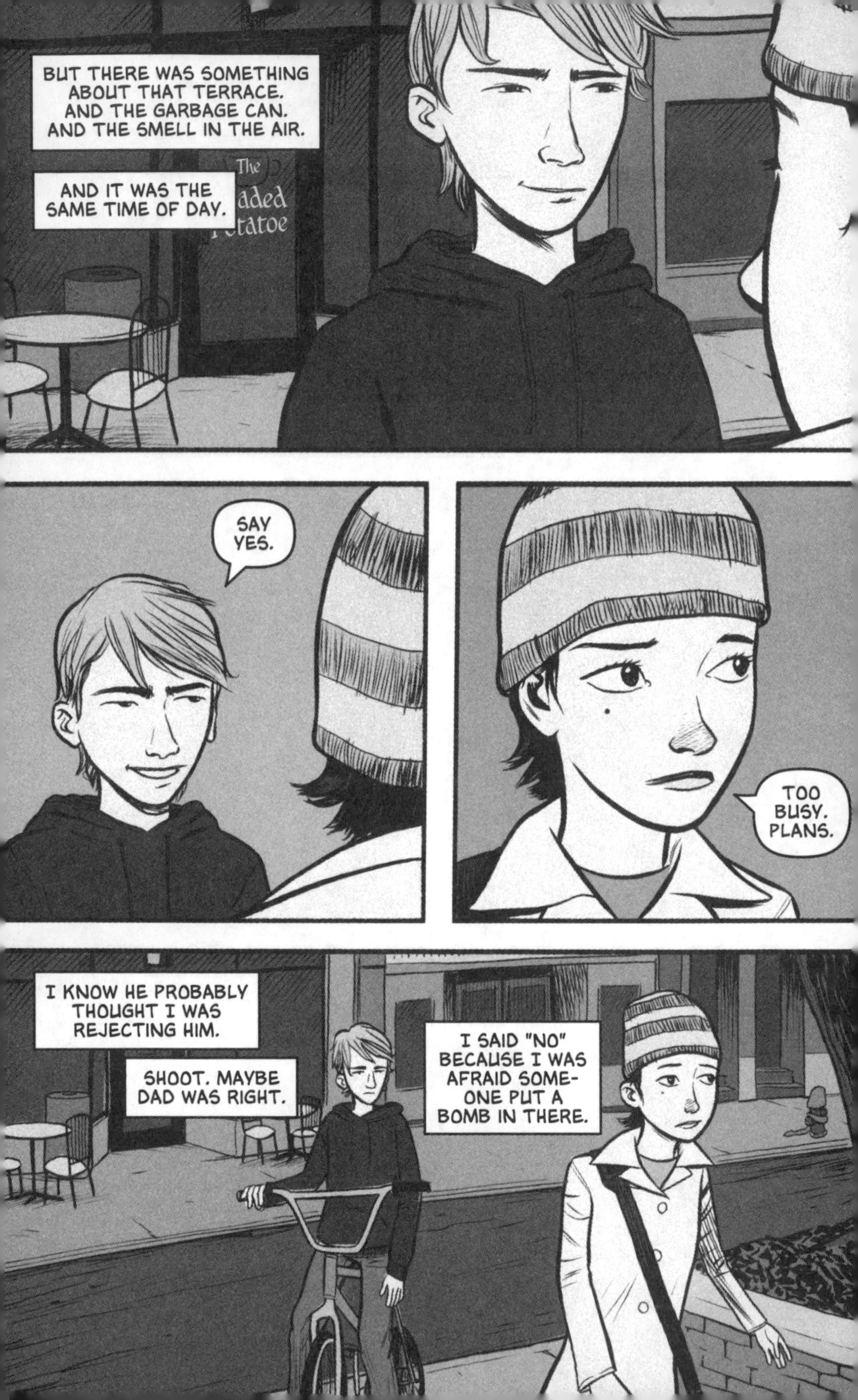
BUT THERE WAS SOMETHING ABOUT THAT TERRACE. AND THE GARBAGE CAN. AND THE SMELL IN THE AIR.
AND IT WAS THE SAME TIME OF DAY.
SAY YES.
TOO BUSY. PLANS.
I KNOW HE PROBABLY THOUGHT I WAS REJECTING HIM.
SHOOT. MAYBE DAD WAS RIGHT.
I SAID "NO" BECAUSE I WAS AFRAID SOME-ONE PUT A BOMB IN THERE.

In which we PLAINly ask that in advance of the Thanksgiving holiday, the town comes together at the hour of noon on Wednesday November 23rd to sing in one voice the song of their choice.

Sing out. Sing strong.
beautiful.

ove you.

A P.L.A.I.N. ANNOUNCEMENT

In which we PLAINly ask that in advance of the Thanksgiving holiday, the town comes together at the hour of noon on Wednesday November 23rd to sing in one voice the song of their choice.

Sing out. Sing strong.
Sing bea-tiful.

We love you.

A P.L.A.I.N. ANNOUCEMENT

In which we PLAINly ask that in advance of the Thanksgiving holiday, the town comes together at the hour of noon on Wednesday Novem to sing in

I DON'T GET IT, JANE. YOU'RE KIND OF *ARTY*. DO *YOU* GET IT?

NOPE.

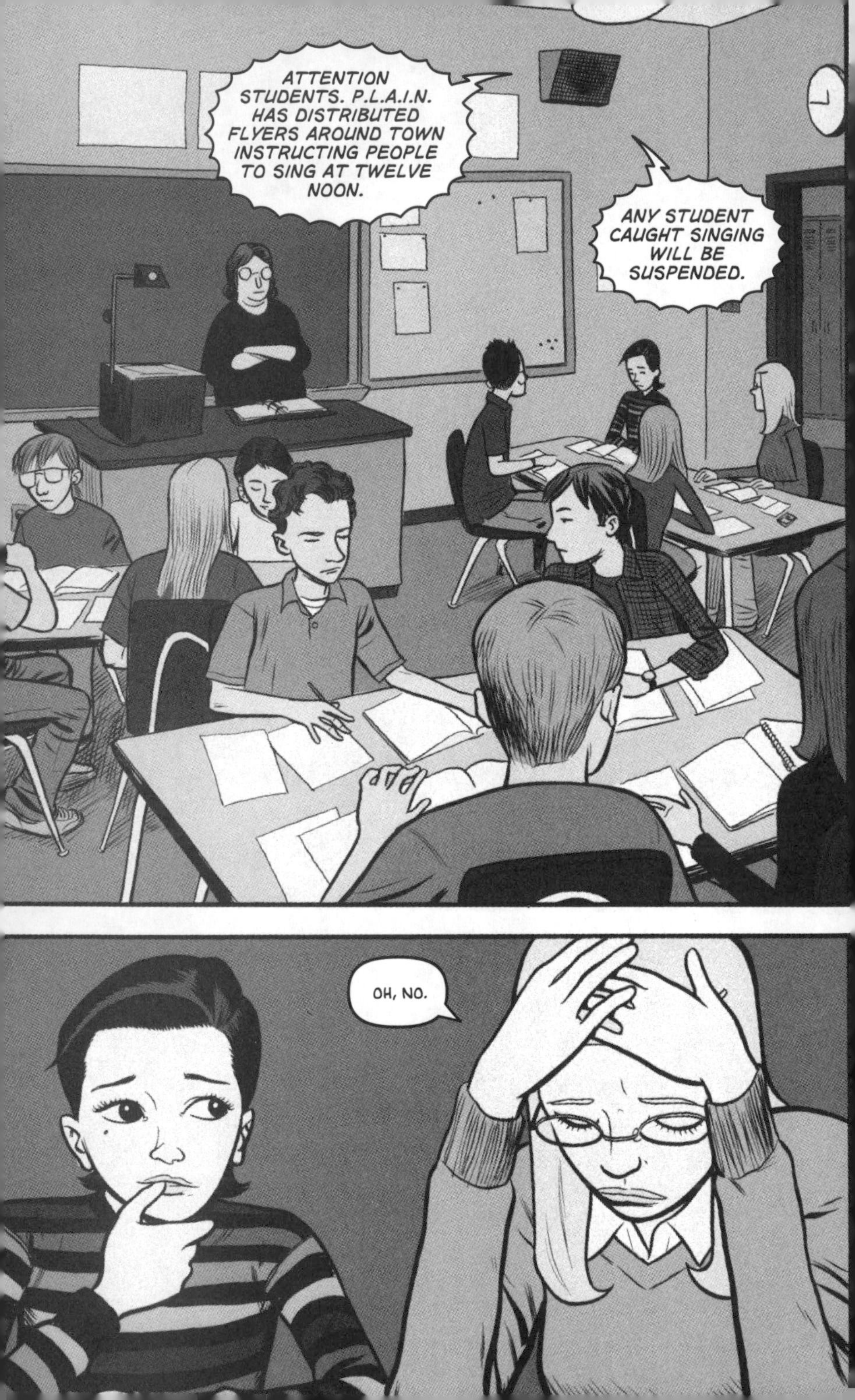
ATTENTION STUDENTS. P.L.A.I.N. HAS DISTRIBUTED FLYERS AROUND TOWN INSTRUCTING PEOPLE TO SING AT TWELVE NOON.
ANY STUDENT CAUGHT SINGING WILL BE SUSPENDED.
OH, NO.

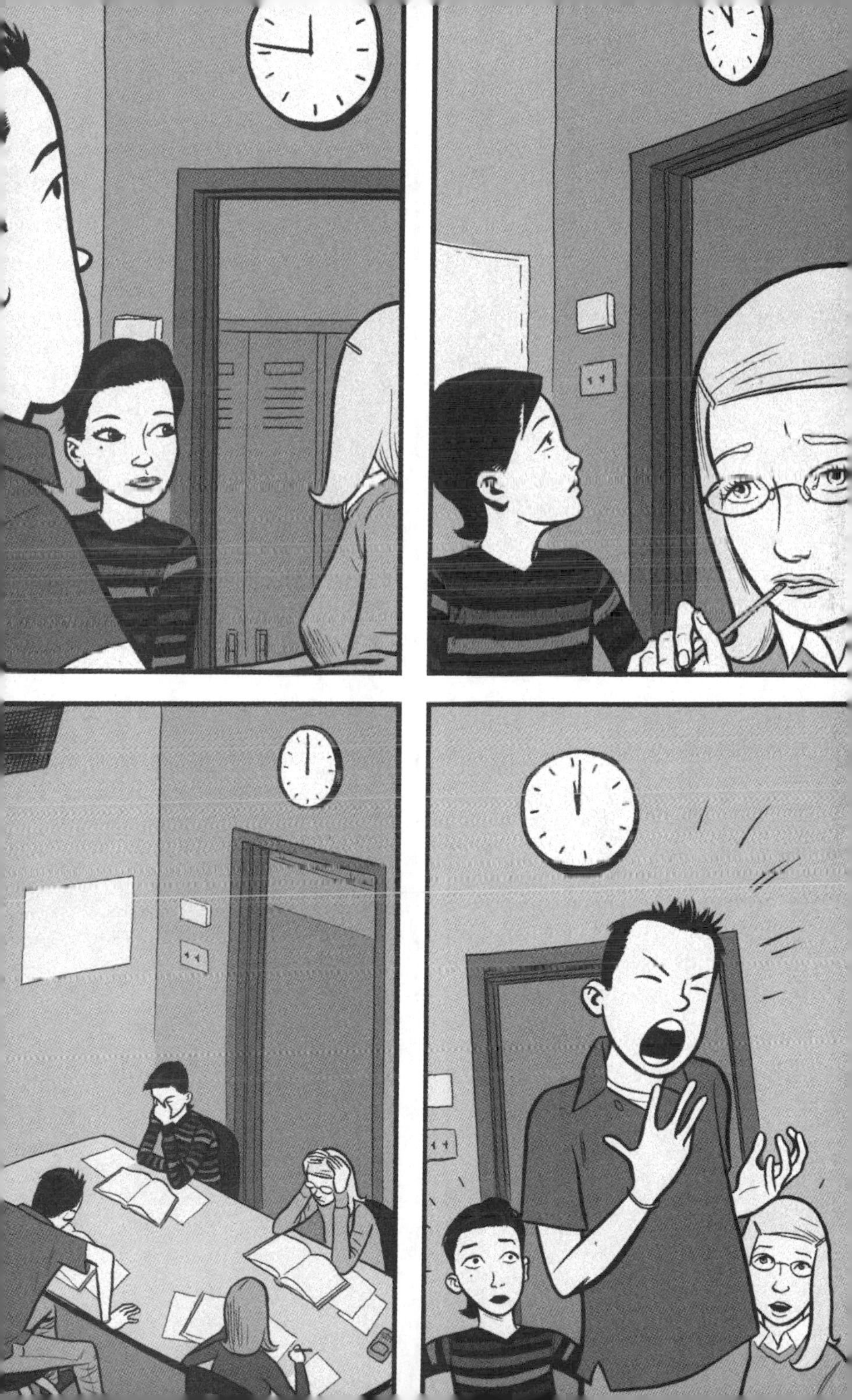

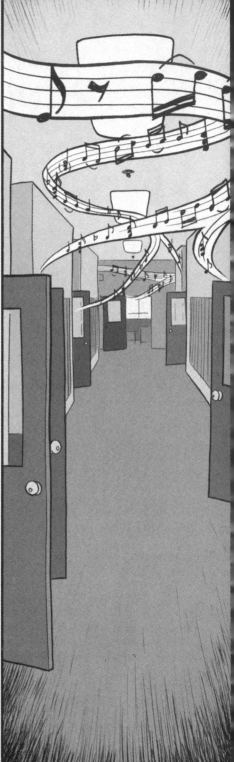

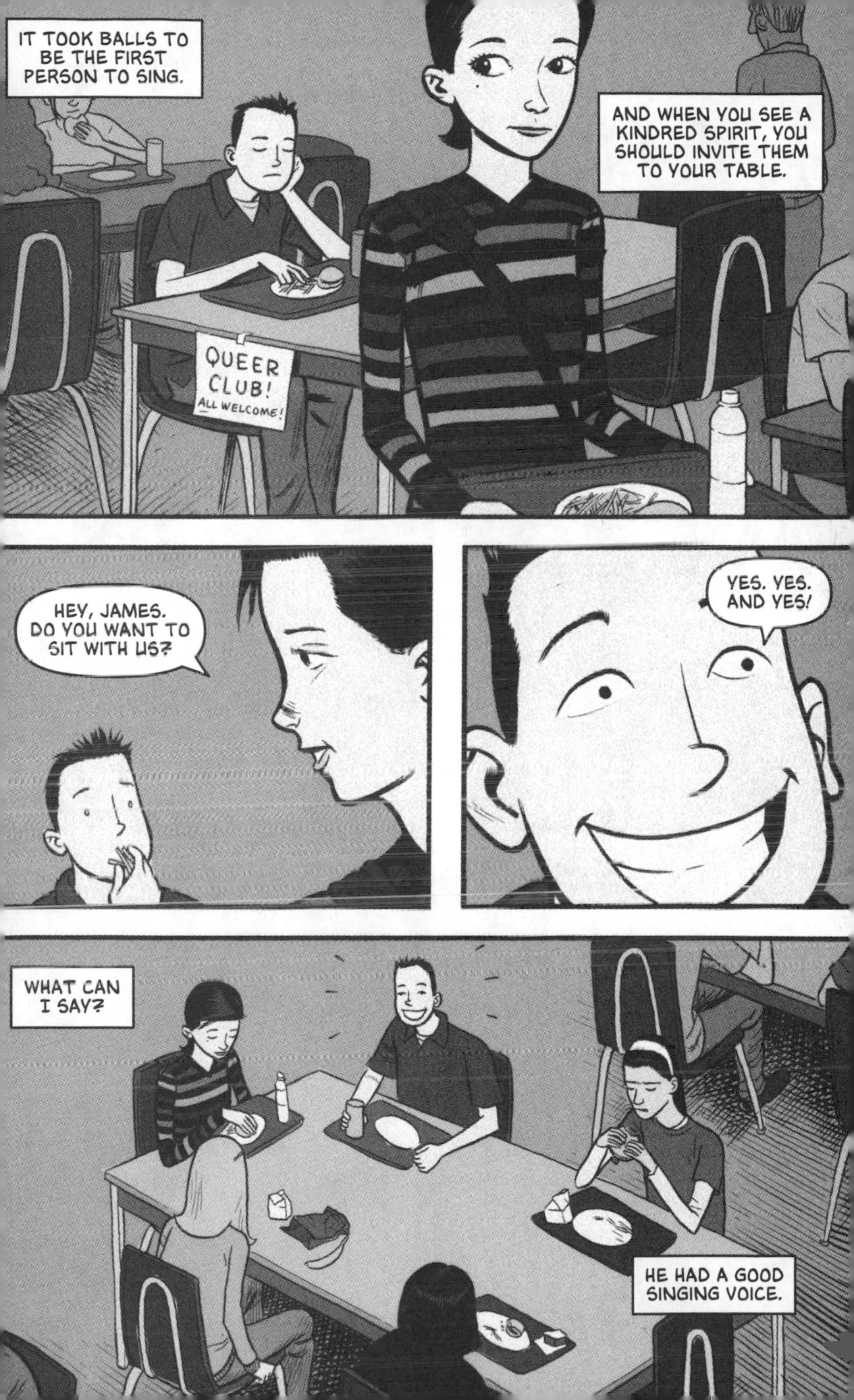
IT TOOK BALLS TO BE THE FIRST PERSON TO SING.
AND WHEN YOU SEE A KINDRED SPIRIT, YOU SHOULD INVITE THEM TO YOUR TABLE.
QUEER CLUB!
ALL WELCOME!
HEY, JAMES. DO YOU WANT TO SIT WITH US?
YES. YES. AND YES!
WHAT CAN I SAY?
HE HAD A GOOD SINGING VOICE.

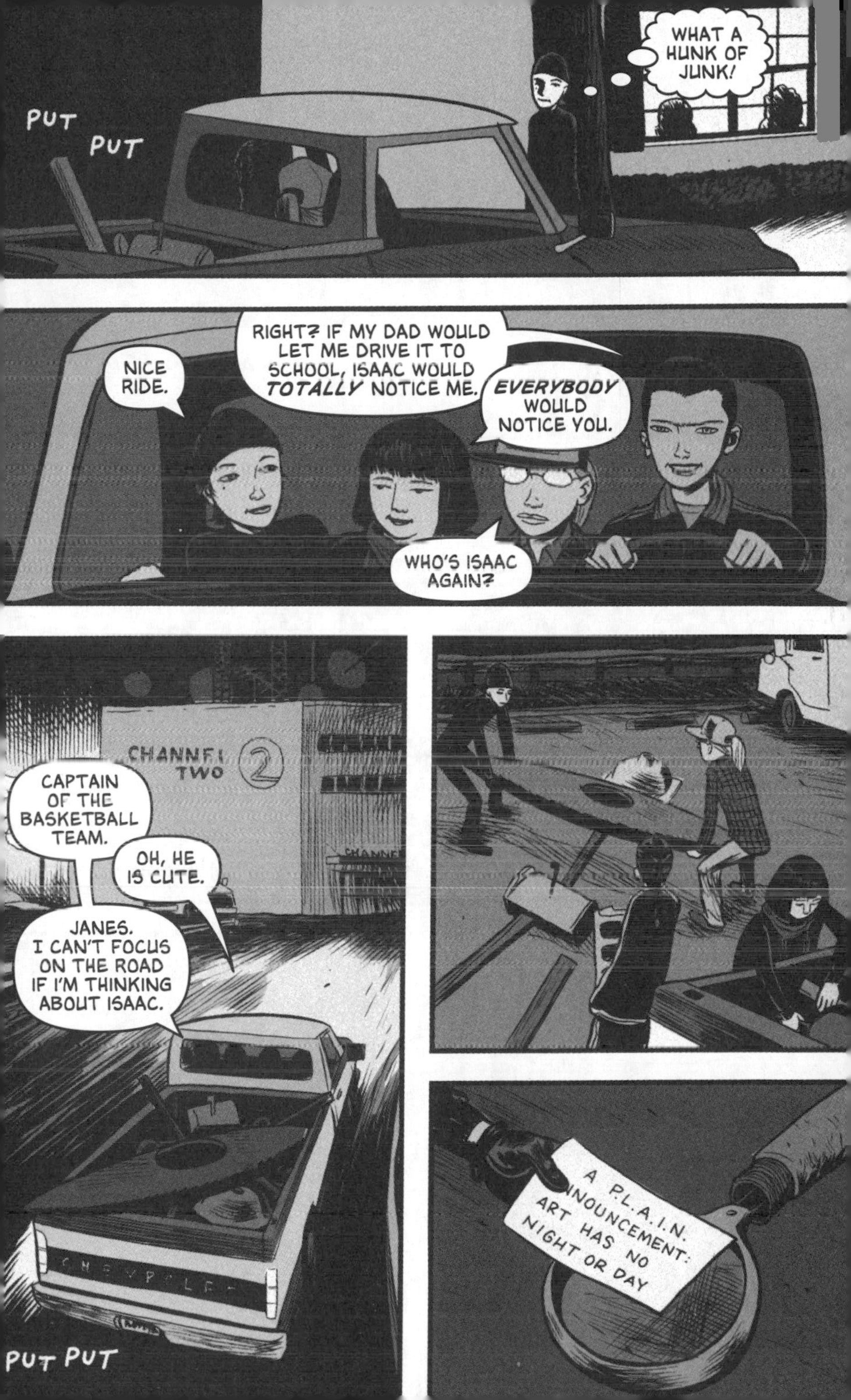
PUT PUT
WHAT A HUNK OF JUNK!
NICE RIDE.
RIGHT? IF MY DAD WOULD LET ME DRIVE IT TO SCHOOL, ISAAC WOULD TOTALLY NOTICE ME.
EVERYBODY WOULD NOTICE YOU.
WHO'S ISAAC AGAIN?
CHANNEL TWO 2
CAPTAIN OF THE BASKETBALL TEAM.
OH, HE IS CUTE.
JANES. I CAN'T FOCUS ON THE ROAD IF I'M THINKING ABOUT ISAAC.
PUT PUT
A P.L.A.I.N. ANNOUNCEMENT: ART HAS NO NIGHT OR DAY

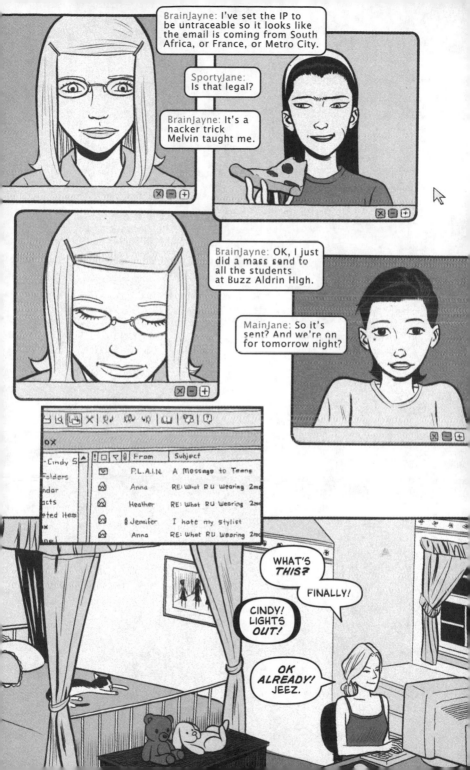

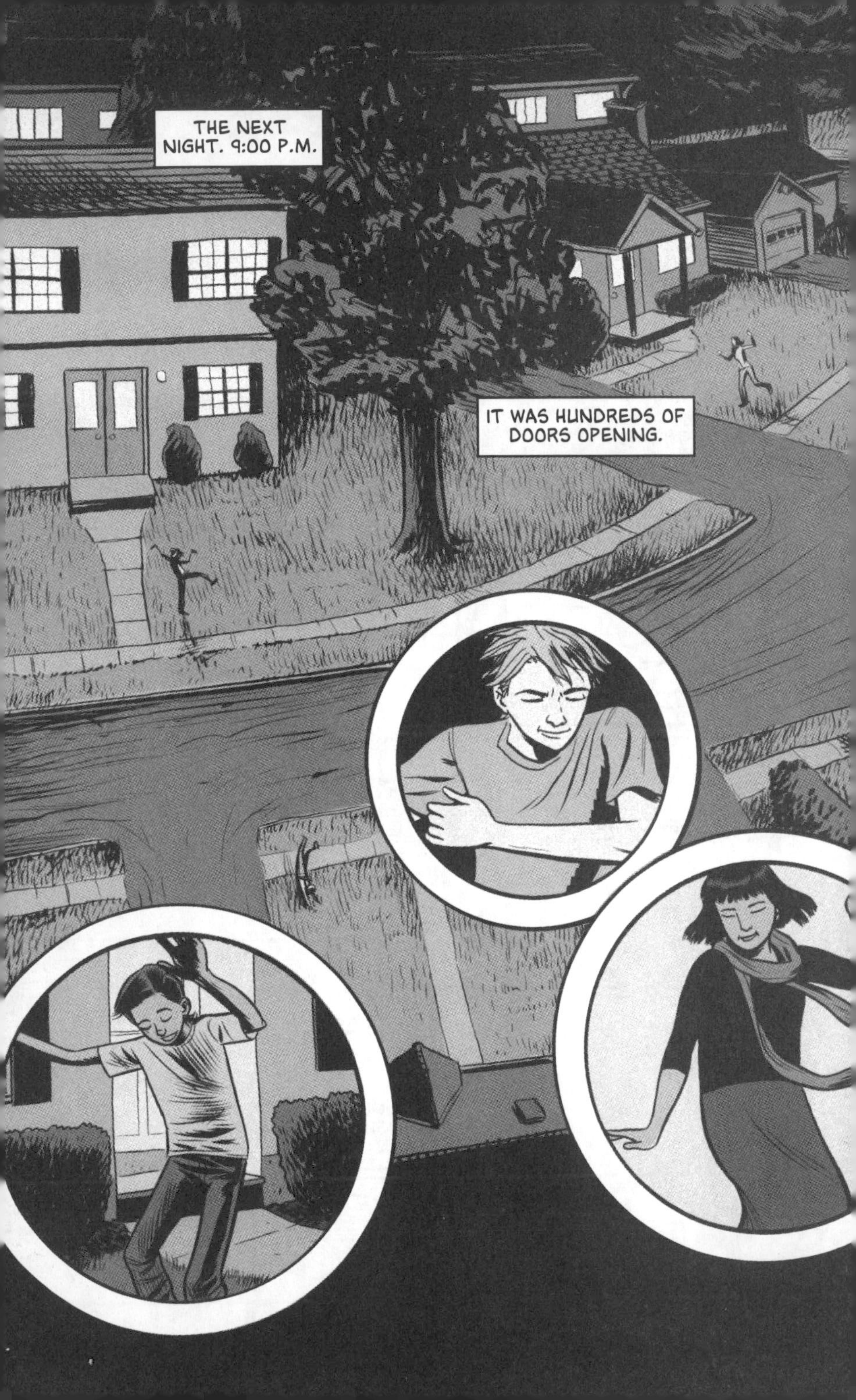
THE NEXT NIGHT. 9:00 P.M.
IT WAS HUNDREDS OF DOORS OPENING.

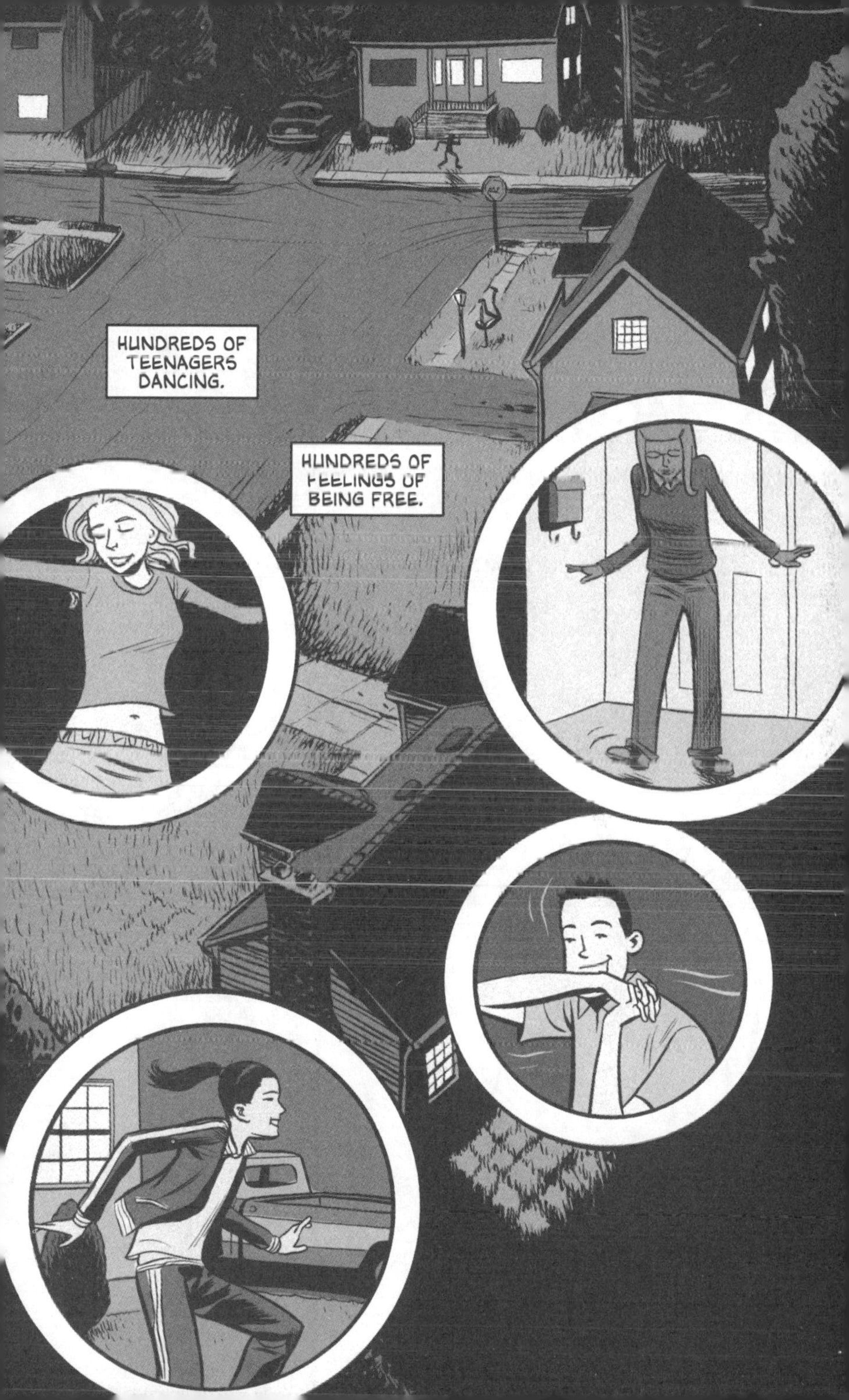
HUNDREDS OF TEENAGERS DANCING.
HUNDREDS OF FEELINGS OF BEING FREE.

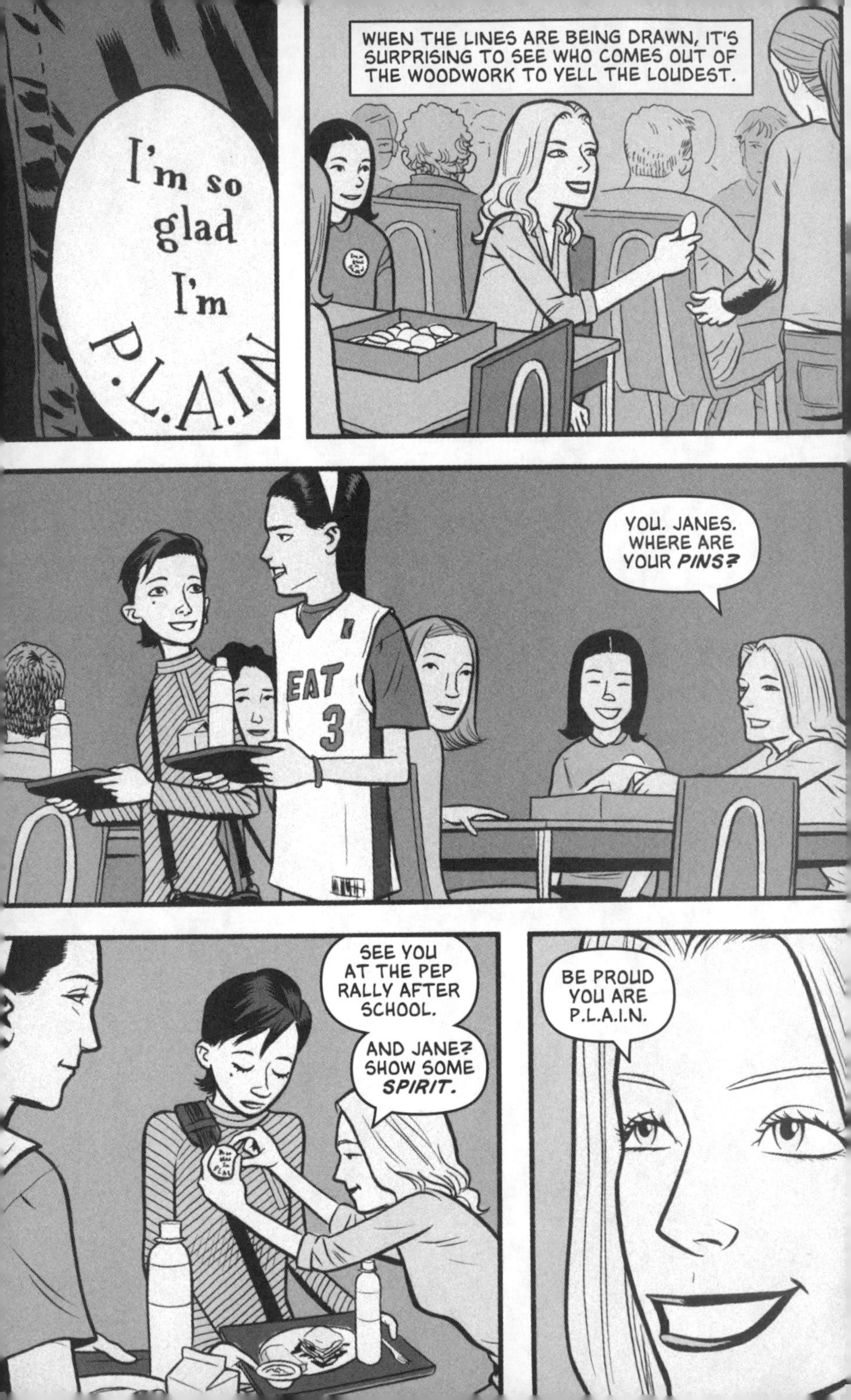
I'm so glad I'm P.L.A.I.N.
WHEN THE LINES ARE BEING DRAWN, IT'S SURPRISING TO SEE WHO COMES OUT OF THE WOODWORK TO YELL THE LOUDEST.
YOU. JANES. WHERE ARE YOUR *PINS?*
EAT 3
SEE YOU AT THE PEP RALLY AFTER SCHOOL.
AND JANE? SHOW SOME *SPIRIT.*
BE PROUD YOU ARE P.L.A.I.N.

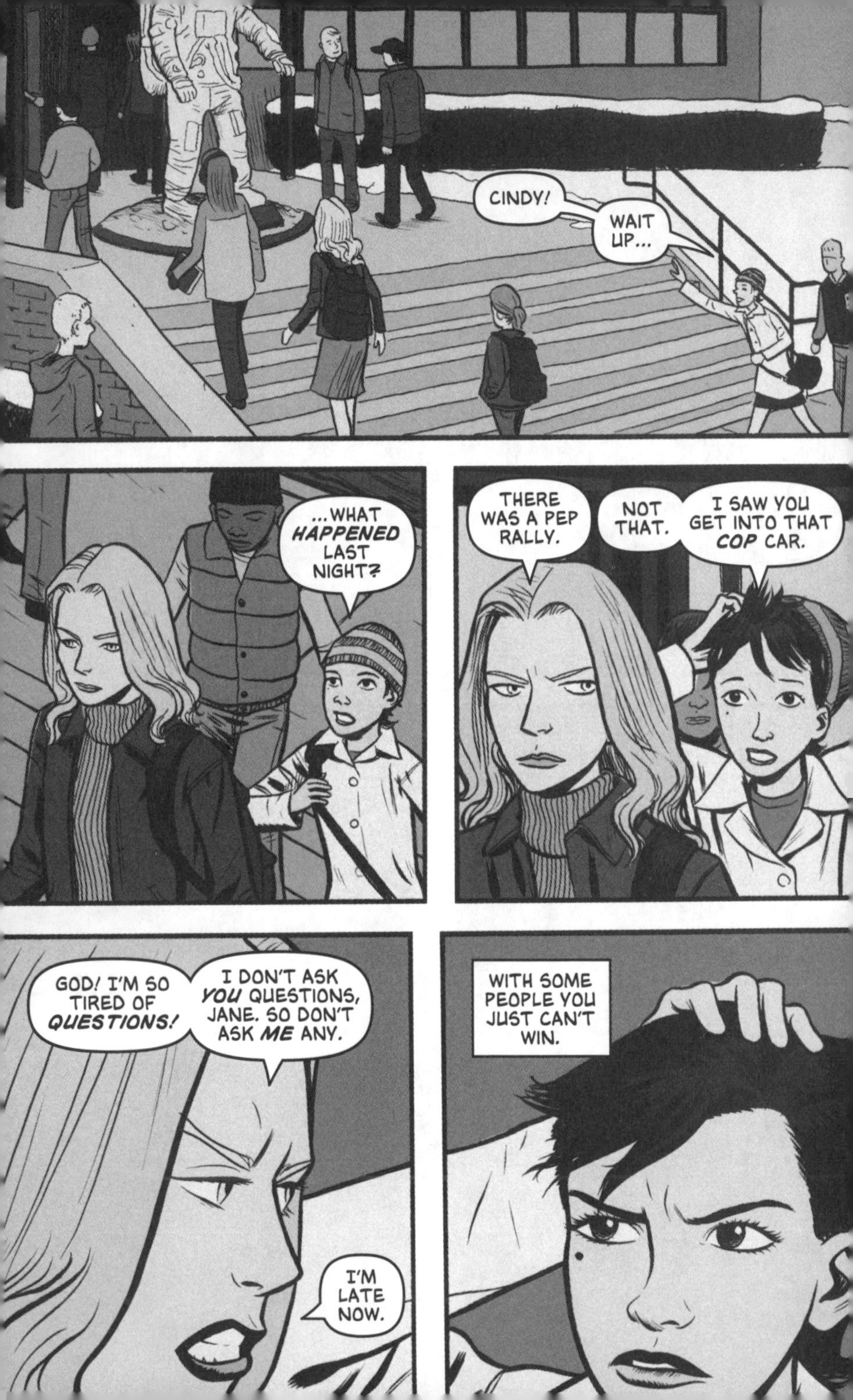
CINDY!
WAIT UP...
...WHAT HAPPENED LAST NIGHT?
THERE WAS A PEP RALLY.
NOT THAT.
I SAW YOU GET INTO THAT COP CAR.
GOD! I'M SO TIRED OF QUESTIONS!
I DON'T ASK YOU QUESTIONS, JANE. SO DON'T ASK ME ANY.
I'M LATE NOW.
WITH SOME PEOPLE YOU JUST CAN'T WIN.

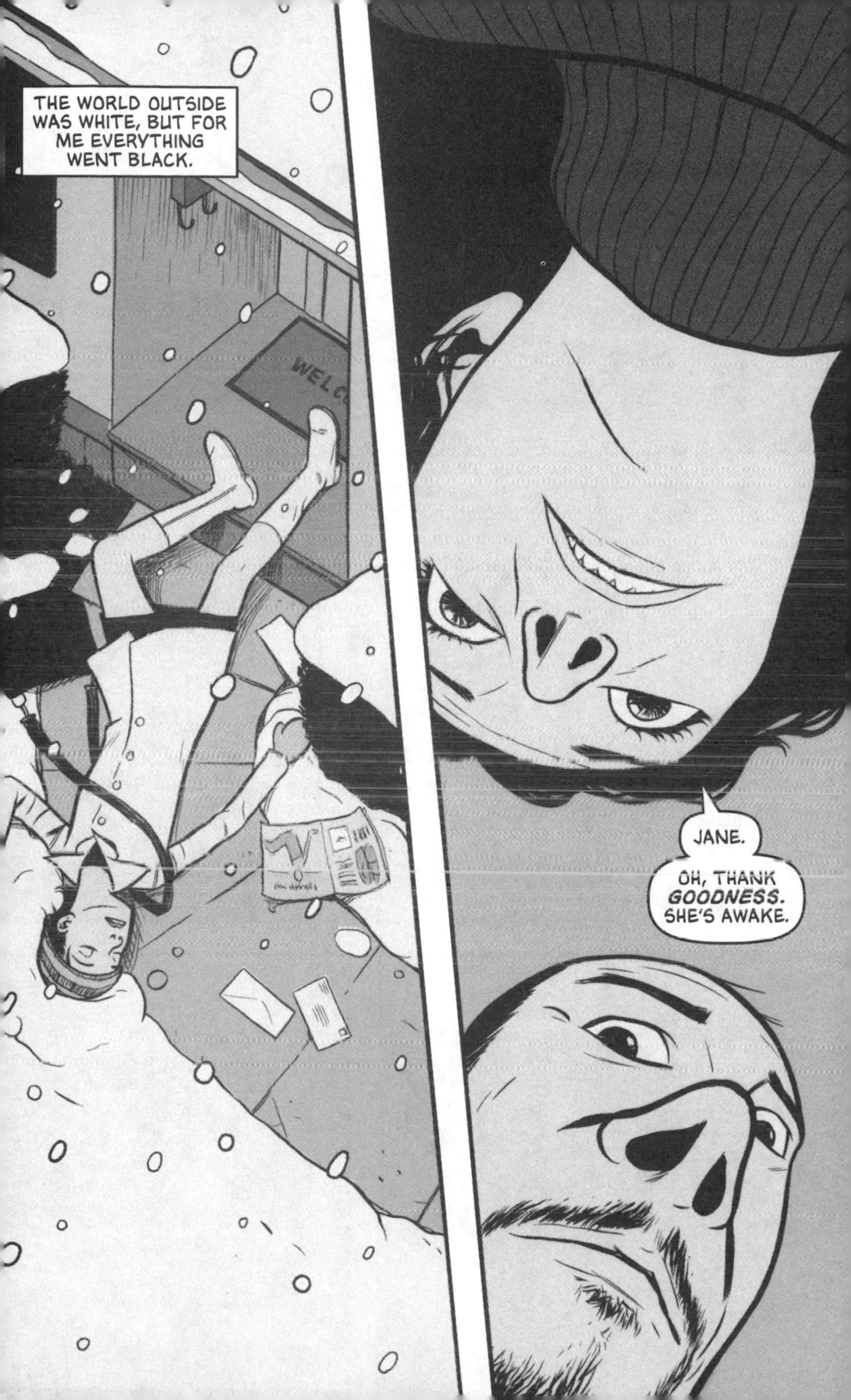
THE WORLD OUTSIDE WAS WHITE, BUT FOR ME EVERYTHING WENT BLACK.
JANE.
OH, THANK *GOODNESS.* SHE'S AWAKE.

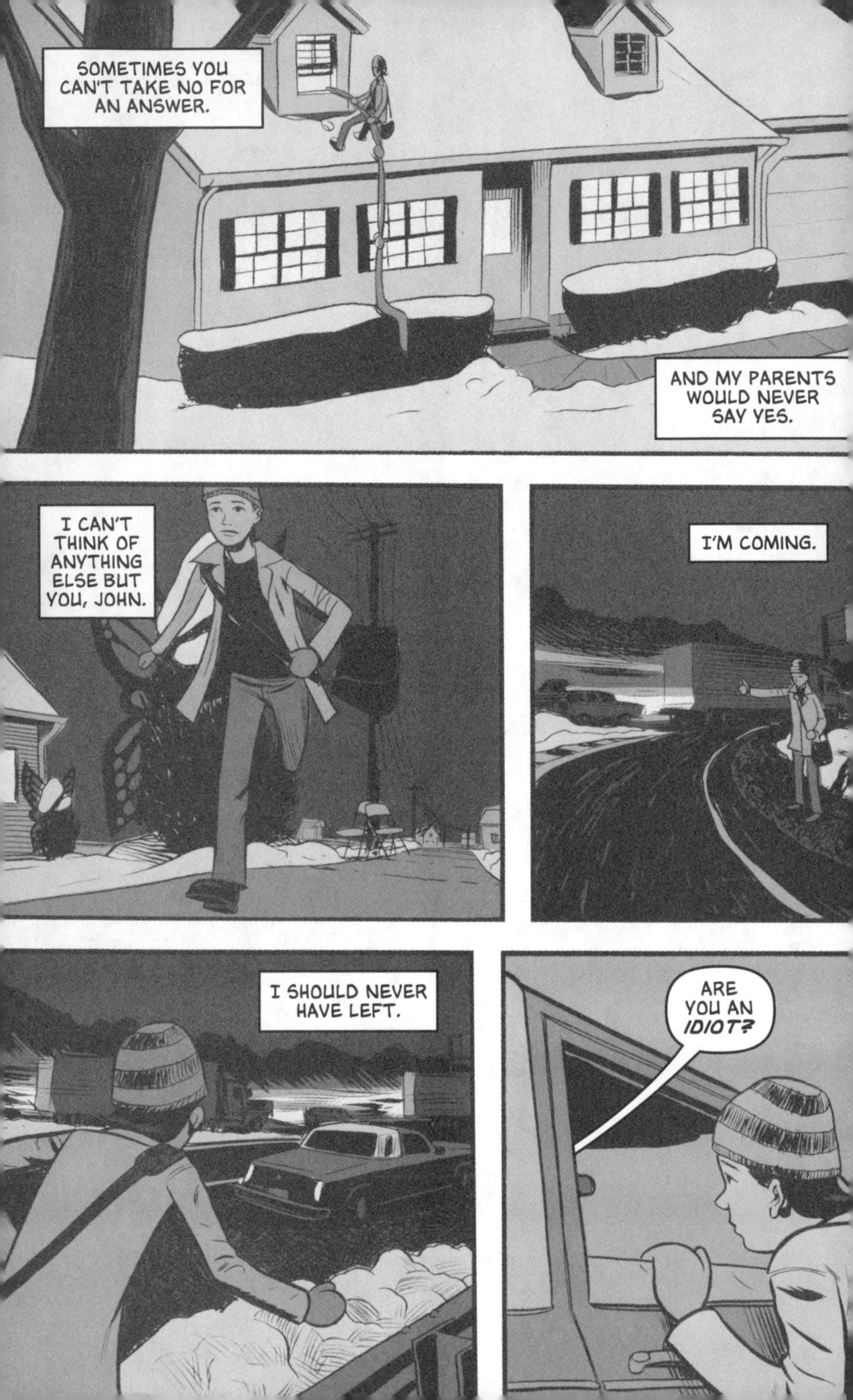
SOMETIMES YOU CAN'T TAKE NO FOR AN ANSWER.
AND MY PARENTS WOULD NEVER SAY YES.
I CAN'T THINK OF ANYTHING ELSE BUT YOU, JOHN.
I'M COMING.
I SHOULD NEVER HAVE LEFT.
ARE YOU AN *IDIOT?*

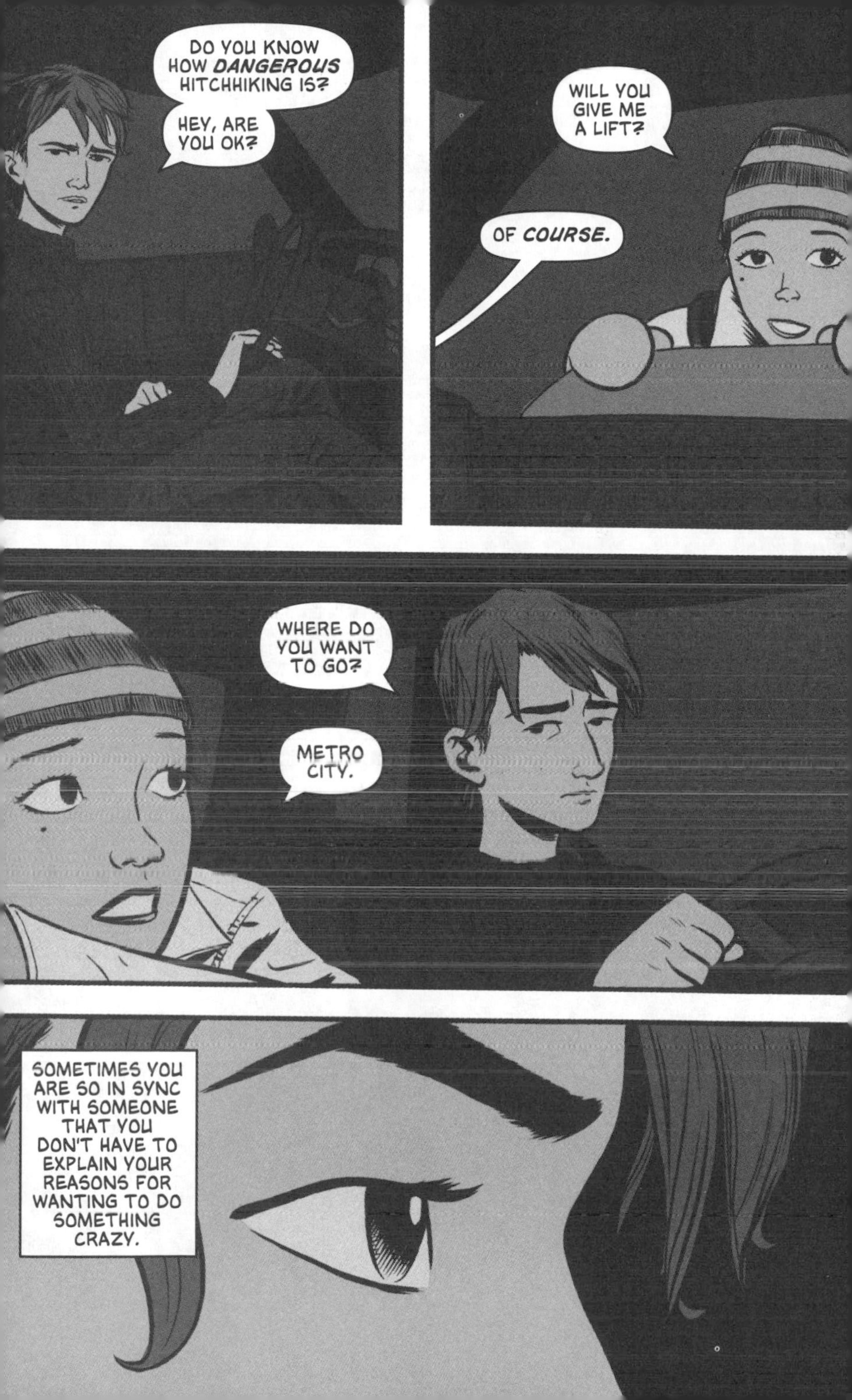
DO YOU KNOW HOW DANGEROUS HITCHHIKING IS?
HEY, ARE YOU OK?
WILL YOU GIVE ME A LIFT?
OF COURSE.
WHERE DO YOU WANT TO GO?
METRO CITY.
SOMETIMES YOU ARE SO IN SYNC WITH SOMEONE THAT YOU DON'T HAVE TO EXPLAIN YOUR REASONS FOR WANTING TO DO SOMETHING CRAZY.

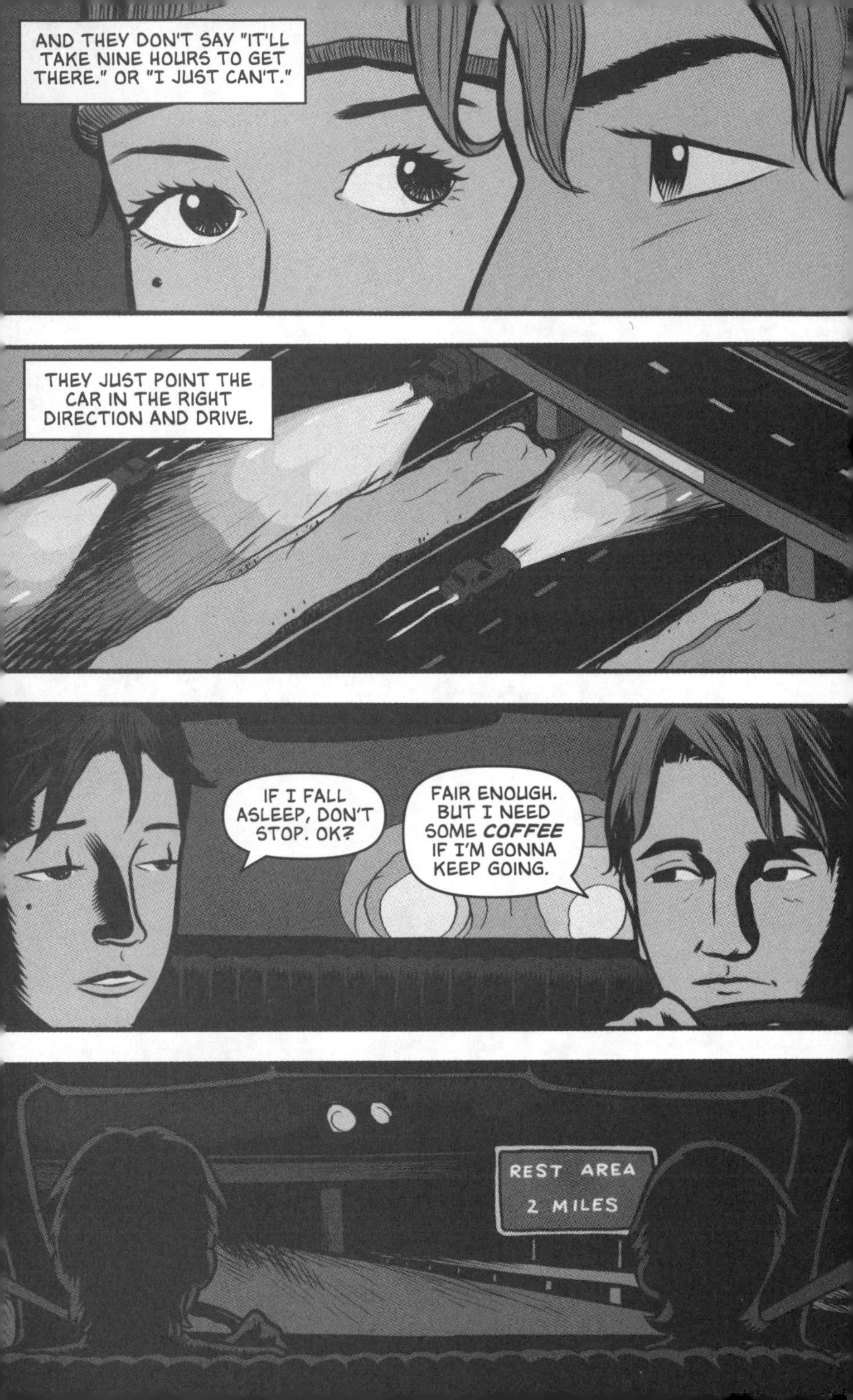
AND THEY DON'T SAY "IT'LL TAKE NINE HOURS TO GET THERE." OR "I JUST CAN'T."
THEY JUST POINT THE CAR IN THE RIGHT DIRECTION AND DRIVE.
IF I FALL ASLEEP, DON'T STOP. OK?
FAIR ENOUGH. BUT I NEED SOME *COFFEE* IF I'M GONNA KEEP GOING.
REST AREA
2 MILES

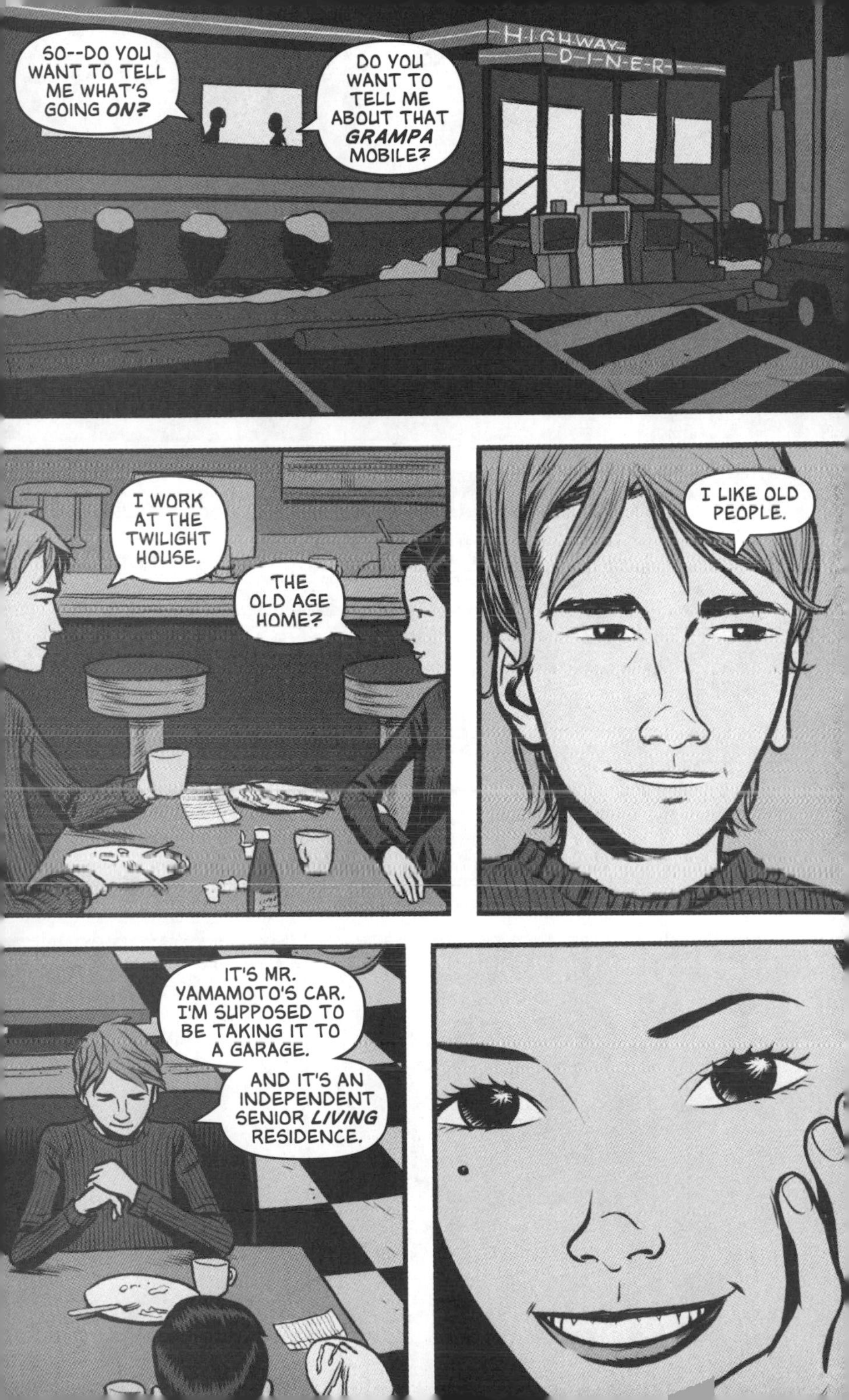
HIGHWAY DINER
SO--DO YOU WANT TO TELL ME WHAT'S GOING *ON?*
DO YOU WANT TO TELL ME ABOUT THAT *GRAMPA* MOBILE?
I WORK AT THE TWILIGHT HOUSE.
THE OLD AGE HOME?
I LIKE OLD PEOPLE.
IT'S MR. YAMAMOTO'S CAR. I'M SUPPOSED TO BE TAKING IT TO A GARAGE.
AND IT'S AN INDEPENDENT SENIOR *LIVING* RESIDENCE.

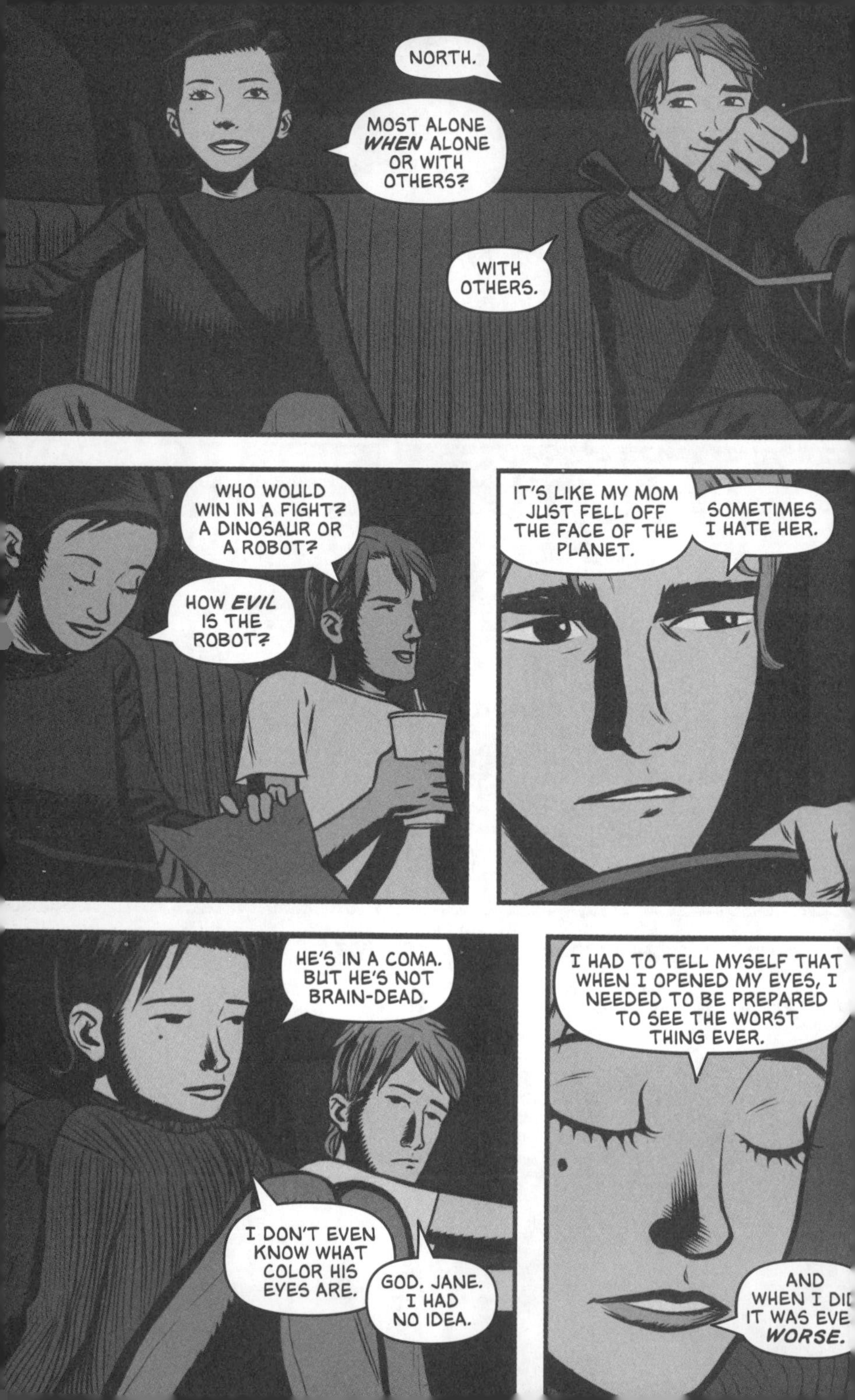

NORTH.
MOST ALONE *WHEN* ALONE OR WITH OTHERS?
WITH OTHERS.
WHO WOULD WIN IN A FIGHT? A DINOSAUR OR A ROBOT?
HOW *EVIL* IS THE ROBOT?
IT'S LIKE MY MOM JUST FELL OFF THE FACE OF THE PLANET.
SOMETIMES I HATE HER.
HE'S IN A COMA. BUT HE'S NOT BRAIN-DEAD.
I DON'T EVEN KNOW WHAT COLOR HIS EYES ARE.
GOD. JANE. I HAD NO IDEA.
I HAD TO TELL MYSELF THAT WHEN I OPENED MY EYES, I NEEDED TO BE PREPARED TO SEE THE WORST THING EVER.
AND WHEN I DI IT WAS EVE *WORSE.*

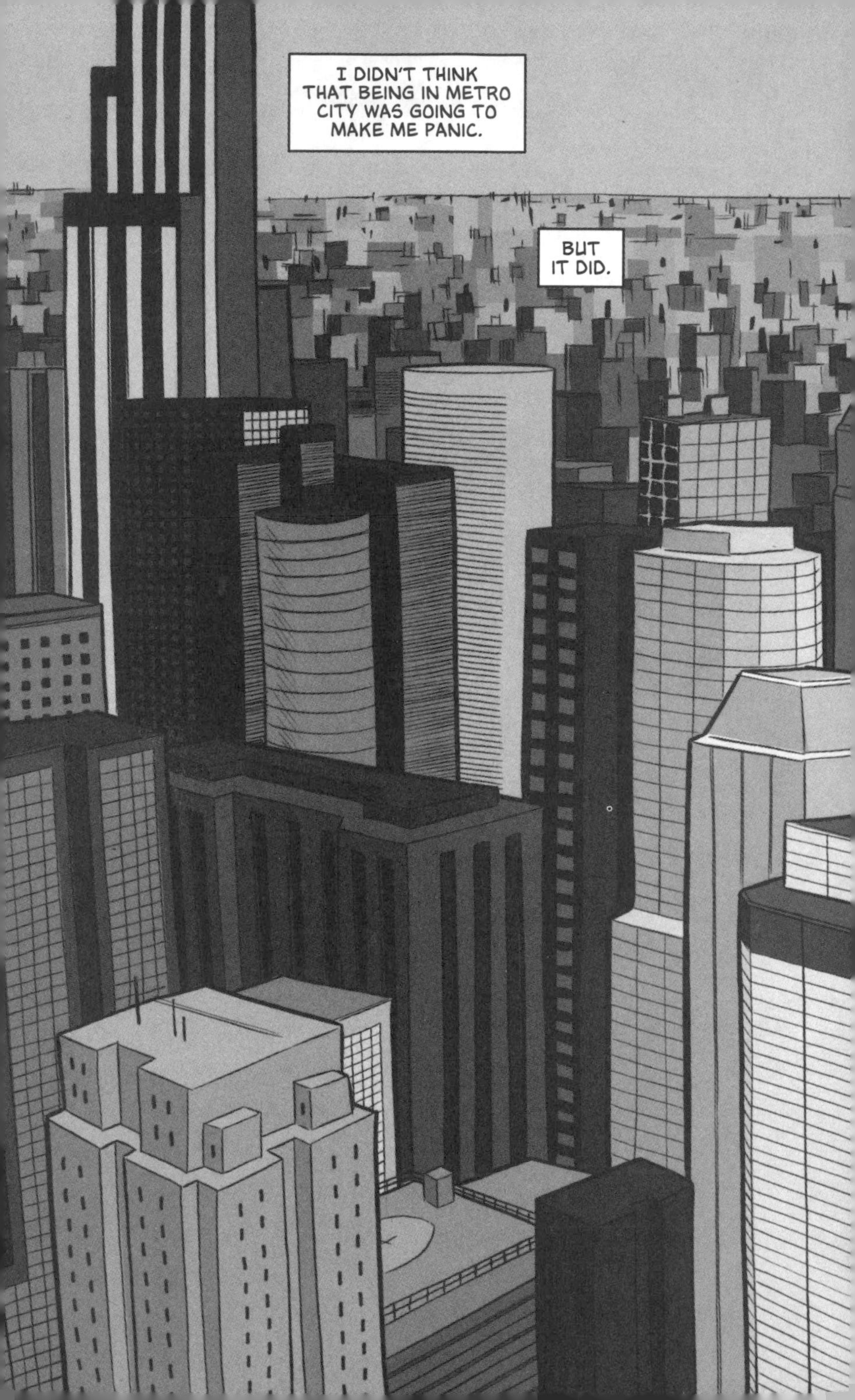
I DIDN'T THINK THAT BEING IN METRO CITY WAS GOING TO MAKE ME PANIC.
BUT IT DID.

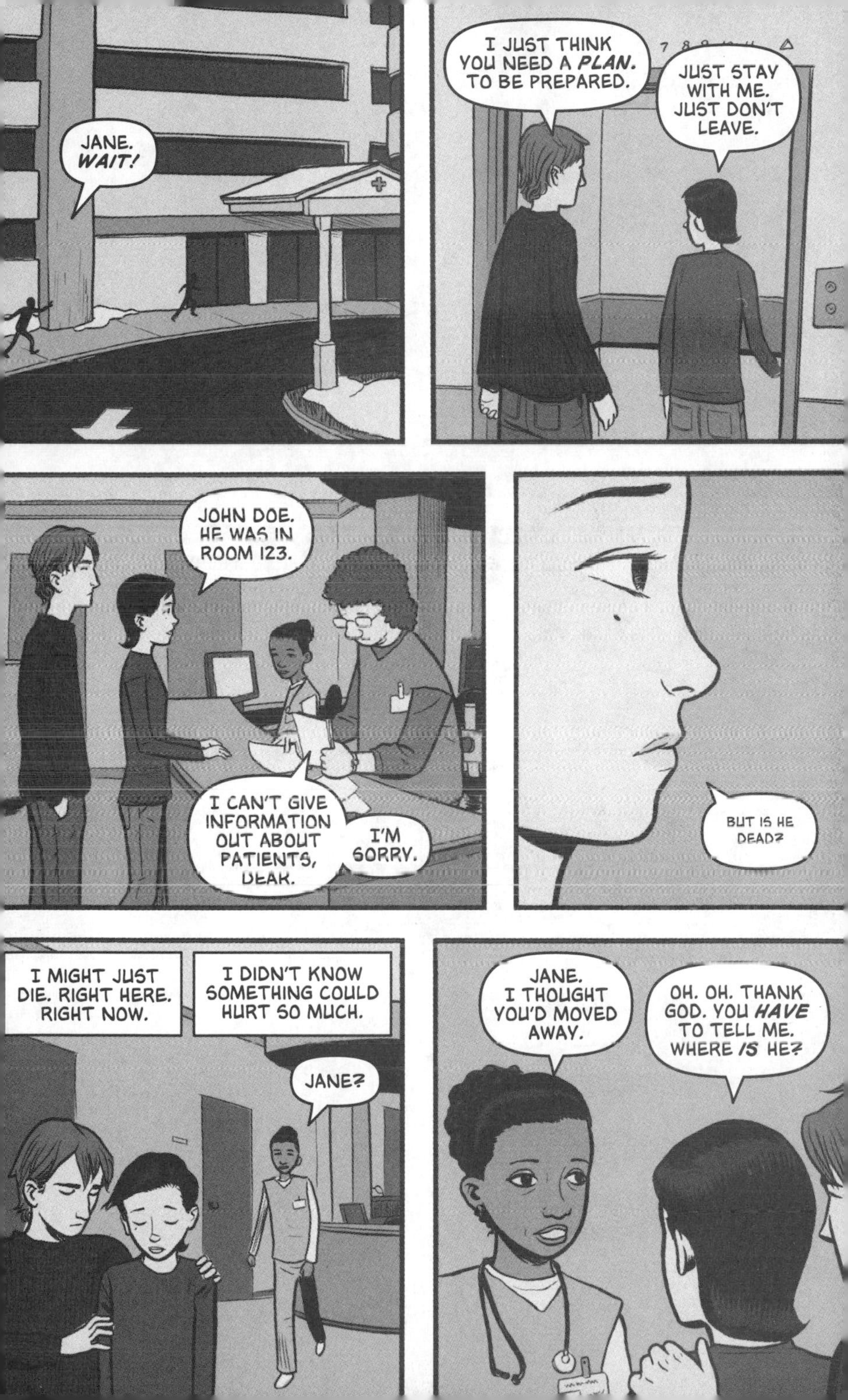
JANE. WAIT!
I JUST THINK YOU NEED A PLAN. TO BE PREPARED.
JUST STAY WITH ME. JUST DON'T LEAVE.
JOHN DOE. HE WAS IN ROOM 123.
I CAN'T GIVE INFORMATION OUT ABOUT PATIENTS, DEAR.
I'M SORRY.
BUT IS HE DEAD?
I MIGHT JUST DIE. RIGHT HERE. RIGHT NOW.
I DIDN'T KNOW SOMETHING COULD HURT SO MUCH.
JANE?
JANE. I THOUGHT YOU'D MOVED AWAY.
OH. OH. THANK GOD. YOU HAVE TO TELL ME. WHERE IS HE?

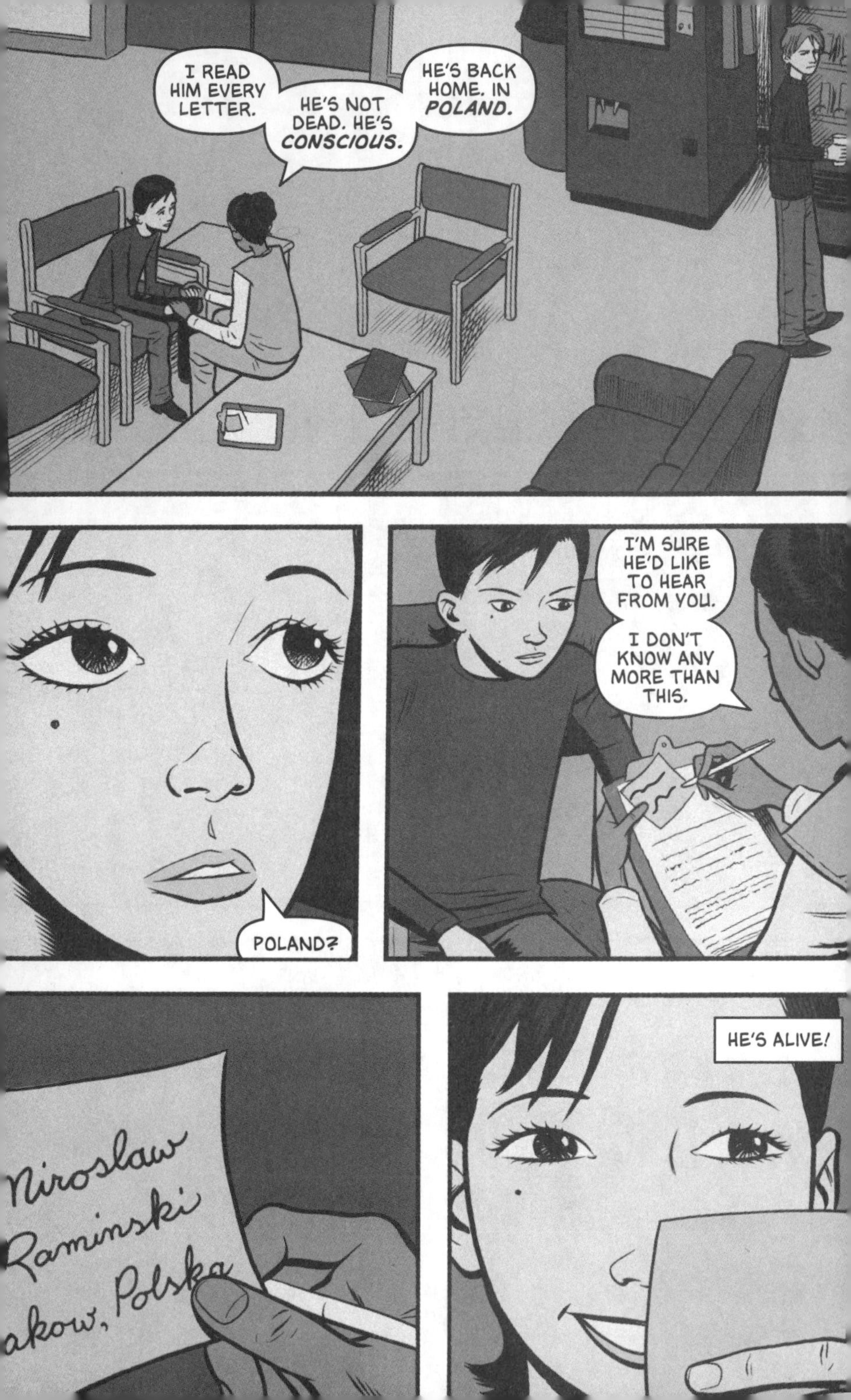
I READ HIM EVERY LETTER.
HE'S NOT DEAD. HE'S *CONSCIOUS.*
HE'S BACK HOME. IN *POLAND.*
POLAND?
I'M SURE HE'D LIKE TO HEAR FROM YOU.
I DON'T KNOW ANY MORE THAN THIS.
Miroslaw
Raminski
akow, Polska
HE'S ALIVE!

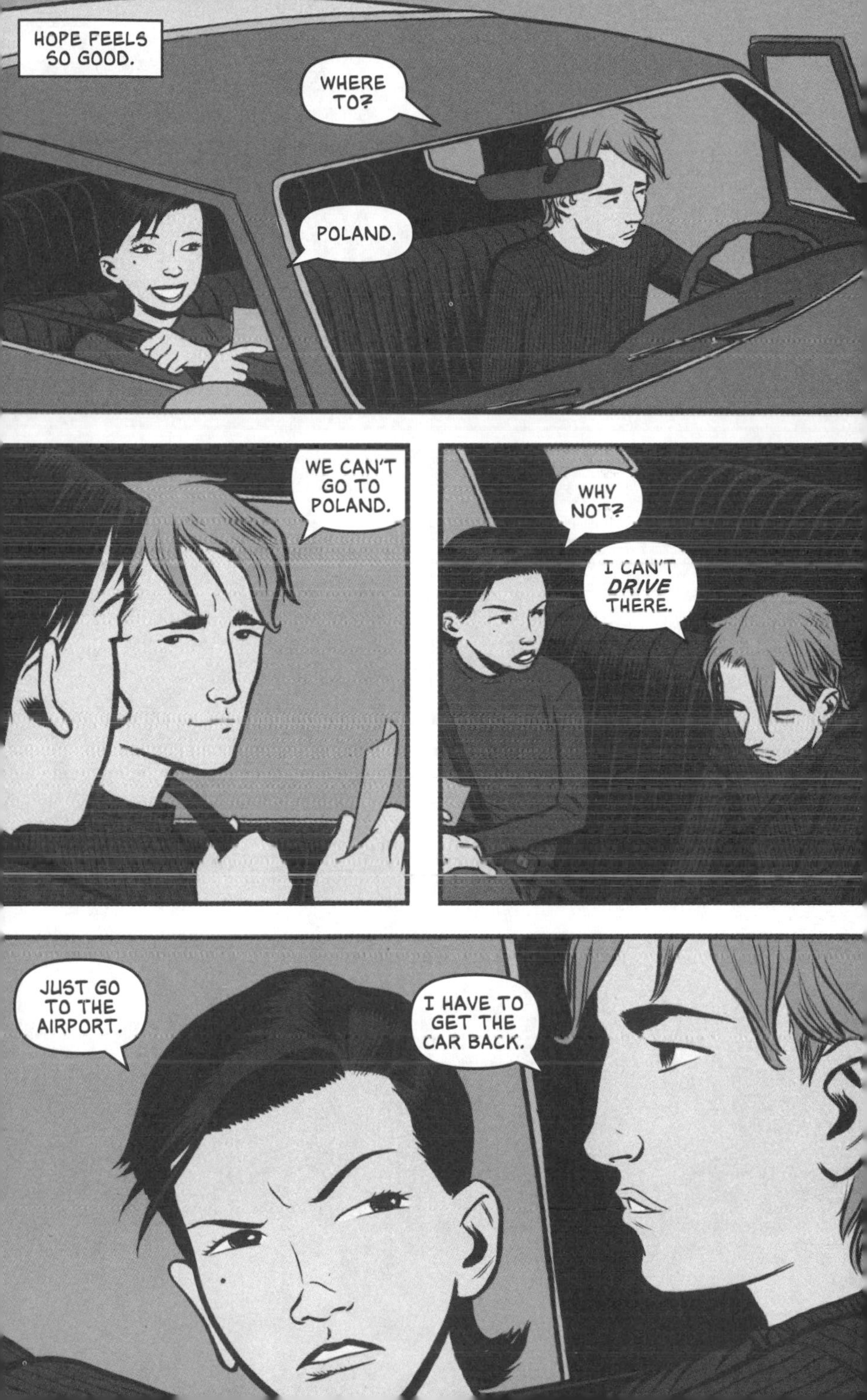
HOPE FEELS SO GOOD.
WHERE TO?
POLAND.
WE CAN'T GO TO POLAND.
WHY NOT?
I CAN'T *DRIVE* THERE.
JUST GO TO THE AIRPORT.
I HAVE TO GET THE CAR BACK.

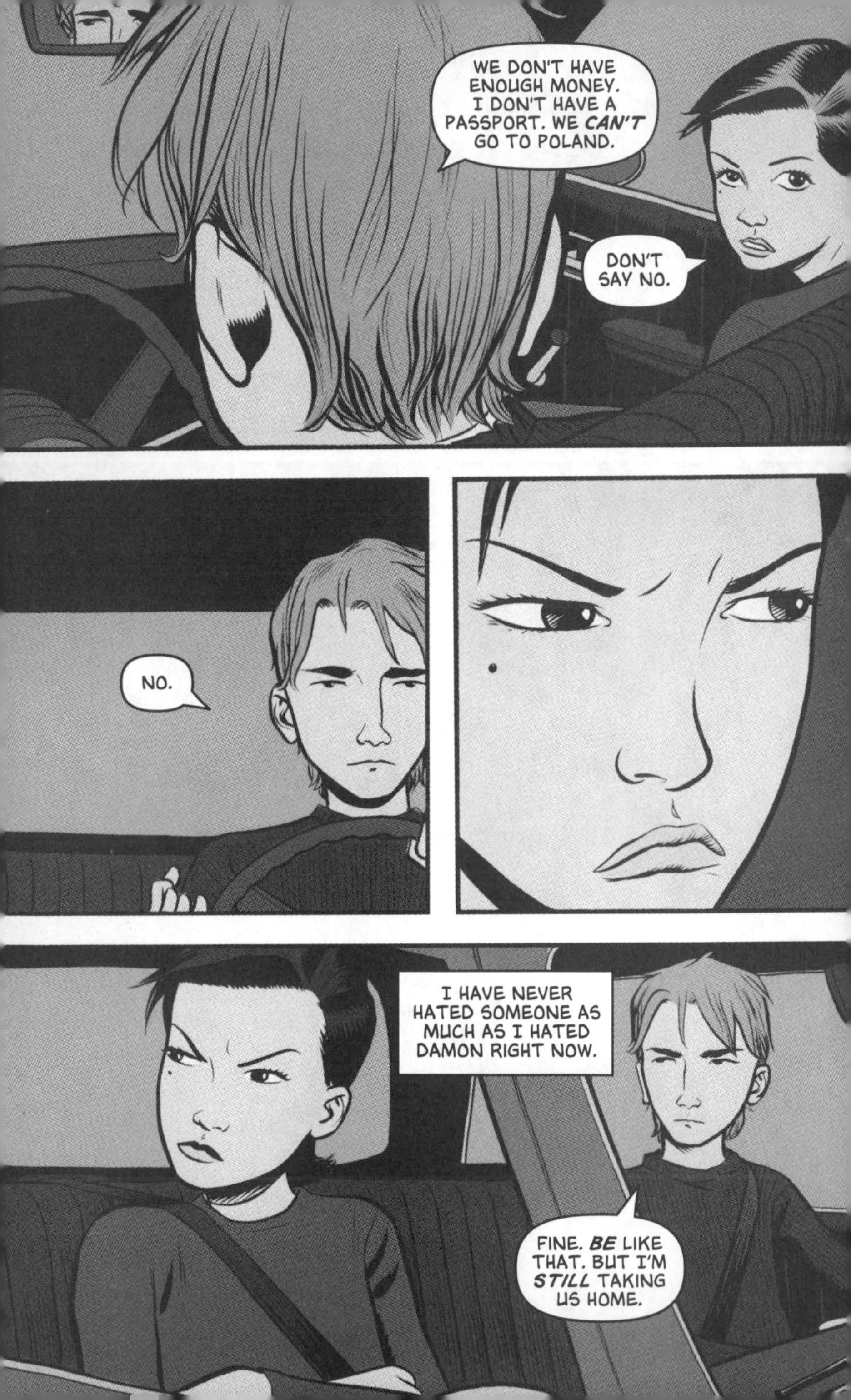
WE DON'T HAVE ENOUGH MONEY. I DON'T HAVE A PASSPORT. WE *CAN'T* GO TO POLAND.
DON'T SAY NO.
NO.
I HAVE NEVER HATED SOMEONE AS MUCH AS I HATED DAMON RIGHT NOW.
FINE. *BE* LIKE THAT. BUT I'M *STILL* TAKING US HOME.

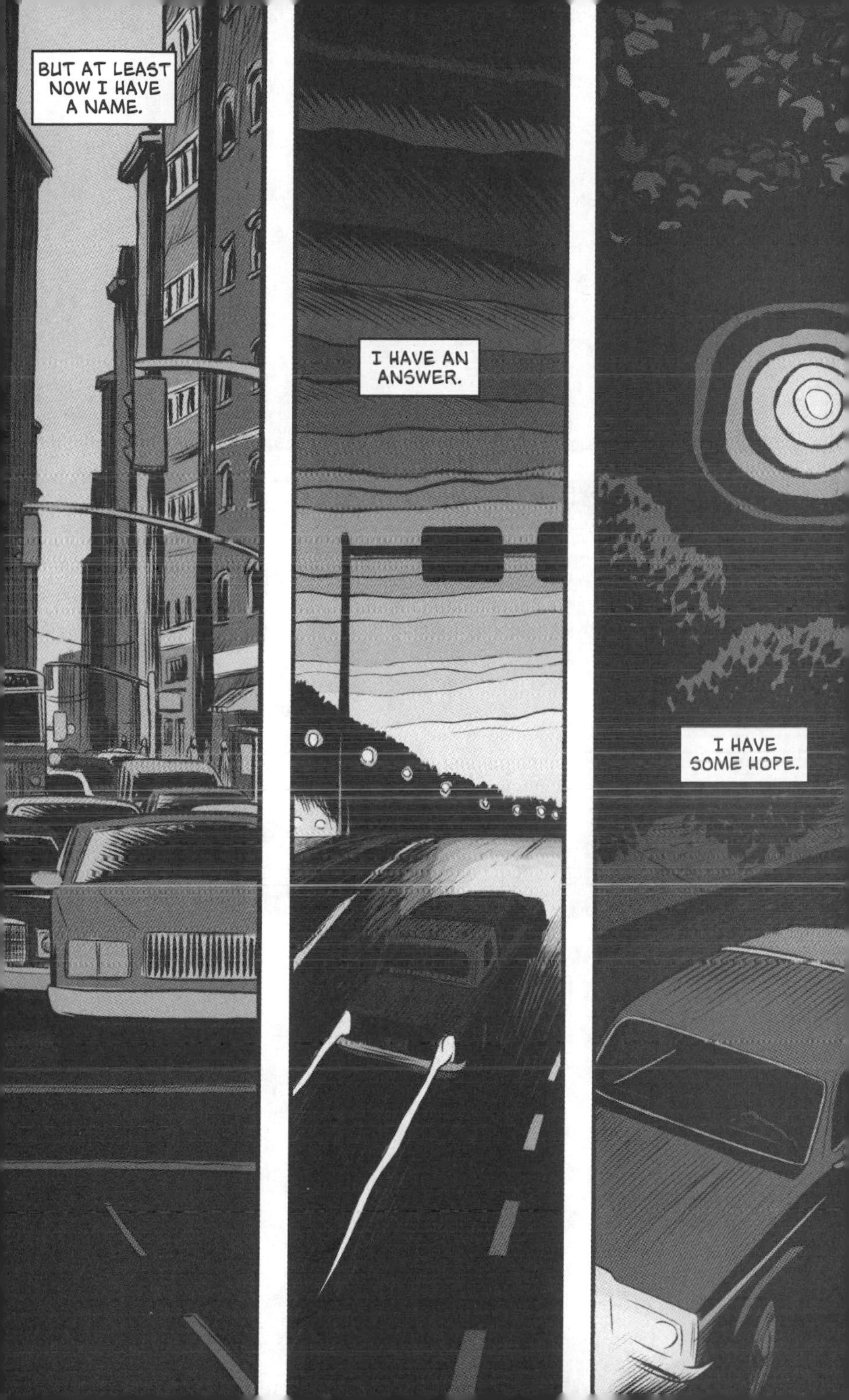
BUT AT LEAST NOW I HAVE A NAME.
I HAVE AN ANSWER.
I HAVE SOME HOPE.

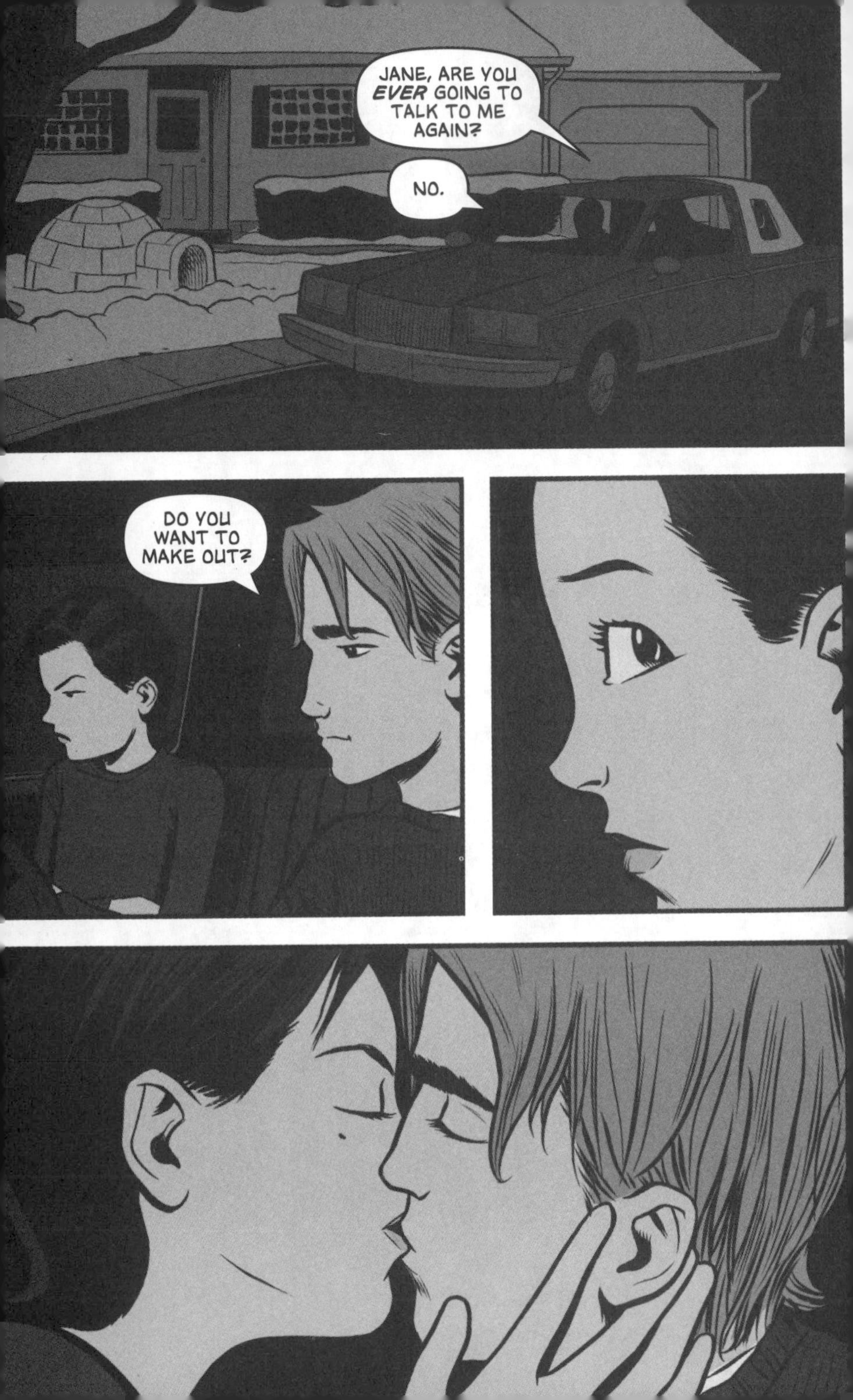
JANE, ARE YOU EVER GOING TO TALK TO ME AGAIN?
NO.
DO YOU WANT TO MAKE OUT?

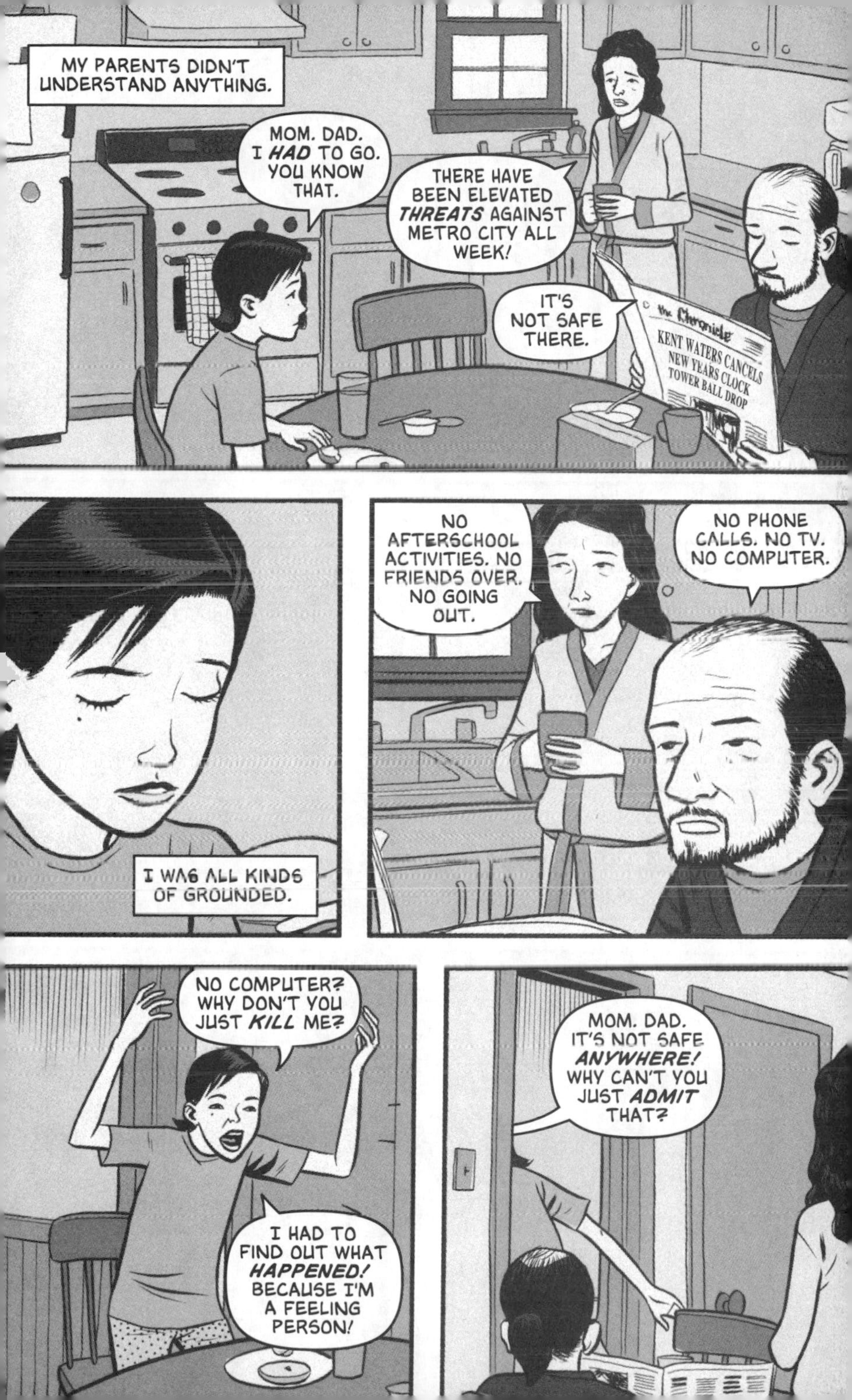
MY PARENTS DIDN'T UNDERSTAND ANYTHING.
MOM. DAD. I *HAD* TO GO. YOU KNOW THAT.
THERE HAVE BEEN ELEVATED *THREATS* AGAINST METRO CITY ALL WEEK!
IT'S NOT SAFE THERE.
the Chronicle
KENT WATERS CANCELS NEW YEARS CLOCK TOWER BALL DROP
I WAS ALL KINDS OF GROUNDED.
NO AFTERSCHOOL ACTIVITIES. NO FRIENDS OVER. NO GOING OUT.
NO PHONE CALLS. NO TV. NO COMPUTER.
NO COMPUTER? WHY DON'T YOU JUST *KILL* ME?
I HAD TO FIND OUT WHAT *HAPPENED!* BECAUSE I'M A FEELING PERSON!
MOM. DAD. IT'S NOT SAFE *ANYWHERE!* WHY CAN'T YOU JUST *ADMIT* THAT?

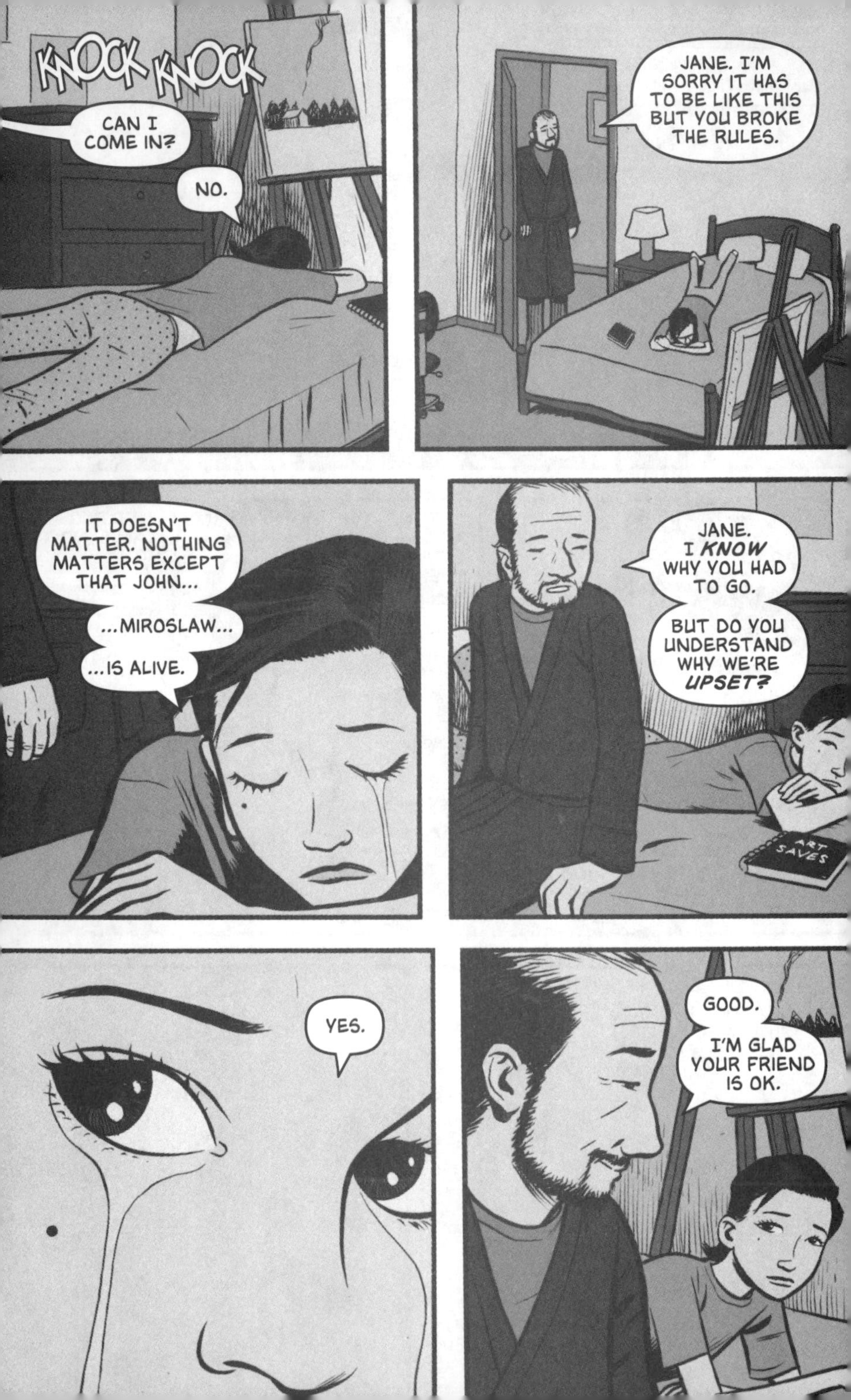
KNOCK KNOCK
CAN I COME IN?
NO.
JANE. I'M SORRY IT HAS TO BE LIKE THIS BUT YOU BROKE THE RULES.
IT DOESN'T MATTER. NOTHING MATTERS EXCEPT THAT JOHN...
...MIROSLAW...
...IS ALIVE.
JANE. I *KNOW* WHY YOU HAD TO GO.
BUT DO YOU UNDERSTAND WHY WE'RE *UPSET?*
ART SAVES
YES.
GOOD.
I'M GLAD YOUR FRIEND IS OK.

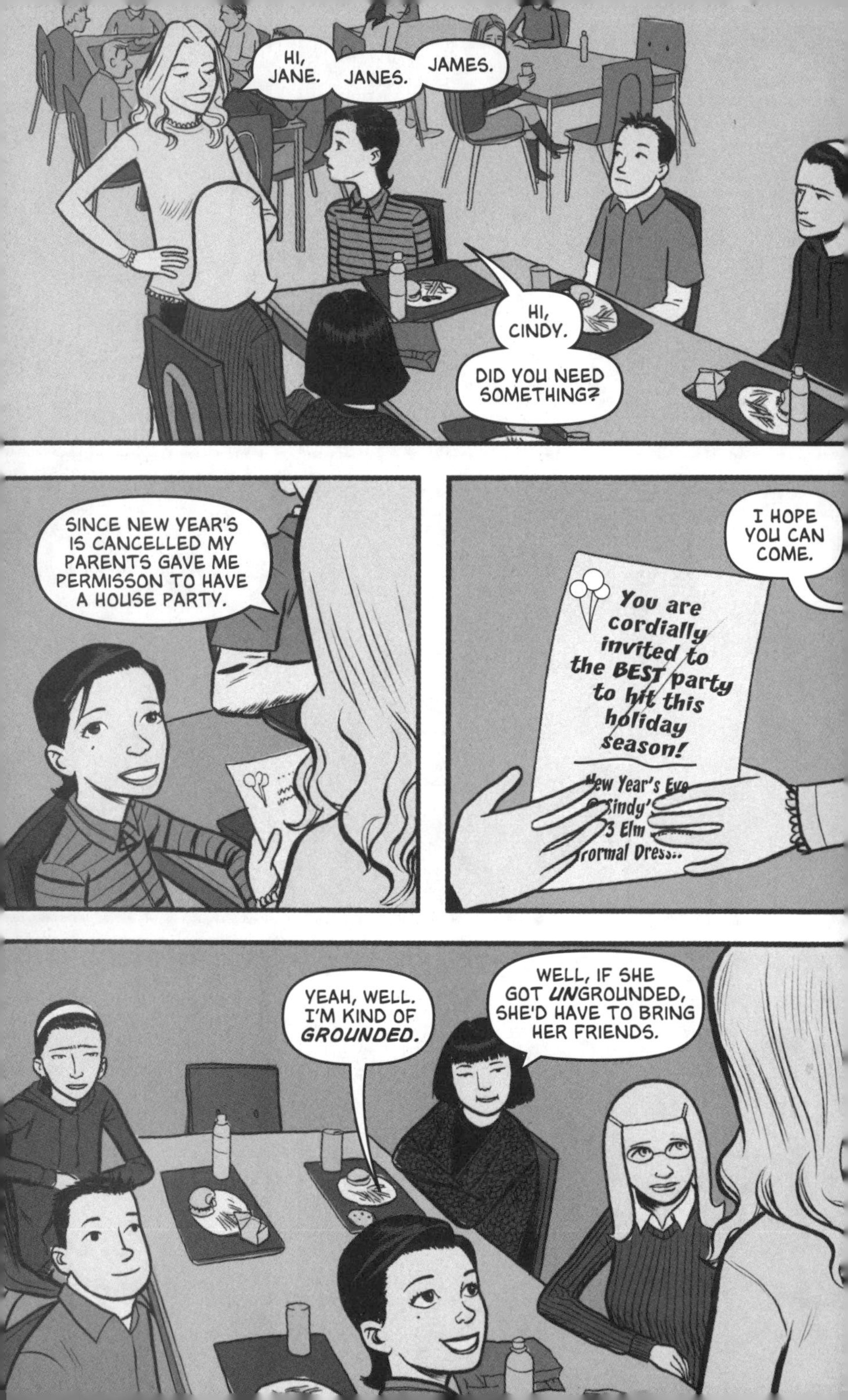
HI, JANE.
JANES.
JAMES.
HI, CINDY.
DID YOU NEED SOMETHING?
SINCE NEW YEAR'S IS CANCELLED MY PARENTS GAVE ME PERMISSON TO HAVE A HOUSE PARTY.
I HOPE YOU CAN COME.
You are cordially invited to the BEST party to hit this holiday season!
YEAH, WELL. I'M KIND OF *GROUNDED.*
WELL, IF SHE GOT *UN*GROUNDED, SHE'D HAVE TO BRING HER FRIENDS.

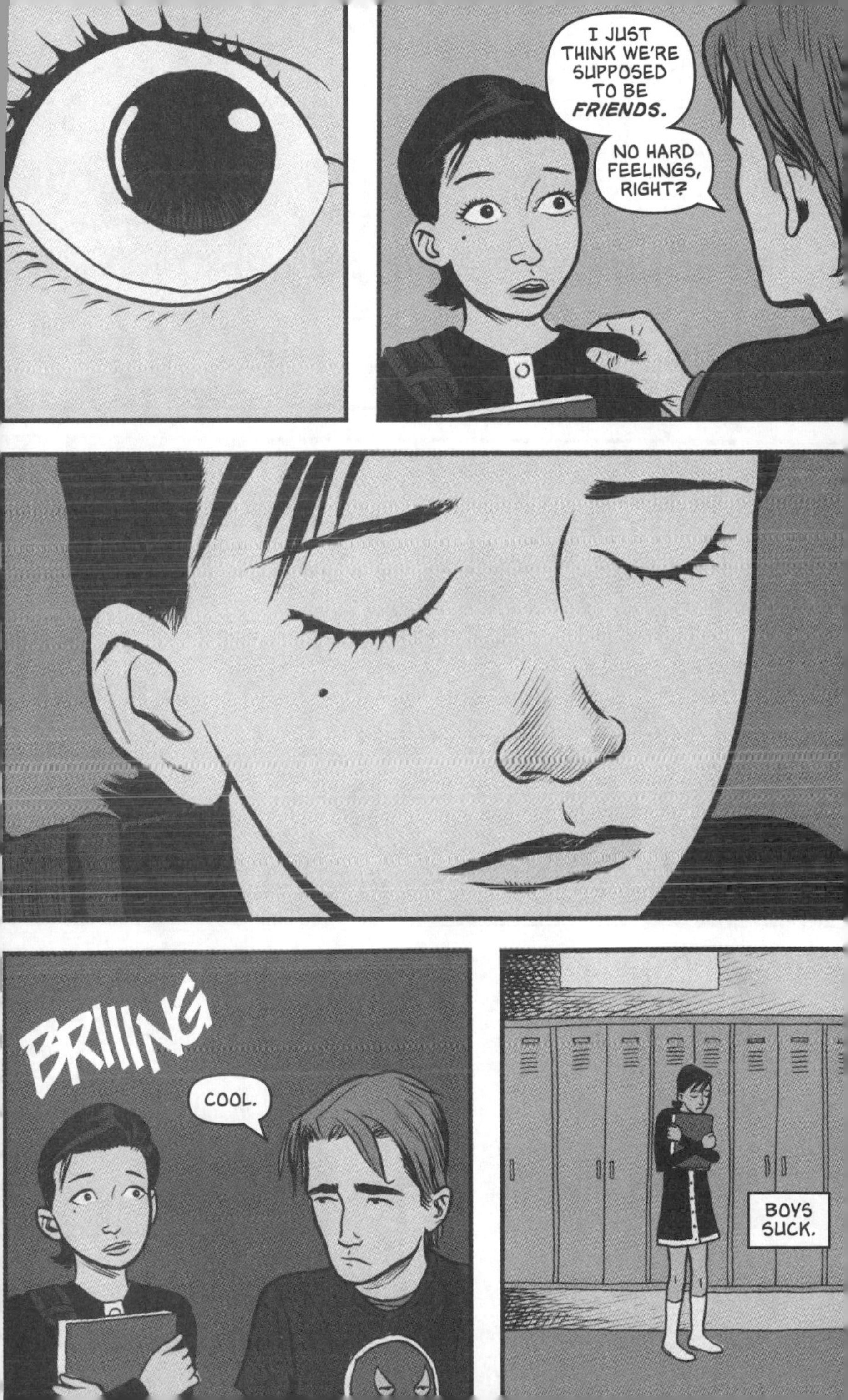
I JUST THINK WE'RE SUPPOSED TO BE FRIENDS.
NO HARD FEELINGS, RIGHT?
BRIIING
COOL.
BOYS SUCK.

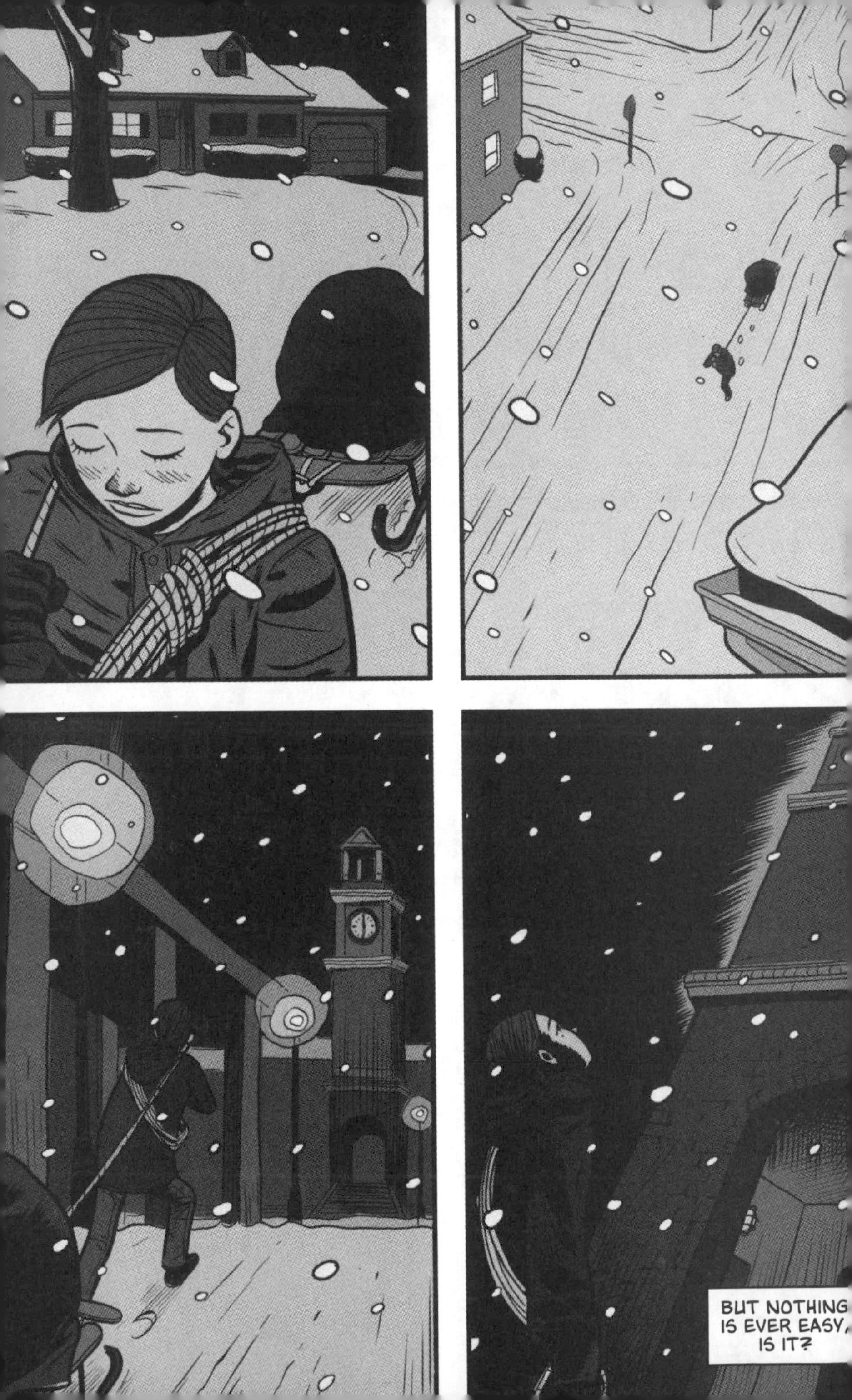
BUT NOTHING IS EVER EASY, IS IT?

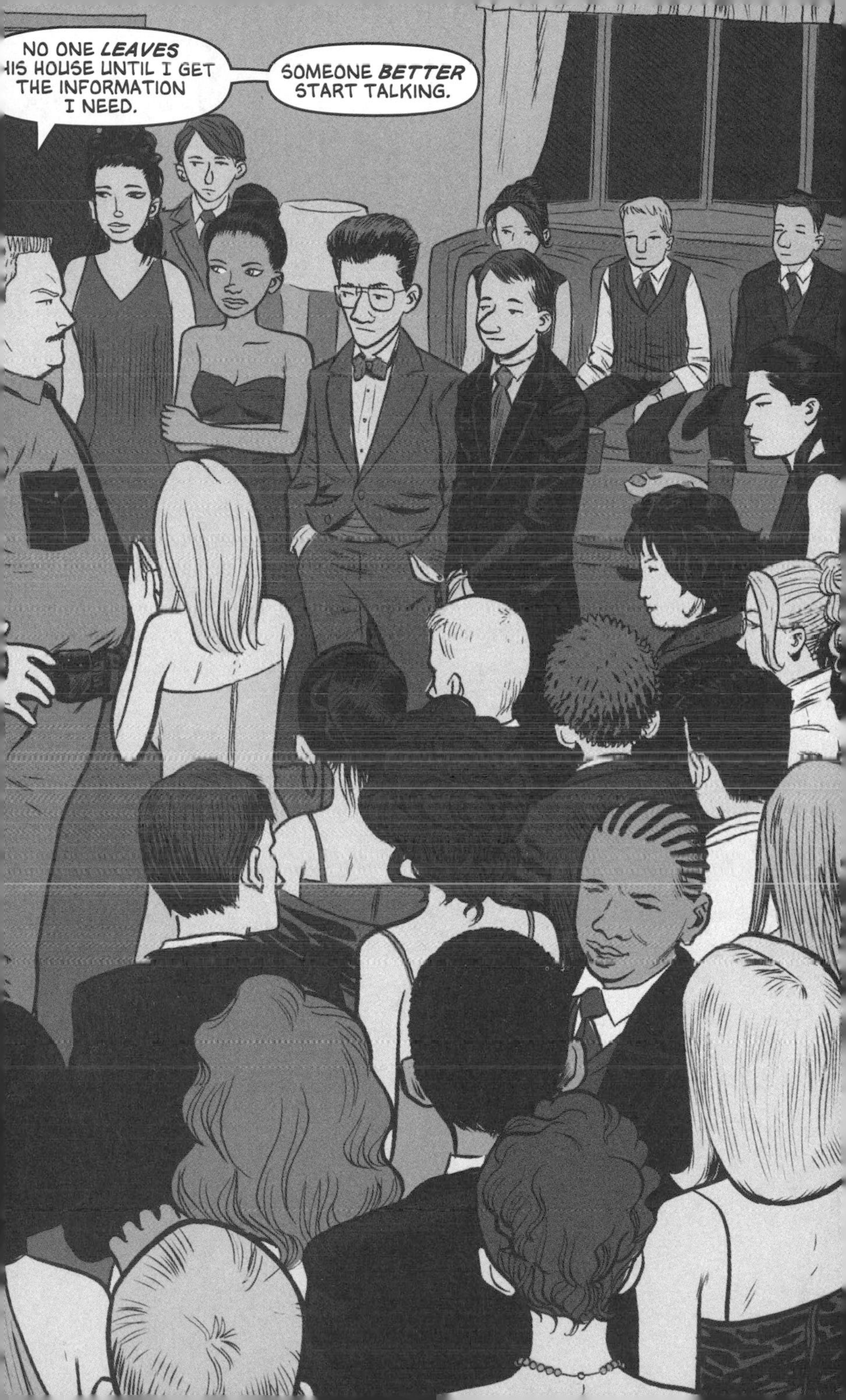
NO ONE *LEAVES* IS HOUSE UNTIL I GET THE INFORMATION I NEED.
SOMEONE *BETTER* START TALKING.

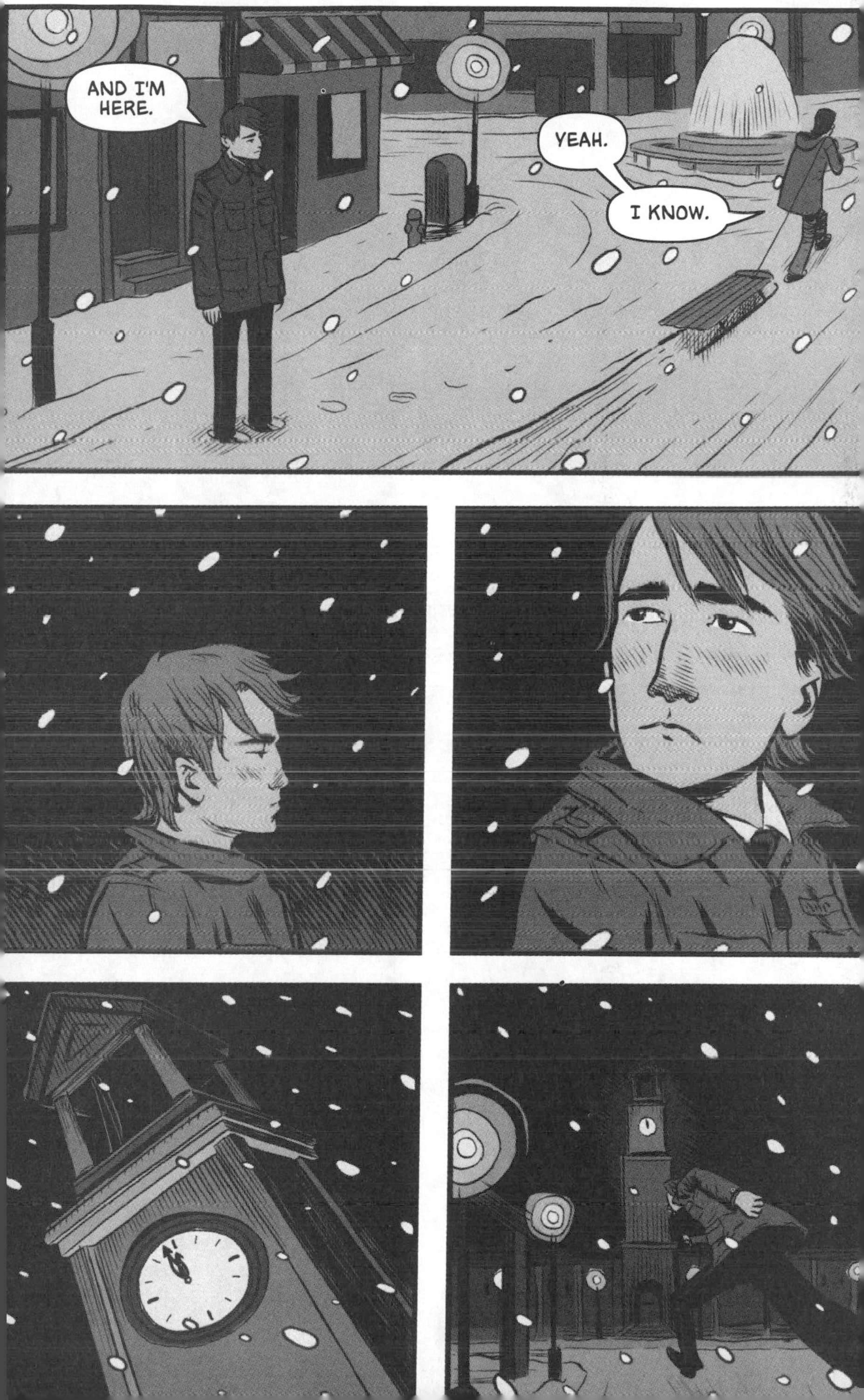
AND I'M HERE.
YEAH.
I KNOW.

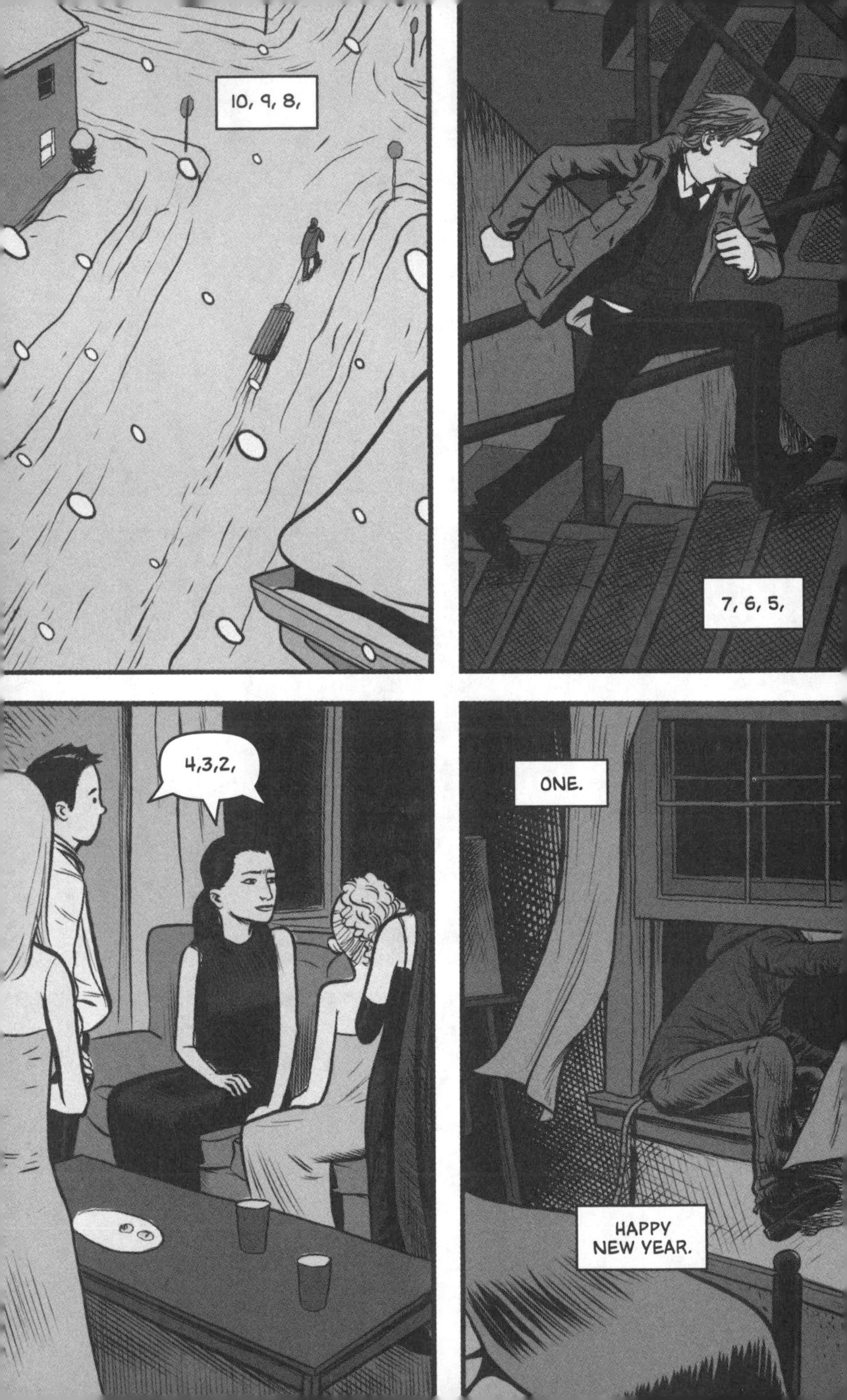
10, 9, 8,
7, 6, 5,
4,3,2,
ONE.
HAPPY NEW YEAR.

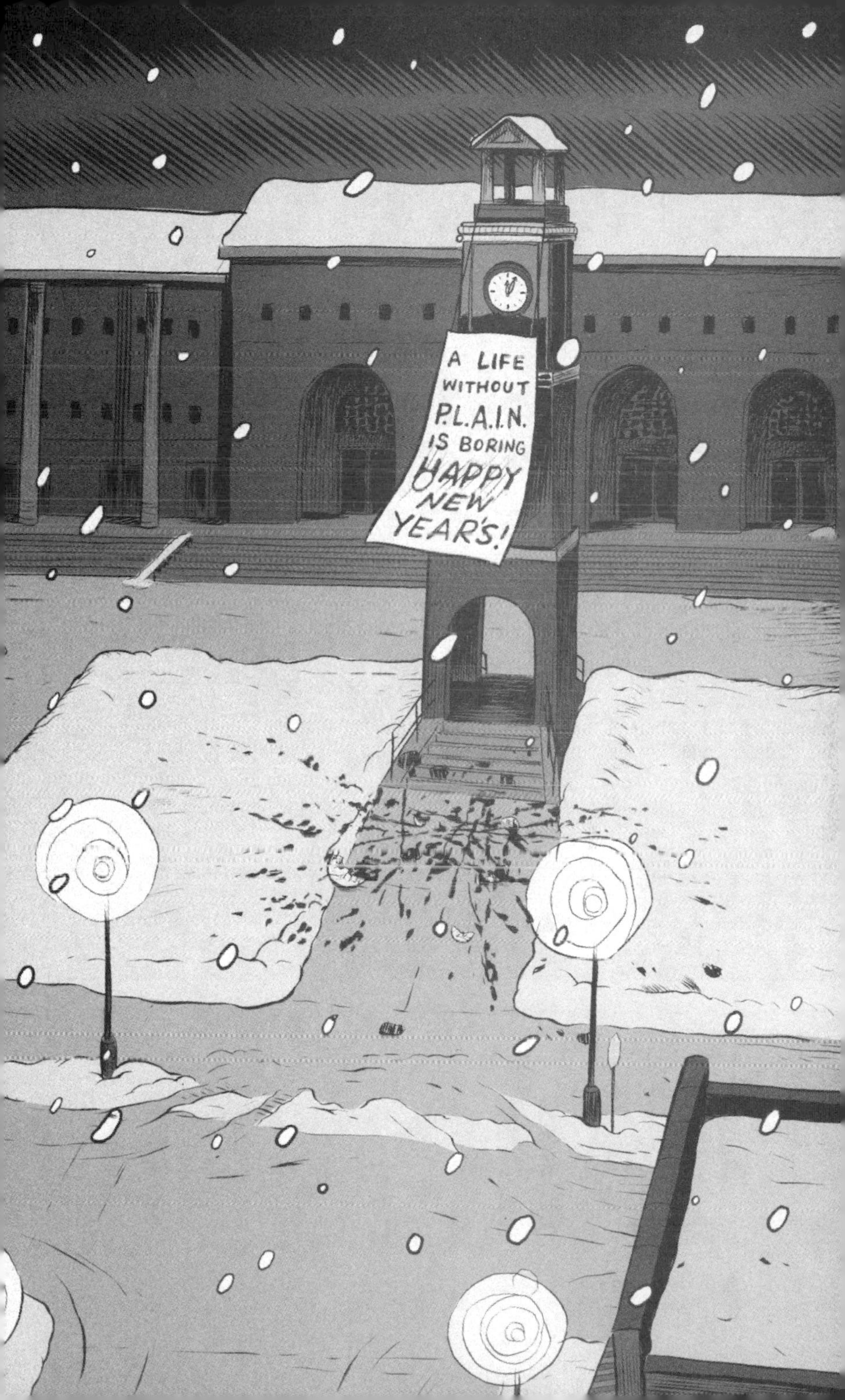
A LIFE WITHOUT P.L.A.I.N. IS BORING
HAPPY NEW YEAR'S!

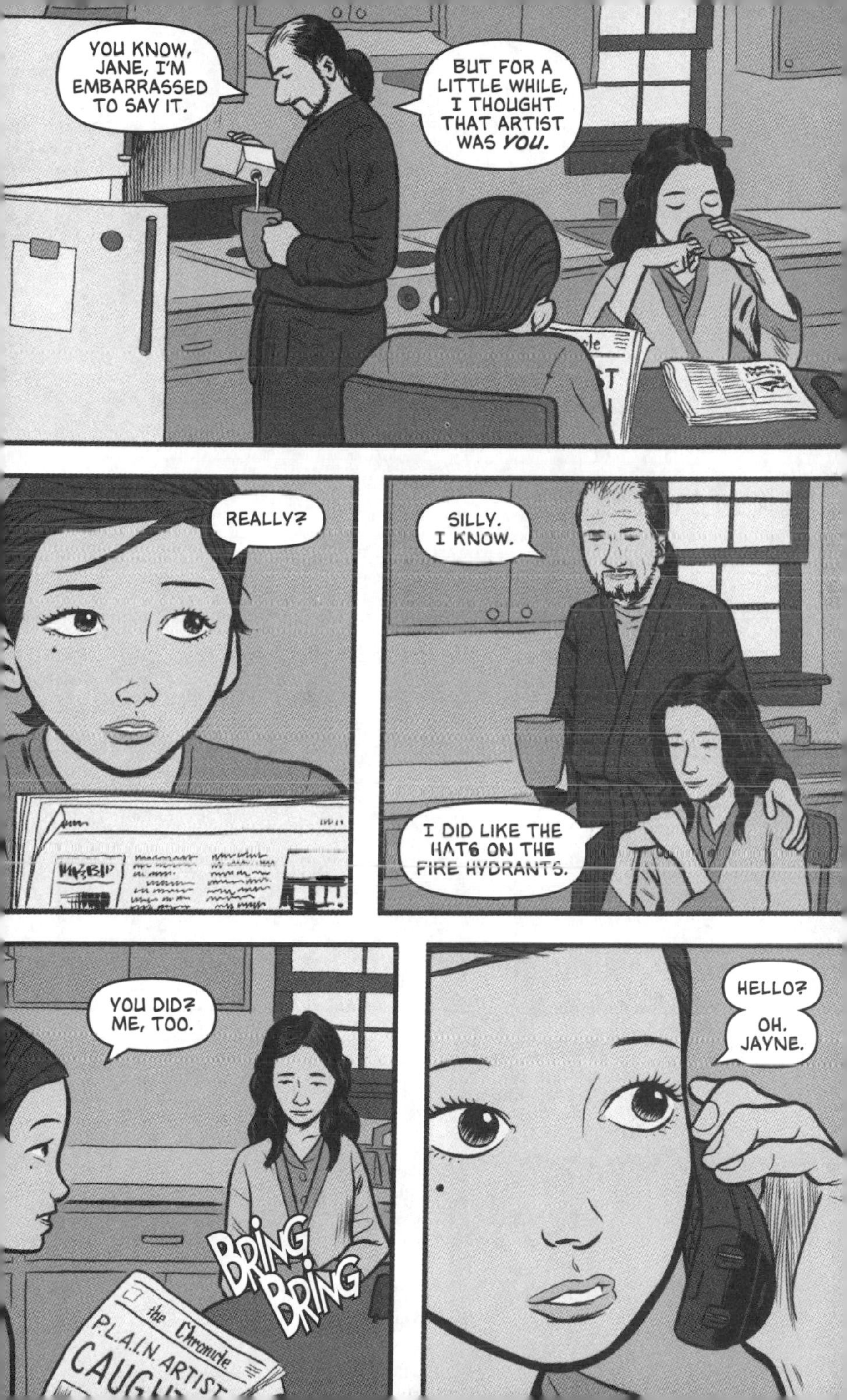
YOU KNOW, JANE, I'M EMBARRASSED TO SAY IT.
BUT FOR A LITTLE WHILE, I THOUGHT THAT ARTIST WAS *YOU.*
REALLY?
SILLY. I KNOW.
I DID LIKE THE HATS ON THE FIRE HYDRANTS.
YOU DID? ME, TOO.
BRING BRING
the Chronicle
P.L.A.I.N. ARTIST
HELLO?
OH. JAYNE.

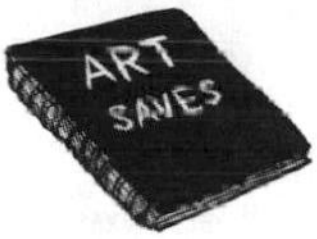
ART
SAVES

The End.

CECIL CASTELLUCCI

Cecil grew up in New York City, is
French Canadian and makes her home in
Los Angeles. She's the author of three
young adult novels, *Boy Proof*,
The Queen of Cool, and the upcoming
Beige. Cecil is also an indie rock
musician, an independent filmmaker
and a playwright. During her years
at the LaGuardia High School of
Performing Arts, she'd see Keith
Haring's drawings in the subways in
New York. She still looks for street
art whenever she's on a walk.

JIM RUGG

Jim is the artist and co-creator of
Street Angel. His comics have also
appeared in anthologies including
Project: Superior, *SPX*, *Orchid*,
and *Meathaus*. He grew up near Pittsburgh
and hasn't come up with a good excuse
to skip town. He's disappointed his
school didn't have a girl gang like
the Janes or the Dagger Debs.

S P E C I A L   B A C K S T A G E   P A S S :

If you liked the story you've just read, fear not: other MINX

books will be available in the months to come. MINX is a line

of books that's designed especially for you — someone who's

a   bit   bored   with   straight   fiction   and   ready   for

stories that are visually exciting beyond words — literally.

In fact, we thought you might like to get in on a secret,

behind-the-scenes look at a few of the new MINX titles that

will aid in your escape to cool places during the long hot

summer. So hurry up and turn the page already! And be

sure   to   check   out   other   exclusive   material   at

minxbooks.net

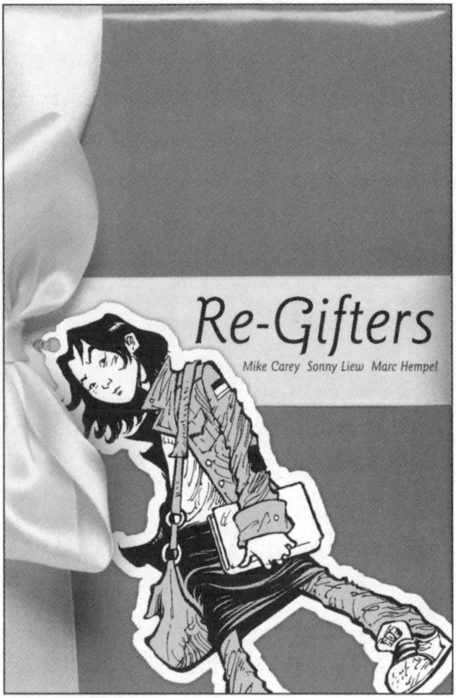
Re-Gifters
Mike Carey Sonny Liew Marc Hempel

A Korean-American California girl who's into martial arts learns that in romance and recycled gifts, what goes around comes around.

COMING IN JUNE 2007 ■ Read on.

*WHAT KOREANS CALL THE RODNEY KING RIOTS--LITERALLY "APRIL 29TH".

A spoiled, rebellious Londoner conquers the

stuffy English countryside when she solves a

murder mystery on the 19th hole of her grandparents'

golf course.

COMING IN JULY 2007 ■ Read on.

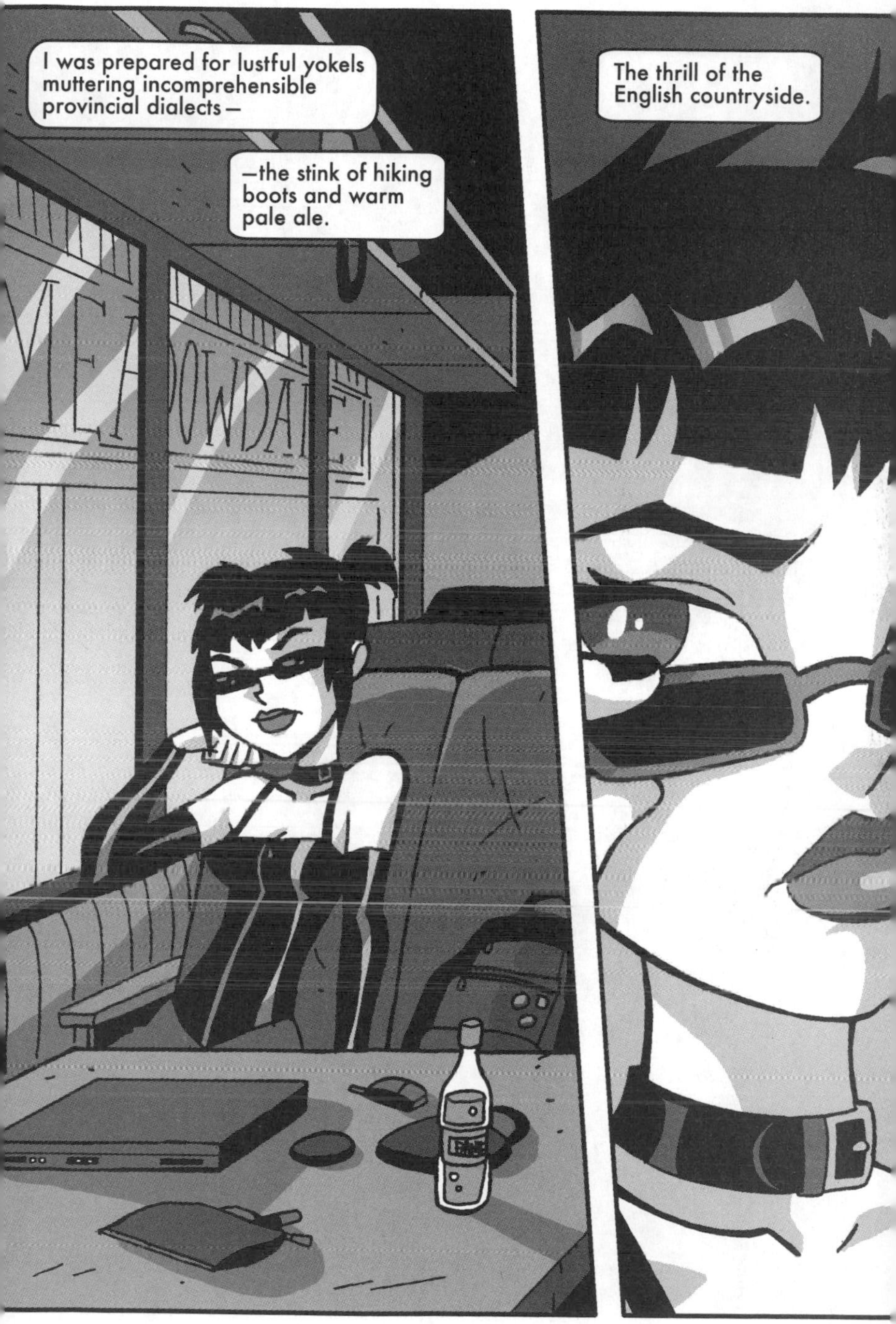
I was prepared for lustful yokels muttering incomprehensible provincial dialects—
—the stink of hiking boots and warm pale ale.
The thrill of the English countryside.

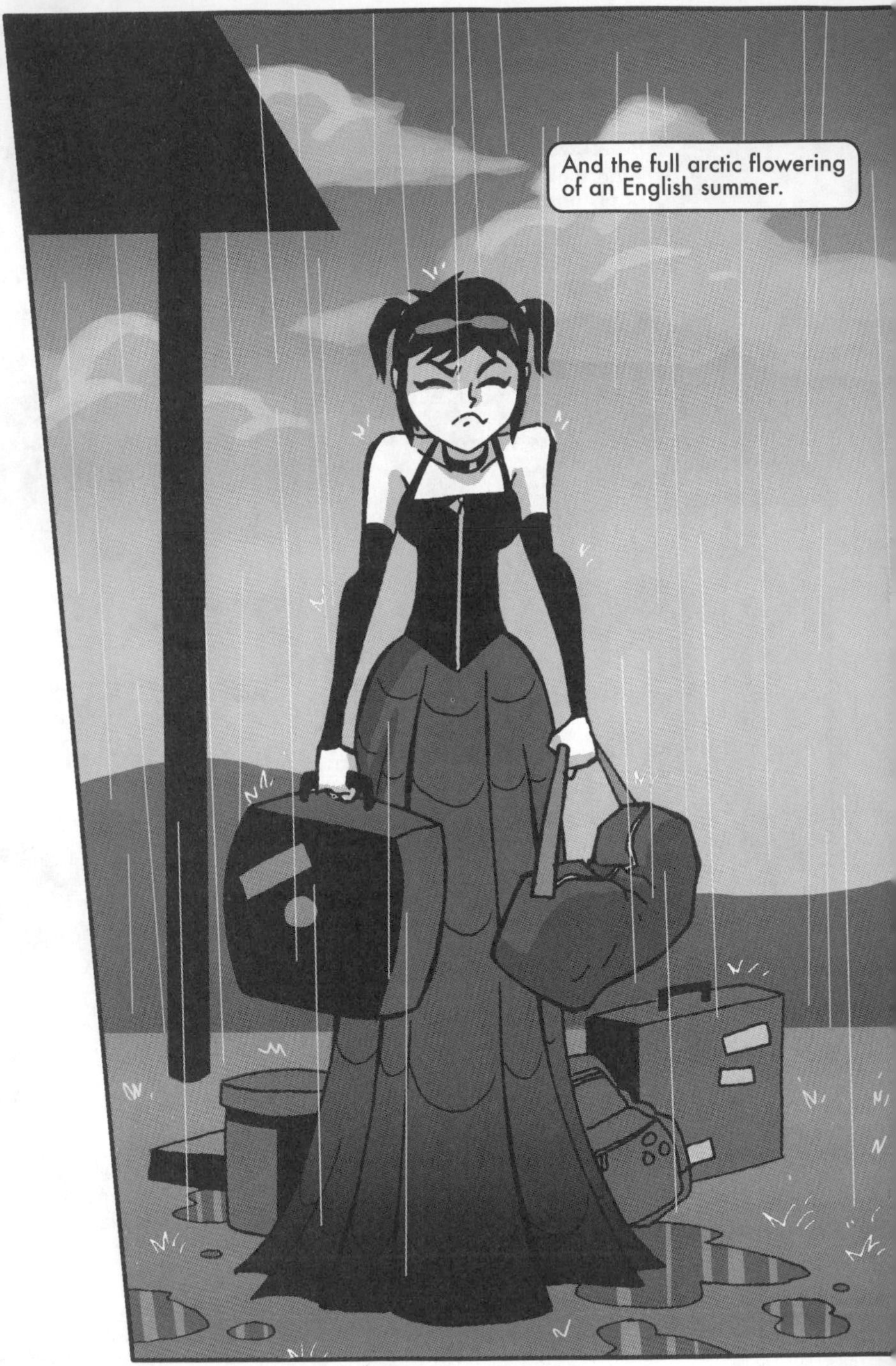
And the full arctic flowering of an English summer.

Good As Lily

What would you do if versions of yourself at ages 6, 29 and 70 suddenly became part of your already complicated high school life?

COMING IN AUGUST 2007 ■ Read on.

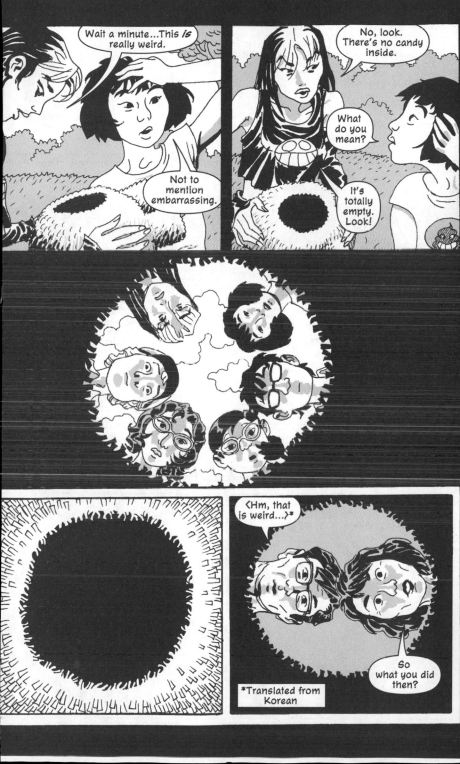

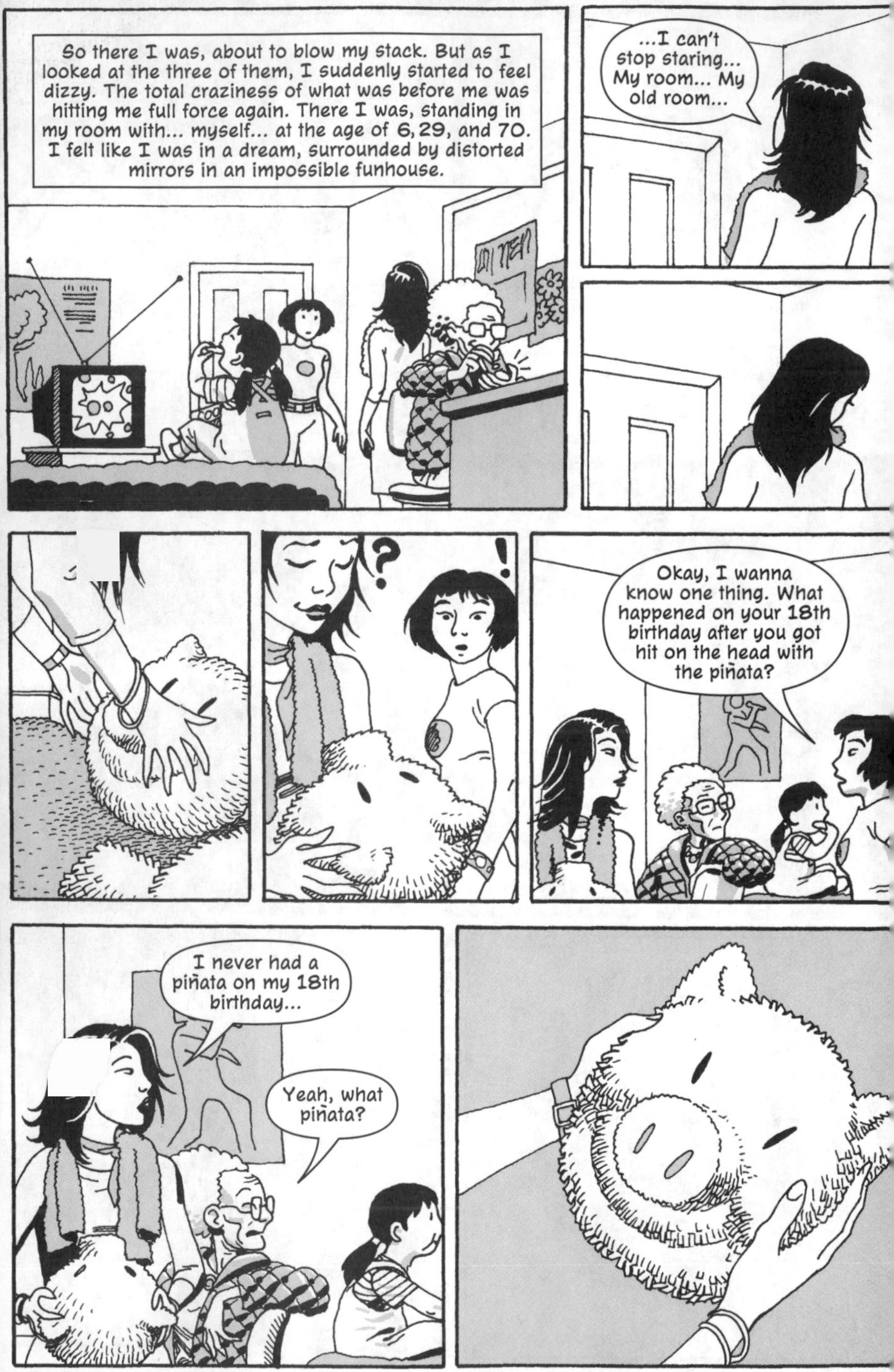
So there I was, about to blow my stack. But as I looked at the three of them, I suddenly started to feel dizzy. The total craziness of what was before me was hitting me full force again. There I was, standing in my room with... myself... at the age of 6, 29, and 70. I felt like I was in a dream, surrounded by distorted mirrors in an impossible funhouse.
...I can't stop staring... My room... My old room...
?
!
Okay, I wanna know one thing. What happened on your 18th birthday after you got hit on the head with the piñata?
I never had a piñata on my 18th birthday...
Yeah, what piñata?

Don't miss any of the upcoming minx books of 2007:

confessions of a
blabbermouth
MIKE CAREY LOUISE CAREY AARON ALEXOVICH

CONFESSIONS OF A BLABBERMOUTH

By Mike and Louise Carey and Aaron Alexovich

September

When Tasha's mom brings home a creepy boyfriend and his deadpan daughter, a dysfunctional family is headed for a complete mental meltdown.

WATER BABY
Ross Campbell

WATER BABY

By Ross Campbell

October

Surfer girl Brody just got her leg bitten off by a shark. What's worse? Her shark of an ex-boyfriend is back, and when it comes to Brody's couch, he's not budging.

kimmie66
AARON ALEXOVICH

KIMMIE66

By Aaron Alexovich

November

This high-velocity, virtual reality ghost story follows a tech-savvy teenager on a dangerous quest to save her best friend, the world's first all-digital girl.

The Face of Modern Fictio